THE EVOLUTION OF INDUSTRIAL SYSTEMS: THE FORKING PATHS

SOCIAL ANALYSIS
A Series in the Social Sciences
Edited by Richard Scase, University of Kent

The Evolution of Industrial Systems

THE FORKING PATHS

Timothy Leggatt

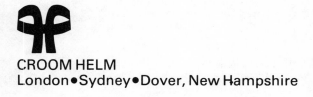

CROOM HELM
London•Sydney•Dover, New Hampshire

© 1985 Timothy Leggatt
Croom Helm Ltd, Provident House, Burrell Row,
Beckenham, Kent BR3 1AT
Croom Helm Australia Pty Ltd, First Floor, 139 King Street,
Sydney, NSW 2001, Australia

British Library Cataloguing in Publication Data

Leggatt, Timothy
  The evolution of industrial systems.
  1. Social change
  I. Title
  303.4   HM101

  ISBN 0-7099-1603-5
  ISBN 0-7099-1670-1 Pbk

Croom Helm, 51 Washington Street, Dover, New Hampshire 03820, USA

Library of Congress Cataloging in Publication Data

Leggatt, T.W. (Timothy W.)
  The evolution of industrial systems.

  (Social analysis)
  Bibliography: p.
  Includes index.
  1. Soviet Union — Industries — History. 2. Japan —
Industries — History. I. Title. II. Series.
HC335.L39   1985   338.09   84-29365
ISBN 0-7099-1603-5
ISBN 0-7099-1670-1 (Pbk.)

Phototypeset by Sunrise Setting, Torquay
Printed and bound in Great Britain

CONTENTS

To Jenny, Emily and William

ACKNOWLEDGEMENTS

Being the consummation of my sixteen years as a practising sociologist, this book is largely idiosyncratic in the focus of its interest and the scope of its concerns. Given this, I would like to record my great debt to Professor Morris Janowitz, my mentor when I was a graduate student at the University of Chicago and for some years afterwards. His chiding inspiration has encouraged me to attempt a piece of work which has both empirical and theoretical relevance. I am grateful to Professor Richard Scase for asking me to write some such book as this, to George Kitson for helping to find the time in which it could be written and to Anne Johnson for expertly converting my manuscript into typescript. Above all, I thank my wife, Jenny, for her support and encouragement in its completion, even when this bit more heavily into family time than any of us would have wished.

Timothy Leggatt
Cambridge

PART ONE

THE FRAMEWORK OF ANALYSIS

1 INTRODUCTION

The subject of this book, and of the studies it contains, is the continuing development of the world's advanced industrial systems. The process of initial industrial development as an issue of general interest or the conditions of industrial take-off are not treated here; they have been the subject of extensive study elsewhere.[1] The title also declares a view of the processes at work that denies the relevance of the rhetoric and symbolism of revolution. The story of evolutionary development contains sufficient surprise and fascination without recourse to the heightened dramatic scenarios of revolution.

Reflections upon human societies and upon their pasts tend, to the sombre analyst, to be bedevilled by dramatic simplicities. It comes to be thought that societies develop in inevitable ways, either according to one plan or according to minor variants of it; that history is full of crossroads or watersheds, vivid disjunctive points punctuating the otherwise largely undifferentiated process of change; that major changes are brought about by single or pre-eminent causes. It is seldom so; indeed perhaps it is never so. But so insistent is the human disposition to simplify the complex flow of historical and contemporary events, to conceptualise with enforced clarity what is normally veiled and obscure, that the simplest patterns of interpretation tend to be the most eagerly grasped.

The evolution of industrial systems does not follow a simple pattern, and this emerges in some detail in the studies that follow. But this does not force us to accept the confessed total ignorance of Heeb: 'whether there are one or many time paths to one or many, or any, end states is unknown'.[2] The way of discretion is surely to assume that there is indeed no end state (short of obliteration) to industrial development but that there are paths, and many of them, into the future. So the study of the Soviet and Japanese industrial systems that follows strongly suggests, in the light of which no simple convergence thesis can remain tenable. The smaller studies of certain issues now of great salience in advanced capitalist systems confirm the complex nature of industrial development.

The argument is also put forward that industrial systems are still very much in *process* of evolution. Little support is found for the idea that to characterise one society as the forerunner of post-industrial

1

development serves to clarify understanding of the changes now taking place. Can we not simply accept, as we do in biological science, 'the continual generation of novel change and the proliferation of diverse genotypes'?[3]

The reader will have recognised that a special claim is being made about the interest and importance to historians and social scientists of 'industrial systems'. This term is chosen to encompass less than 'industrial societies', with all the social institutions and relationships that they comprise. It also affirms the belief that what goes on in these societies and how their futures evolve are dependent, more than upon any other features, upon the complex of institutions, relationships, practices and other factors that make up their industrial systems: upon, for example, the organisation of industry, the nature of work, relations between managers and workers, the place of trade unions, the control of large companies and the applications of advanced technology.

The object of the studies, for both historians and social scientists, is twofold: to throw more light on areas that have hitherto been only fitfully and inadequately illuminated; and to try to identify the principal features of advanced industrial systems that will shape their continuing evolution. In Chapter 2 the ideas of leading social theorists, both classical and contemporary, are investigated in order to provide a theoretical frame of reference for what follows. Our concern is primarily with those of their ideas that relate to the nature of industrial systems and the experience of industrial life, but so large is this subject already that wider issues, related to possible developments in advanced industrial societies, are also germane to the discussion. In Part Two certain critical issues for capitalist systems are comprehensively treated: in Chapter 3, the complex issue of the control of corporate power, with some special reference to multinational companies; and in Chapter 4 the impact of automation upon work and employment and the implications of the shift to service employment. These issues are relevant to all advanced capitalist systems but the focus is upon Britain and the USA from which the evidence discussed is drawn.

In Parts Three and Four the focus shifts first to the Soviet Union and then to Japan, the two pre-eminent nations to industrialise in the twentieth century. Both nations were deliberate followers of the first industrialising nations and deliberate borrowers from them. In the case of the Soviet Union we have a society which, as Russia, for some hundreds of years aspired to be Western but which for ideological reasons chose a different industrial system and a different path of development. In the case of Japan we have a society which never wished to be Western but has deliberately sought to borrow from the West and to adapt to its own cultural traditions whatever was necessary to emulate the industrial development of the West. Each society has found its own path to, and form of, industrial evolution that is distinct from that trodden by the Western pioneers of industrialisation.

But the Western reader's knowledge and needs are so different in the two cases that the treatments of the two societies are equally different. Although the social system of the USSR is frequently thought of as alien, because characterised as Communist or despotic or both, all the ideas upon which it is based are of European origin and Russia, as it then was, shared its earlier phases of social and economic development with the remainder of Europe. Hence the exposition of the Soviet industrial system in Part Three is not historical but is concerned with recent developments, with only passing reference to the period before 1945. The focus is upon the planning system, examined within its institutional and governmental framework. Customarily, economists ignore the political and social context of economic behaviour, while non-economists concern themselves with this context, leaving scrutiny of economic behaviour to the specialists. Here a broader, more comprehensive analysis is attempted.

In the Japanese case, while capitalist institutions are familiar to the Western reader, the history is not. Usually, what is surprising about Japanese practices — for example, the employment system — is treated in a few paragraphs of historical explanation. The approach in Part Four, however, is unashamedly historical, and in order to place in context the discontinuities of the Meiji period of modernisation and the aftermath of World War II the account starts with the Tokugawa regime. Only in an historical framework, however brief, can the process of development be properly examined.

In Part Five are put forward the writer's views as to the main factors and issues that are even now shaping the evolution of the advanced industrial societies.

Notes

1. The economic literature starts with Colin Clark, *The Conditions of Economic Progress* (Macmillan, London, 1951) and W.W. Rostow, *The Stages of Economic Growth: A Non-Communist Manifesto* (Cambridge University Press, 1971); the historical literature starts with Alexander Gerschenkron, *Economic Backwardness in Historical Perspective* (Harvard University Press, 1962) and David S. Landes, *The Unbound Prometheus: Technological Change and Industrial Development in Western Europe from 1750 to the Present* (Cambridge University Press, 1972).

2. Quoted in Leon N. Lindberg, 'Introduction: Politics and the Future of Industrial Society', Ch. 1 of Lindberg (ed.), *Politics and the Future of Industrial Society* (David McKay Co., New York, 1976), p. 6.

3. James R. Millar, 'On the Merits of the Convergence Hypothesis', *Journal of Economic Issues*, vol. II, no. 1 (1968), pp. 60–8. The quotation is from p. 68.

2 THEORIES OF INDUSTRIAL CHANGE

The purpose of this chapter is to review the work of leading social theorists where they have touched upon theories related to the process of industrialisation and the development of industrial societies. These issues became of central importance in the nineteenth century with the industrialisation of Britain and of the other leading European nations. The chapter therefore starts with a survey of the ideas of Marx, Weber and Durkheim and sets out their great insights into the process of industrial development. It is at once apparent that their conceptualisations of the process remain the starting point of any study even in the closing years of the twentieth century.

The chapter continues with an exposition of the analyses of industrial society of six leading social thinkers in the period since the Second World War: Aron, Galbraith, Bell, Habermas, Mandel and Marcuse. Their relevant ideas are set out as fully as possible given the summary nature of the exposition.

The chapter is completed by a discussion of the main issues raised, the object being to bring together the thoughts of the theorists who have been considered, in order to draw out the questions of common concern. This discussion provides both a framework for consideration of the empirical material of the following six chapters and a point of reference for the theoretical concerns of the final chapter.

The Classical Legacy

The great trinity of classical sociological thinkers, Marx, Weber and Durkheim, were all deeply concerned about the nature and direction of change of the industrialising societies of their time. They were aware that the changes brought about by what is now termed the industrial revolution were quite without precedent in their powers of destruction of the former, traditional ways of living associated with agrarian society and in their promise of a different society in the future. They all had different ideas as to what was most significant in the processes of change and therefore also as to what social factors would pre-eminently shape the future.

No one can predict the future in any kind of detail, but it is possible to point to the key factors in its unfolding or to attempt to do so. The classical thinkers were not 'right' in their examination of trends. Their claim to greatness rests upon their identification of factors and forces that have aided man's understanding of the processes of social change and their concern with issues that have proved to be general and enduring.

Even if they did not focus on industrial societies by that name, their concern was with the societies of their day whose destiny was evidently being shaped by developments in science, technology and manufacturing industry.

Marx and the Analysis of Capitalism

Marx is acknowledged everywhere as the most provocative of social thinkers but he was just as unequivocally one of the most original. Unfortunately for later social critics reared in the heritage of positivism it has not always been easy to treat fairly someone who did not divorce thought and philosophy and science from action, and whose passionate humanism led him to marry his concern for the realisation of man's essential nature to his analysis of contemporary society. But here we are solely concerned with his social analysis.[1]

In this domain Marx offered three profound insights that have had an enduring influence on the study of industrial society.[2] The first was to single out the economic sphere from every other sphere of social behaviour and to give it priority. Thus Marx analytically separated the economic substructure from all other elements in society, from the superstructure which included other social institutions (political, legal, cultural, etc.), beliefs and forms of consciousness and pointed to the economic substructure as the principal determining feature of any society.

Within the economic substructure Marx identified the forces of production, the current state of production technology, as giving rise to the relations of production, the prevailing property relations and the social division of labour, which in turn determined corresponding forms of social consciousness. Thus the institutions of slavery, serfdom and wage labour were seen as the product of the prevailing technology, as were, indirectly, the modes of thought, justification and belief associated with these developments.

Dispute has fastened upon whether economic factors are always of prior importance in social analysis or whether, if they are, they have an exclusive position or whether elements of consciousness (ideas) do not at times precede social structures. Yet the central insight is

.untouched: to understand a social situation or a social change, ask first about economic forces and economic relations.

Marx's second insight concerned the nature of work in a capitalist society.[3] To him, natural labour was the realisation of the essence of man through physical commerce with nature. Unfortunately, in a capitalist society an unnatural division of labour prevailed whereby those who owned the means of production (property-owners, capitalists) were separated from those who did not (the propertyless labourers) and who owned only their own labour. As a result the owners treated labour as just another commodity, thus exploiting the worker and giving him a sense of himself as a thing. This is the genesis of alienation: the worker's sense of estrangement from his product, the work process and himself. The organisation of work also separates material and mental labour (practical and intellectual activity), production and consumption, labour and enjoyment. Thus the peculiar division of labour that emerged under capitalism produced social division, alienation, exploitation and a variety of forms of contradiction and conflict.

Marx's third great insight built upon Hegel's notion of dialectic: that every idea gives rise to its opposite and an ensuing contradiction that eventually leads to the emergence of a new idea that resolves the contradiction; the new idea is opposed and contradicted in its turn and a further resolution emerges. Marx brought Hegel's notion down to the material level and observed that every social force, whether an abstract idea or a material act, is subject to the process of dialectic. He further identified social formations related to the means of production (social classes) as the significant forces, throughout recorded history, in bringing about social change. Thus class conflict is the prime motor of societal change.

Marx's analysis of social classes has a further original element. He recognised that while a social class could have objective existence, identified by observing the relationship to the means of production that members of a group have in common, it would not act as a social entity unless the group members also shared awareness of the common features of their situation and of the opposition of their interests to those of another class. Thus an objectively identifiable category takes on subjective existence as a social class with the addition of class consciousness. Marx's profound point is that a group is only significant for social life when it acts upon its shared consciousness of its existence and common plight.

A class society is a society full of contradictions. Class conflict of a kind that may seriously change a society arises after two principal classes have emerged and become increasingly polarised and politically mobilised against each other, to the virtual exclusion of other classes. In the capitalist society of his day Marx predicted that the state of class conflict between the capitalist property-owners (the bourgeoisie) and the propertyless industrial workers (the proletariat) could only be resolved by a social and political revolution as a result of which private property would be abolished, all citizens would have the same relationship to the means of production and, consequently, class conflict as the pre-eminent form of social contradiction would cease to exist. This state of society, with common ownership of the means of production, distribution and exchange, would be socialist.

This brief exposition of Marx's most profound ideas by no means exhausts the fecundity of his thinking. They are, however, the ideas that any examination of industrial society must take into account. They will be referred to later in this study. There are also three ancillary ideas that deserve further notice in what follows: the place of ideology, the role of the state and the importance of revolution.

Ideologies, to Marx, were ideas (views, convictions, philosophies), especially about social life, that appear to exist in the mind in their own right. The subject may thus be unaware of their origin in social conditions and of the part they play in maintaining those conditions. The leading ideas in a society will be those promulgated by the ruling class; those of other classes may be influenced by them without recognising their origin and that they serve the interests of the ruling class. Ideologies are of special importance in disguising social contradictions and equally in mobilising parties in class conflict.

The state, that is, the central organs of administration and government, is not neutral but has a role in defending privileged classes and vested interests; it is, like other superstructural institutions, a product of the social relations of production. Its fate is therefore to be abolished, following the expected social revolution. Finally, revolution (brought about by the uprising of the industrial working class whose interest in social justice is equated with the long-term interest of society as a whole) is indispensable to overthrow the ruling classes who will never voluntarily relinquish the power that they possess and the political institutions which protect them. Reform (incremental, piecemeal, evolutionary change) merely expresses the ideas of a minority which perceives needs for change. It is only partial and inadequate.

Marx's ideas possess singular power and interest for political analysts as well as for political activists. They form a point of departure for any study of industrial societies and their future development.

Weber and the Process of Rationalisation

Weber was not overly concerned with industry as such but the major part of his work arose from an absorbing interest in economic development and scientific progress: specifically, in how it was that the societies of the West, rather than others, had initiated the scientific and industrial revolution.

In the context of this study we may select two major insights of Weber as having special importance. First, Weber focused on the process of rationalisation as the characteristic feature of Western development. It is the disenchantment (*Entzauberung*) of the West, its freedom from the thrall of magic and superstition, its embrace of rationality, that has given it its lead in economic development and scientific progress. This insight is of course in deliberate and sharp contrast to Marx's analysis. Whereas Marx identified material forces as the determinants of social change, Weber offered the power of ideas, concepts and values.

For Weber, the spirit and the original impulse of capitalism whereby 'Man is dominated by acquisition as the purpose of his life'[4] did not derive from the state of technology or the organisation of relations of production. It arose from the ethic of ascetic Protestantism (especially Calvinism), that is, the belief in the value of efficient performance in a chosen vocation as a duty and a virtue. Since performance of good works could be a sign of being among God's chosen, Protestants engaged in intense worldly activity. This spirit led to the application of rational calculation in all spheres — in science, in book-keeping and elsewhere. Given the generation of this spirit, even if the originating, religious impulse grows weak, the future development of modern society, implies Weber, is best accounted for in terms of the continuing application of rational calculation to man and nature.

Weber's second great insight (which also provided persuasive evidence for his first) was to discern the working-out of the rationalising spirit in the social and political sphere in the peculiarly modern, rational-legal form of domination, known since Weber as bureaucracy. The context of Weber's exposition of bureaucracy was indeed a discussion of forms of domination, in which he contrasted the rational-legal form with the traditional and the charismatic.[5] This context turns out not to be adventitious but highly relevant to an assessment of the implications of the process of bureaucratisation.

Rational-legal principles applied to social organisation give the bureaucratic form, in a word, bureaucracy, which is typically characterised by the following five features: a hierarchy of authority with clear accountability of offices; the differentiation of tasks and duties; a system of rules, regulations and records to give uniformity of performance and standards, between officials and over time; impersonality, impartiality and lack of personal interest — in contrast to the traditional form of organisation based on patronage and favour; and the employment of officials, according to qualification, in secure, salaried careers in which promotion is by seniority (that is, accumulated local expertise).

Bureaucratic administration was to Weber the most efficient and 'the most rational known means of carrying out imperative control over human beings',[6] because it comprises the exercise of control on the basis of knowledge, and knowledge that is the most technically relevant to the task in hand and added to through experience. It takes the machine as its model and treats its human officers as interchangeable cogs. In Weber's words, 'The choice is only that between bureaucracy and dilettantism in the field of adminis-tration'.[7] For all that is has been found wanting by modern critics Weber's ideal type has enduring value because of these features.[8]

Modern theorists of organisation have commented that Weber's ideal type is not well suited to environments characterised by turbulence and uncertainty where greater flexibility and adaptability are needed than are allowed by Weber's model. We merely note that this means that the bureaucratic is not always the most rational form of organisation. The criticism is itself testimony to the enduring spirit of rational calculation.

Weber himself observed the long-term contradiction at the heart of bureaucracy which historically developed in tandem with modern political democracy, both embodying the idea of equality of treatment for the individual and the denial of favour and privilege. He saw that, because its officials have assured positions beyond the reach of privileged individuals and even groups, and a more inclusive range of administrative power than officials had historically possessed before, bureaucracy was profoundly antagonistic to democracy[9] and to the freedom and humanity of the individual. In an unusually vivid passage he wrote: 'Together with the machine the bureaucratic organisation is engaged in building the houses of bondage of the future, in which perhaps men will one day be like peasants in the ancient Egyptian state, acquiescent and powerless, while a purely technical good, that is rational, official administration and provision becomes the sole, final value, which sovereignly decides the direction of their affairs'.[10] Elsewhere he noted, 'Only by reversion in every field — political, religious, etc — to small-scale organisation would it be possible to any considerable extent to escape its influence'.[11] We may note the connection Weber makes between the process of bureaucratisation and large-scale organisation.

We may carry forward with us not only Weber's insight into the process of rationalisation as the dominant tendency in a modern, no longer traditional, society and its embodiment in bureaucratic organisation, but also his sense of foreboding.

Durkheim and the Crisis of Moral Regulation

Durkheim was a social theorist one of whose abiding concerns was the moral regulation of society, the only defence, as he saw it, against the flood of the individual's otherwise unrestrained passions and desires. He observed that the process of industrialisation had moved men away from the traditional, 'mechanical', form of social solidarity in which each individual was immediately, wholly and directly dependent on a collective type of society, that is, 'the totality of beliefs and sentiments common to average citizens'.[12] The major cause of change was the division of labour, but its progression also brought about a new, 'organic', form of social solidarity founded on the necessary interdependence of those whose labour was distinct and complementary and a society that was 'a system of different, special functions which definite relations unite'.[13] Thus Durkheim's interests were tied to the progress of industrialisation.

The *natural* form of the division of labour in society, according to Durkheim, does not bring about fragmented, repetitive and meaningless work 'degrading the individual by making him a machine', and causing a situation characterised by *anomie*, the normlessness and moral helplessness that is induced by a lack of social solidarity and social integration. On the contrary, 'The division of labour presumes that the worker, far from being hemmed in by his task, does not lose sight of his collaborators, that he acts upon them and reacts to them. He is, then, not a machine who repeats his movements without knowing their meaning, but he knows that they tend, in some way, towards an end that he conceives

more or less distinctly. He feels that he is serving something'. And
. . . 'as special and uniform as his activity may be, it is that of an
intelligent being, for it has direction, and he knows it'. The natural
form of the division of labour is thus not 'merely a means of
increasing the produce of social forces . . . it is above all a source of
solidarity'.[14] It is the pathological form, the *forced* division of labour,
that leads to a debasement of human nature precisely because in this
form the need to provide a source of solidarity through work is
ignored.

The division of labour in an industrialised nation is thus, for
Durkheim, both a hope — of a new form of interdependence and
solidarity — and a threat — of anomie and social disintegration. But
there were other sources of moral regulation outside the
organisation of work. There was the 'corporation' or occupational
group, there was the state, and there was the moral consensus of
society as a whole.

Durkheim looked to trade unions as the first form of occupational
organisation, closest, and directly related, to the work place; and he
then advocated a common organisation to bring together employers'
associations and employees' unions and to become a defined and
recognised public institution.[15] At all costs 'the framework of the
occupational group must always have relations with the framework
of economic life'. Eventually with the emergence of local, regional
and national industrial organisations, and possibly a single agency to
co-ordinate them all, capable of influencing society as a whole, the
state must become involved. But industrial organisation and
government must remain distinct, neither dominating the other.
'Economic life would thus be regulated and determined without
losing any of its diversity'.[16] Durkheim continues, 'A nation can be
maintained only if, between the State and the individual, there is
intercalated a whole series of secondary groups near enough to the
individuals to attract them strongly in their sphere of action and drag
them, in this way, into the torrent of social life. We have . . . shown
how occupational groups are suited to fill this role, and that is their
destiny'.[17]

Durkheim at this point allows prediction to become prescription.
However, we need take from this brief exposition of some of his
leading ideas just two profound insights. First is his insight that what
matters humanly about work as the division of labour progresses is its
organisation and the spirit in which it is organised: anomie is an ever-
present danger but it can be held at bay. The division of labour brings

with it new forms of interdependence which, in the proper social framework, will lead to a new form of solidarity which yet protects the diversity of individuals. His second insight is the need for a plurality of groups to offer to individuals social support and moral regulation in a socially dense and culturally diverse society. The complex structure of these overlapping and interdependent groups provides a network of norms and values from which may in due course arise a new moral consensus of society as a whole.

Contemporary Approaches

Aron and Industrial Society

With the emergence of the Soviet Union and its rapid progress into a fully industrialised society it was no longer possible to refer to all economically developed post-agrarian societies as capitalist. At the same time, to refer to such societies as simply industrial made no distinction of political systems. To critics on either side of the ideological divide the concept of industrial society omitted precisely what was most significant in societal development. Yet to the social commentator concerned precisely with the outcomes of industrial development, with societies advancing economically beyond dependence on subsistence agriculture, the term is entirely meaningful.

Raymond Aron has shrewdly observed that the idea of industrial society becomes prominent in times of economic adversity or warmth in international relations when economists and politicians may wish to play down the overall significance of economic and political systems. It recedes from use when prosperity returns and when again the political system may be given credit for its return.

Aron's point depends upon breaking Marx's causal connection between the forces of production and the social relations of production. He simply notes that the forces of production, the technological and economic structure, can reach the identical stage of development within wholly different economic systems; there is thus no necessary connection or one-to-one correspondence between the two and they can, and do, vary independently. He goes on to separate, within the idea of the relations of production, the property system and the method of economic regulation. The property system may be one of exclusively private ownership or exclusively state ownership; there may also be forms of co-operative and collective ownership; and there may be, and are, mixtures of these forms of ownership. Economic regulation may be by the interplay of market forces or by state planning or by some planning-market intermixture. And the forms of property ownership and the forms of economic regulation may vary independently. In this way, Aron unpacks Marx's idea of economic substructure and leaves it in separate pieces.

But Aron goes further when he turns to Marx's superstructure. He rejects the idea of a clear-cut, unambiguous distinction of substructure and superstructure. A certain state of the forces of production, given that development of the forces of production is a product of the development of science and technology, assumes a certain state of science and technology; it also assumes 'a certain social or even political organisation of production'. Thus, argues Aron, 'these forces of production, which are held to be the foundation of society, contain a part of what may be called the superstructure'. He goes on:

> . . . the whole social reality in my opinion is in the same plane. There is not a material reality on one side and an ideological reality on the other. The economic organisation which is said to be the foundation of society already contains a certain scientific knowledge and also very often a certain way of envisaging the world. Therefore all human activities must be considered significant and one must not try to oppose a foundation of a material nature to a superstructure of an ideological kind.[18]

Aron also observes that just as the forces of production do not determine the relations of production so the relations of production do not imply any specific political regime or any distinct ideology.[19] Industrial societies differ visibly in their political forms and scales of values as in other respects.[20]

Having separated aspects of developed economic systems that Marx had causally linked, Aron proceeds to characterise an industrial society. It has five defining features: the economic enterprise is completely separated from the family; there is a technological division of labour within the firm; there is capital accumulation; the idea of rational calculation is prevalent; and labour is concentrated in the workplace. Any society with these characteristics, whatever its political system or ideology, is an industrial society.

Aron is not offering a convergence thesis.[21] He is at pains to note how industrial societies differ, principally according to two features — the ownership of the means of production and the methods of economic regulation. In other words, once a nation in its economic development has reached the plateau of industrialisation, its organisation of economic life may be characterised by private ownership or by state ownership and by planned distribution· of resources or by distribution through the market. Both apparently congruent types, capitalist and socialist, exist and both are equally viable. There is no reason to suppose convergence: 'It is no more necessary for the Soviet economies to develop into neo-capitalist economies than for the latter to develop into Soviet type systems'.[22] Further, there is no necessary association of a planned economy and state ownership. Aron argues that a system of private ownership is compatible with a planned economy and that state ownership may use market devices to find out what the people want. Mixed systems are as compatible with the industrial society as the 'pure' types that have hitherto been prevalent. The Soviet Union could adopt the lineaments of a market economy and do so without undermining the system of one-party rule and ideological monopoly.[23] Thus convergence in one (substantial) sphere need not imply convergence of societies taken as wholes.

Aron goes on to point out that industrial societies have three main forms of social differentiation: 'through the division of labour, through the hierarchy of wealth, power and prestige, and through the plurality of groups which are formed and come into conflict with each other within the society as a whole',[24] and that all these phenomena may vary greatly in industrial societies at comparable stages of technological development (development of the forces of production). Indeed, given that different types of society are compatible with similar development it is highly improbable that forms of social differentiation will be the same. Aron in fact allows that the division of labour, because of its close dependence on technological structure, may be similar in different societies but that differentiation of resources and competing groups (sometimes social classes) will only improbably be so. Observation fully confirms this thesis and indeed gives it strength. The evidence is that even the division of labour takes different forms, at least in workers' subjective experience in different societies; even this is not techno-logically determined but depends in part on forms of organisation which manifestly vary with different forms of ownership and economic regulation.

Finally, Aron notes the need in all industrial societies for an ideology 'to fill the gap between men's actual experience and what their lives might be in terms of the prevailing ideas'. It is indeed the role of ideology to make sense of the world, especially in those spheres in which the endeavours of science cannot do so,[25] and necessarily to encompass also the contradictions and paradoxes that men encounter in modern society. Aron notes that ideology must reconcile the egalitarian ideas and the hierarchical structures, both generated in industrial societies. 'Such societies', he points out, 'proclaim an egalitarian conception of society, and at the same time give rise to even larger collective organisations in which the individual is increasingly absorbed'.[26] Perhaps this is a significant insight into the principal human problem of industrial societies. It is one to which we shall return.

We take with us from this brief look at Aron's analysis three elements. First, his critique of Marx. Second, two hypotheses: that different political, economic and social systems evolve with the achievement of industrialisation, all of them equally stable, and that just as there is no necessary path of industrial development or growth, there is no necessary path beyond the industrial stage. Third, the insight into the necessity of ideology to resolve the contradictions of industrial society and especially to reconcile its ideal values of freedom and equality with the reality of experience in large organisations.

Galbraith and the New Industrial State

John Kenneth Galbraith is the sole economist among the social theorists whose ideas are examined in this study. Galbraith takes delight in portraying himself as the black sheep of the economic community in writing not merely about economic change and for the narrow specialist but about 'the complex of change', for all students of society, and in easy prose.[27] He invites his readers to accept that there have been numerous interrelated changes in the advanced industrial society that should bring a new understanding of the course of its development.

Like other theorists Galbraith finds a relationship between the advance of technology, the division of labour, the growth of firms and the increasingly interventionist role of the state, but the interest of his analysis lies in two intermediate factors, the necessity for planning and the emergence at the heart of the modern organisation of a group of specialists, called by Galbraith 'the technostructure'.

According to Galbraith, 'Technology means the systematic application of scientific or other organised knowledge to practical tasks. Its most important consequence . . . is in fixing the division and subdivision of any such task into its component parts. Thus, and only thus, can organised knowledge be brought to bear on performance'.[28]

There are a number of consequences of advancing technology: an increasing commitment of capital to production, an increased commitment of resources to defined projects, a larger time span required for the completion of specific tasks, a need for specialised manpower, a need for organisation and, as a result of all these, the necessity for planning. This combination of developments tends to lead to organisations of growing size, a trend also brought about by the industrial enterprise's wish to reduce the uncertainties of the market. The control, supersession or suspension (by the development of government contracts) of the market only becomes possible for large firms in positions of oligopoly. From this in turn arises the development of close collaborative relationships with the government that eventually become symbiotic. The government then becomes involved in a national programme of research and development which feeds back into the evolution of new technology, and, through its responsibility for the education system, in the generation of professionals, scientists and other specialists to fill the manpower needs of industry. And so the cycle continues.

The group of specialists, called by Galbraith the technostructure, is 'the association of men of diverse technical knowledge, experience or other talent which modern industrial technology and planning require.'[29] The requirements of technology, the massive deployment of capital and the need for planning and co-ordination, in short, the complexities of decision-making, have ousted the single decision-maker of the past, the entrepreneur, and enthroned the group of technical and planning staff. Just as the basis of power once shifted from land to capital, it has shifted again, to organised intelligence; the technostructure, not management, is sovereign.[30]

The technostructure now uses the corporation and the state to promote its own interests by wholesale manipulation of needs, attitudes, perceptions and beliefs. 'The corporation becomes . . . an instrument', avers Galbraith, 'for attributing social purpose to the goals of those who comprise it. Social purpose becomes by this process of adaptation what serves the goals of members of the technostructure'.[31] Members of the technostructure are motivated by identification with the organisation and by adaptation (association in the hope of influencing the organisation's goals). The goals of the organisation, now that profit maximisation is no longer obligatory once market instabilities are controlled, become those of the technostructure: first, survival (to maintain the autonomy of the technostructure); second, growth, measured in sales; third, technical virtuosity; fourth, an increase in shareholders' dividends. The achievement of these goals may suffice to give the technostructure the protection it needs from informed outsiders: owners, creditors, workers, consumers and government. But ideology is also used to this end: for example, the propagation of the beliefs that the consumer is king, that government intervention is meddlesome and bad, that trade unions should leave decisions to management.

Beyond the organisation, in the economy at large, the technostructure comes to define the public interest. 'What serves the technostructure — the protection of its autonomy of decision, the promotion of economic growth, the stabilisation of aggregate demand, the acceptance of its claim to superior income, the provision of qualified manpower, the government service and investment that it requires, the other requisites of its success — *is* the public interest'.[32] Even the state itself is somewhat in thrall. 'The modern state . . . is not the executive committee of the bourgeoisie, but it *is* more nearly the executive committee of the technostructure'.[33]

Apart from the technostructure, Galbraith's other key idea, and hardly to be differentiated from it, is that of the necessity for planning.[34] It is the necessity for planning that gives rise to at least part of the technostructure and the growth of large firms that can be assured of the stability that planning requires. The necessity for planning, therefore, is the intermediate term between the use of advanced technology, the commitment of massive outlays of capital and the development of complex organisation on the one hand and the need for the psychological control of the consumer and a symbiotic relation with the state on the other.

Out of the necessity for planning comes Galbraith's dual US economy split between a thousand giant firms that constitute 'the planning system' and twelve million small firms that make up the residual market system. In the planning system the giant firms control costs and prices, consumers, and even raw materials. Prices, says Galbraith, in a long planning cycle may even be fixed before production; wage costs are inconsequential (since profits are not of central importance), they are simply passed on to the customer. The consumer is controlled by the double-headed device of market research and advertising. Innovation is no longer a new way of satisfying an old need but a means of creating new needs upon which the organisation depends for its continuance. Raw material control is achieved by firms going multinational and reducing the uncertainties of the international market.

But beyond the reach of its own power and influence the planning system still needs and depends upon the state, and — this is Galbraith's insight — the state also needs the planning system. Both have an interest in economic stability, economic growth and scientific advance. Both also have an interest in defence:[35] the government for national protection, the planning system for the size, time span and stability of government contracts. The planning system relies on government for the provision of educated manpower, for investment in social infrastructure (for example, in support of road, rail, and air transport systems) and for coping with the ill effects of inflation.[36] The interdependence of the state and the planning system is evident to the clear-sighted analyst. It could even be, or become, conspiratorial. Galbraith comments, 'The damage to liberty lies in the subordination of belief to the needs of the industrial system. In this the state and the industrial system will be partners'.[37]

Galbraith is no harbinger of revolution in so stable a situation, nor its advocate. But he strongly espouses change away from the situation in which the goals of the industrial system 'are co-ordinate with life' and 'what is consistent with these ends we shall have or be allowed; all else will be off-limits'.[38] He sees two contradictions that could herald it. First, he is renowned as the critic of 'private affluence and public squalor'. He constantly stresses the inadequate expenditure on housing, medicine, transportation, parks, the arts etc. He observes, 'the poor . . . are outside the industrial system. They are those who have not been drawn into its service or who cannot qualify'.[39] Second, while he notes the importance for the technostructure of 'the educational and scientific estate' which gives access to scientific innovation, this estate also has the political initiative to press for public, aesthetic and intellectual priorities. The industrial system is intellectually demanding and hence 'It brings into existence, to serve its intellectual and scientific needs, the community that, hopefully, will reject its monopoly of social purpose'.[40] Thus Galbraith looks, though with only moderate confidence, to students and intellectuals to usher in the successor to the new industrial state.

Bell and the Post-Industrial Society

Daniel Bell is foremost among the prophets of the post-industrial society, which is to say a society that is as qualitatively different from industrial society as industrial society is from pre-industrial society or agrarian society. The model for the post-industrial society is provided by the United States, the first society to attain this stage of development. However, the stage of post-industrialism (assuming this to be the new stage that supersedes industrialism) has still to show its full development. Bell, therefore, both characterises the new society and identifies the key factors in its evolution.[41]

Bell characterises the post-industrial society first by the shift in the balance of employment to the service economy and second by a cluster of features associated with the advance of science: the pre-eminence of a professional and technical class; the primacy of technical, and especially theoretical, knowledge; the planning and control of technology; and the rise of intellectual technology.[42]

The growth of service employment is shown by the rise of the service-producing labour force in the USA from 49 per cent of the total labour force in 1949 to 64 per cent in 1968 and by the growth of the service component in the labour force in manufacturing and construction, to 31 per cent in 1970. Bell also noted that in 1968 white collar workers were 47 per cent of the US labour force.[43] Bell has observed that there was a shift within service employment away from those ancillary to goods-producing industries towards personal (education, health and social services) and information services. By 1960 professional and technical workers amounted to 10.8 per cent of the labour force.

In the arena of science and technology, Bell links together the emergence of new knowledge, new technology, new industry, a new class and a new emphasis on planning and control. Whereas, in the past, industrial development was at least in part founded on workbench and applied scientific innovation, in the post-industrial society industrial and technological development is based on *theoretical* knowledge. This brings universities and research institutions into new prominence, it requires massive and long-term funding, it puts a premium on intellectual and technical work, it generates new industries and it has produced new technology to revolutionise information-gathering and decision-making. Theoretical knowledge now affects the bases of economic growth, the system of stratification, and government policy-making. 'Science as a "collective good" has become the major productive force in society'.[44] It is a source of value, alongside land, capital and labour, and a source of power.

Bell documents the growing salience of science, research and education. In the USA in 1947 there were 3.8 million professional and technical personnel and in 1964 8.5 million; his estimate for 1975 was 13.2 million.[45] Bell quotes Machlup's (1958) estimates that 31 per cent of the US labour force worked in the 'knowledge sector' and that 31 per cent of GNP was spent on 'knowledge'; Burck's (1963) estimate that 'knowledge' gave rise to 33 per cent of GNP; and Marschak's (1968) estimate that in the 1970s knowledge industries would contribute approximately 40 per cent of GNP.[46]

In 1964 the USA spent 3.4 per cent of GNP on research and development (as compared with 1.4 per cent, 1.5 per cent and 2.3 per cent spent, respectively, by West Germany, Japan and the United Kingdom). Of this research effort 64 per cent was funded by government in 1965. By 1968 50 per cent of the 18–19 age group in the USA were in college; and 30 per cent of the 18–24 age group in institutions of higher learning. So Bell establishes the salience of research and higher education,[47] and the fact that the universities and research institutes are the significant locations of the new knowledge resource.

In this situation technical knowledge and skill are the new bases of power which give rise to the new dominance of scientists and research personnel and the emergence of a new professional and technical stratum and a diffuse knowledge elite.[48] The balance of power is now a balance of technical-political forces; and knowledge and planning are now the basic requisites for action in the post-industrial society. Finally, however, the politician remains sovereign: 'the power to say yes or no . . . is a political power that belongs, inevitably, to the politician rather than to the scientist or economist. In this sense, the idea that the knowledge elite will become a new power elite seems to me to be exaggerated'.[49]

Accompanying the development of this post-industrial society, Bell observes changes in business, in the polity and in ideology. He has least to say about business. He duly notes the emergence of managers as the controllers of business so that now ownership is largely a legal fiction, and the concentration of economic dominance in a few firms; and that property remains one of the bases of power in society. The economic function is subordinated to the political order. He finds changes in the political and socio-cultural spheres to be of greater interest.

The polity in the post-industrial society has been transformed through the increase of state bureaucracy and the rise of political technocrats (the counterpart of the technocrats outside industrial circles). But at the same time there has been a growth of participatory politics: interest groups demanding public mechanisms for decision-making, open politics, more participation. The result has been to make more public group influence in politics, to generate conflict, to promote bargaining rather than rationality as a means of problem-solving and political mobilisation as a source of power, and to lower consensus.[50] This has provoked a crisis of political legitimacy. The society is state-managed but there is no political philosophy to justify the rules for establishing priorities and for social allocations. Capital accumulation and a measure of governmental direction of the economy are sanctioned, while there is a 'revolution of rising entitlements', a growth of private and group claims to the satisfaction of wants without a recognised mode of adjudication between them. Trust and faith in the political system are diminished.[51]

The counterpart of this tension within the political system Bell finds in an ideological tension between what he calls the 'economising' and the 'sociologising' modes of thought. 'Economising', the product of engineering and economics, is concerned with the best allocation of scarce resources among competing ends; ends are given, what is at issue is rationality in the choice of means. The product of this approach is the modern corporation which embodies functional rationality and the economic ordering of social relations and whose aim is to satisfy the private wants of the individual for the consumption of economic goods. In contrast has arisen the 'sociologising' mode of thought concerned with the social — social justice and social goods — and energising the drive for greater political participation.[52]

Bell does not regard the techno-economic realm and the political realm as wholly distinct. They have become in the USA progressively intermingled as the post-industrial society has emerged. In the 1930s a normative economic policy of government intervention was established; in the 1950s the development of science and technology was underwritten by the state; and in the 1960s there came a commitment to a normative social policy (embracing health, housing, environmental matters and civil rights) to redress social and economic inequalities. This trend has produced what Bell has termed the 'public household', a third sphere of economic management, alongside the market economy and the domestic household, for the management of state revenues and expenditure for the satisfaction of public needs and wants.[53] Perhaps an intermingling of economising and sociologising may arise in relation to the public household.

However, Bell finds a third source of tension[54] in capitalist society between the culture, becoming anti-institutional and antinomian, and the economising and technocratic social structure; between the goals of self-enhancement and those of rationality and efficiency. The conjunction of the economic and cultural realms achieved under Puritanism has now been undone, resulting in a spiritual crisis, a lack of moral consensus or agreed meanings of human existence necessary to sustain society and to motivate individuals.[55]

In a later development of his conceptualisation of the post-industrial society Bell has emphasised the key role of information. He now distinguishes between knowledge as the strategic resource of the post-industrial society (as against raw materials and financial capital in the pre-industrial and industrial societies) and information as the transforming resource (as against natural power and created energy).

Information, in the form of computer and data-transmission systems, is the new form of power. Bell writes, 'Information is power. Control over communications services is a source of power. Access to communication is a condition of freedom'. Even now, however, it is still not the scientists and the professionals who are the power-holders. Bell still concedes that 'ultimately the power is governmental'.[56] Bell also refines his categorisation of services into the tertiary, quaternary and quinary sectors and thus shows how the full elaboration of the post-industrial society is still in process of development.[57]

Habermas and Advanced Capitalism

Jurgen Habermas offers an analysis of advanced capitalism (which he terms, interchangeably, 'late' or 'state-regulated' capitalism) in contrast to the preceding phase of 'liberal' or 'competitive' capitalism. Following in the footsteps of both Marx and Weber, Habermas sees this new phase of development as being characterised by the growth and concentration of large economic enterprises, by state intervention in the economy to secure the stability of the system, and by the increasing interdependence of science, technology and industry which has turned the sciences into the leading productive and rationalising force. Between them these trends have transformed the character of the class struggle on the one hand and the development of bureaucracy and the process of rationalisation on the other. The overall results, according to Habermas, are the emergence of an ideology whereby political decisions seem 'to be determined by the logic of scientific-technical progress',[58] and a permanent crisis of legitimacy.[59]

The economy of the advanced capitalist society has three sectors: the private, labour-intensive, market-oriented sector; the monopolistic sector of highly capitalised large firms, largely independent of the market and largely dependent on government contracts; and the public (state-owned) sector. Government, 'the administrative system', both regulates the economic system (by fiscal policy, etc.) in order to 'correct' the effects of the free market, and replaces the market mechanism in certain spheres such as education, research and development, housing, regional policy, and defence. It acts in order to improve the conditions of the exploitation of capital and to prevent the recurrent crises forecast by Marx. In the earlier form of competitive capitalism no such government intervention took place. As Held puts it, 'the "hand of the state" is more visible and intelligible than "the invisible hand" of liberal capitalism'.[60]

This major development calls into question the legitimacy of government. Under competitive capitalism, government of a non-interventionist kind, providing a neutral, non-political framework for economic activity, was granted legitimacy on the basis of formal democracy (every adult citizen having a periodic and not infrequent vote) and this was justified by the tenets of nineteenth century liberalism. Under advanced capitalism the government takes greater powers, and demands greater loyalty, than formerly, without any new ideology or theory being developed to justify its wider claims.

The fundamental contradiction of capitalist society — social production versus private appropriation — remains, but class conflict now becomes latent and concealed. With the government shouldering even wider responsibilities for society's economic life, the inequalities of class have become *submerged* under permanent inflation, unequal sectoral and regional economic development, crises in government financial policies, and discussions of wage structure and price setting; and *diffused* over weak and powerless groups. The old, the young, the sick, the unemployed, consumers, public-transport users and others who are not directly 'lived off' or exploited do not form a class. Hence class consciousness is fragmented although it is still present in latent form. Hence also, when class struggle is manifested, it is likely to be against the government.

The tendency to crisis of advanced capitalist societies is, according to Habermas, fourfold. First there is an economic crisis because the economic sphere has been politicised and there is no accepted theory under capitalism as to how government should behave in the management of the economy. Old-fashioned economic exploitation of man by man has been replaced by a system in which advantage goes to the best organised and most effective pressure groups, regardless of class. Government behaviour is characterised most aptly as 'reactive avoidance of crisis', and this reveals the second crisis, the rationality crisis. The activities of government are incompletely co-ordinated and its efforts at crisis management only fitfully successful, its administration is deficient in rationality as it arbitrarily allows power and influence to pressure groups, and it continues to sustain its planning and interventionist policies while the prevailing ideology still advocates reduced intervention.

The third crisis is the crisis of legitimation in the minds of citizens, which arises from this contradiction, from the government's failures in crisis management, and from the occasional recognition that the government has a hand in, and responsibility for, the still inequitable distribution of the social product. Thus the more government takes responsibility for crisis management, the more it loses legitimacy; while the more it cleaves to legitimacy, the more fitful and ineffective are its interventions. In this situation the administrative system seeks to make itself independent of the available bases of legitimacy by various devices: by converting policy issues into personality issues or into administratively soluble technical problems, by calling in 'experts', by organising public hearings, by the use of advertising. Citizens then organise in groups and take initiatives, demanding substantive (not merely formal) democracy and a say in decision-making. This is both a threat to the system and not sanctioned by the ideology. Further, it breaches the conventionally accepted roles of contented consumer and private family person.

The fourth crisis is the crisis of motivation. Changes in, even collapses of, traditions, world-views and moral systems as a consequence of the secularisation of knowledge following the advance of science have resulted in widespread feelings of a lack of meaning in life. This is critical because the need of people to be motivated (for example, within the educational system or in their jobs) is as great as ever while the sources of motivation are weak if not absent.

In these circumstances acceptable motivation is for what Habermas terms civic and familial-vocational privatism: that is, an interest, but low participation, in the administrative system, an orientation to private consumption and leisure, and dedication to a personal career in a context of status competition. However, adherence to and satisfaction with this pattern of motivation is undermined by products of the secular trends of society: by the expansion of the social services, the commercialisation of culture and politics, the scientisation of professional practice, the formalisation of political and social intercourse, and the psychologising of child-rearing. These have the effect of undermining the individual's independent judgement, self-reliance and sense of identity, and increasing the sense of being a digit and being manipulated. Further, notes Habermas, the traditional creed of possessive individualism cannot promote provision for collective needs, such as public transport, health and education.

At the same time there are positive forces demanding changes. New patterns of adolescent socialisation, new social movements (especially the students' and women's movements) and pressure groups have created new levels of consciousness involving a universalistic and communicative ethic. Individuals increasingly demand rational and coherent explanations and justifications.

Although the progress of science and technology, including the spread of the scientific and rationalising approach from the natural sphere to the social, is closely associated with developments in the economy and in the role of government, its effects are so wide as to hold Habermas's constant attention: it could be claimed that the 'scientisation' of society is the object of his greatest concern.[61]

In this sphere he offers insights of major relevance to this study. He observes that the process of rationalisation noted by Weber has moved into a second stage in which the provision of decision-makers with objective information and technical advice is tending to evolve to a point at which the technology of the expert adviser has almost ousted the decision-maker himself. In this technocratic situation, writes Habermas, 'Systems analysis and especially decision theory do not merely make new technologies available . . . they also rationalise choice as such by means of calculated strategies and automatic decision procedures. To this extent the objective necessity disclosed by the specialists seems to assert itself over the leaders' decision'.[62]

This might appear to be a watershed because if it were possible more fully to rationalise decisions about practical questions the politician would become dependent on the professional, 'the mere agent of a scientific intelligentsia', left with nothing but 'a fictitious decision-making power', 'a stop-gap in a still imperfect rationalisation of power, in which the initiative has in any case passed to scientific analysis and technical planning'; and the state would become 'the organ of thoroughly rational administration'.[63]

Habermas, however, rejects this technocratic model of decision-making, which he considers to be flawed on the one hand by its technological determinism in that technical progress has historically *appeared* to have immanent necessity and on the other by its false assumption that the process of rationalisation brings about 'the disappearance of the problem-complex connected with the decision of practical issues'. Habermas continues, 'Either there are still other forms of decision than the theoretical-technical for the rational clarification of practical issues that cannot be completely answered by technologies and strategies, or no reasons can be given for decisions in such issues'.

Against this technocratic model of decision-making Habermas puts forward a pragmatistic alternative. In this the functions of the expert and the decision-maker are no longer strictly separated as in Weber's model[64] nor are those of the second subordinated to the first as in the technocratic mode but the two are placed in critical interaction. There is reciprocal consultation whereby on the one hand 'the development of new techniques is governed by a horizon of needs and historically determined interpretations of these needs, in other words, of value systems' and on the other 'these social interests, as reflected in the value systems, are regulated by being tested with regard to the technical possibilities and strategic means for their gratification. In this manner they are partly confirmed, partly rejected, articulated, and reformulated, or denuded of their ideologically transfigured and compelling character'.[65]

Only the pragmatistic model is necessarily related to substantive democracy. In the Weberian situation in which values and technical considerations are strictly separate, democratic choice merely takes the form of the acclamation of alternating elites since 'choice applies only to those who occupy positions with decision-making power and not to guidelines of future decisions themselves'; the exercise of power is legitimate but not made rational because of the non-involvement of the public in technical debate. In the hypothetical technocratic situation technique is sovereign, administration is wholly rational and the processes of democracy are irrelevant; the exercise of power is rational but not legitimate. In the pragmatistic case values and techniques interact and there is the possibility of substantive democracy; the exercise of power is scientised and could be both rational and legitimate *given the necessary degree of participation of the public.*

Unfortunately, notes Habermas, the proper conditions for the pragmatistic model, for 'the mediation of technological progress with the conduct of life in large industrial societies' do not at present exist. Neither the social basis for broad public discussion nor the provision of relevant scientific information currently exists. The social basis for discussion will not be promoted under a system of domination supported by the depoliticisation of the mass of the population, the decline of the public realm ('confined to spectacles and acclamation') and the bureaucratised exercise of power. The provision of the relevant information is blocked by the contractual organisation of modern science, the bureaucratic encapsulation of the research process, and the increasing specialisation within the scientific community itself. The task therefore remains of equipping and activating the public, the citizens at large, to initiate and sustain critical reflection and unrestricted discussion in order to control the transposition of the fruits of advancing technology into political and social practice. The public sphere must be reclaimed from being an arena for interest group conflict and be reconstituted as the locus for citizens at large to engage in general debate. 'Our only hope', warns Habermas, 'for the rationalisation of the power structure lies in conditions that favour political power for thought developing through dialogue. The redeeming power of reflection cannot be supplanted by the extension of technically exploitable knowledge'.[66]

Neo-Marxist Perspectives

The contemporary theorists whose ideas have been explored thus far have all been sharply aware of Marxist analytical thinking and have knowingly borrowed or assimilated or distanced themselves from elements of that tradition. We now turn to examine directly the theories of two neo-Marxist thinkers in so far as they bear upon the central themes of this study.[67]

Mandel and Late Capitalism

In his non-economic analysis of what he terms 'late capitalism' Ernest Mandel has attached prime importance to the greatly developed role of the State. Since parliaments are no longer the exclusive preserve of the bourgeois class, he argues, the political domination of capital is now transferred to, and mediated by, 'the upper levels of the State administration'; and this political development coincides with the State's increasing involvement in economic affairs.[68]

There are tendencies in late capitalist society towards an increase in State economic planning and towards absorption by the State, through nationalisation, of the costs and losses of a growing number of productive processes. State budgets cover R and D costs more widely, and the financing of, for example, large industrial projects and the development of nuclear power stations. The State is responsible for crisis management of the economy, for guarantees of capital investment in the armaments industry and for ensuring 'general conditions of production' by the provision of law and order and a sufficient degree of societal integration of workers, consumers and citizens at large.

There are three major behavioural consequences, according to Mandel, of the greatly enhanced power of the State.[69] First, the need of the capitalist class to retain control of government agencies leads to the emergence of a new device for the exertion of influence: the private lobby. Private lobbies, employers' organisations and commercial monopolies vie with think-tanks, foundations and political party groupings in the competition to bend the ear and actions of government. Second, this politics of influence succeeding the politics of the ballot box and the increasing centralisation of political decisions in the technical administrative apparatus of the State brings about the closer union of top government and the large corporations. Third, it becomes important to the bourgeois class that the professional bureaucracy of government administration is staffed by those loyal to bourgeois norms, has some degree of independence from the other powers of the polity (and thus freedom from the direct influence of non-bourgeois interests) and acts to incorporate working class and trade union cadres into the system by drawing them into joint committees, quasi-governmental agencies and similar bodies.

Finally there is the consequence of the new role of the State for the ideology of late capitalist society. In Mandel's words, 'belief in the omnipotence of technology is the specific form of bourgeois ideology in late capitalism'. The power of an inexorable yet neutral technology is exalted above the machinations of mere classes or other interest groups (to which Marxist analysis might be applied), and the State propagates 'the myth of a technologically determined, omnipotent economy which can allegedly overcome class antagonisms, ensure uninterrupted growth, steadily raise consumption and thereby bring forth a "pluralistic" society'.[70] Technological rationalisation tends to what is called de-ideologisation.

Mandel is not of course a neutral observer of the society that he describes, and he points to the enduring hegemony of capital and the bourgeois class under the veil held before it by the State and at a time of what he terms the 'reprivatisation' of collective interests. He finds the ideology of technological rationality to be both false and a source of mystification. The more decisions are taken by the administrative bureaucracy away from the domain of public debate (away from elected representatives), argues Mandel, the more the articulation of bourgeois class interests becomes 'reprivatised'; and the more the cultural needs and leisure activities of the proletariat are commercialised and reabsorbed into the capitalist process of commodity production and circulation (for example, through the expansion of television, including cable television, and video technology), the more the recreational life of the working class with its traditional opportunities for collective activity and the enhancement of solidarity is also 'reprivatised'. In such circumstances the unwieldy organisation of the many is no match for the more manageable co-ordination of the few; and the bourgeois class inexorably gains more purchase on the system than the proletariat.

To Mandel the ideology of technological rationality is false because damage to the environment is caused not by technology but by harmful decisions taken by private interests; because there are no technical solutions to society's crises, contradictions and disorders, only social and political solutions; and because 'the character of labour is not determined *directly* by technology, nor the stage of development reached by the forces of production'[71] but by social interests and social decisions. It is mystifying because despite its falsity the ideology claims that the system of late capitalism can overcome all fundamental socio-economic contradictions while the traditional theory of democracy continues to exalt the personal interests of the citizens at the point of voting over their collective interests. Thus the legitimacy of the system of late capitalism which has already, through the interventions of the State and monopolistic business, voided the ideology of nineteenth century capitalism that proclaimed the formal equality of independent, competitive entrepreneurs, is not secured by a new ideology. The corruption of the Watergate and Tanaka scandals shows the values of the system to be a sham.

As might be expected, Mandel proclaims the demise of late capitalism. He predicts the *long-run* inability of monopolistic capital to secure stable profits, the limits of the system perhaps being reached when capital is yet more fully internationalised, through expansion of the activities of multinational companies, than it is today. He predicts the global spread of threats to the environment. He predicts the rising level of education and the average qualifications of the typical workers which will in due course make the subordination of wage-earners to capital intolerable and shift the emphasis of class struggle to issues of control (of machines and labour power). Then these factors from within the capitalist system will meet the vast and unsatisfied needs of the semi-colonial masses, and the world-wide planning of the basic economic resources of the planet will become imperative.

For a Marxist this is a cautious prophecy. Mandel knows that the capitalist system is doomed, that a socialist society must succeed it and that the solidaristic values of that society are to be generated from the collective experience of associated workers. But he supposes that it may still take time for the capitalist system to reach its final limits. His communistic vision is as follows:

> if the producers henceforth organise, plan, discuss and realise their process of labour in common, in *voluntary* association, then naturally the mystery of the *social* force of production disappears, and the latter no longer seems to adhere to things, as a collective force 'external' to the producers, but is seen to be the result of the common, commonly planned and commonly organised labour capacity of all workers.[72]

Marcuse and the One-dimensional Society

Although not an analyst of economic and industrial development, Herbert Marcuse was passionately concerned with the condition of advanced capitalist society and with the possibilities for its transformation. Unlike the other theorists that we have examined, to Marcuse the question of how far in the prevailing social conditions man can fulfill his essential nature was of central significance. Yet the search for answers led him to analyse the objective state of the affluent society, the individual's perception of it and the role of technical rationality in sustaining it. He also considered which groups in an advanced capitalist society were the victims of the system and which might be the harbingers of its transcendence.[73]

Marcuse's principal contention is that in the affluent conditions of the consumer society man's awareness of the true quality of his social life and of the true nature of his needs is mystified. With a comfortable standard of living and the continued production of new goods and services, the people indeed have a good life and are content. But this does not, asserts Marcuse, give 'the real fulfilment of everything that man desires to be when he understands himself in terms of his potentialities'.[74] Thus the contentment is a sham; it is merely with the fulfilment of needs, which are false, imposed by the system. The system, in other words (or the apparatus, in Marcuse's term), not only provides the goods but also determines the needs. 'The products indoctrinate and manipulate; they promote a false consciousness which is immune against falsehood',[75] and the result is what Marcuse terms 'the universal servitude, the loss of human dignity in a prefabricated freedom of choice'.[76]

At times Marcuse sees no way to change. 'There is no personal escape from the apparatus which has mechanised and standardised the world. It is a rational apparatus, combining utmost expediency with utmost convenience, saving time and energy, removing waste, adapting all means to the end, anticipating consequences, sustaining calculability and security'.[77] At the same time Marcuse says clearly that human needs are historical needs, the product of their time; false needs are those imposed by powers outside individuals and beyond their control while true needs are those identified by the individuals themselves — 'but only in the last analysis; that is, if and when they are free to give their own analysis'.[78]

This vision of advanced capitalist society is in strange contrast to Marx's vision of nineteenth century capitalism, for while to Marx capitalist society was one riven by class conflict between a fattening bourgeoisie and an increasingly pauperised proletariat to which he announced the promise of transformative change, to Marcuse it has become one of material abundance for all classes for whom there is virtually no hope of liberation from spiritual degradation and servitude.[79]

A number of objective changes have occurred to baulk Marx's revolutionary programme. First, the working class is no longer the revolutionary subject. In advanced capitalist societies 'the radicalization of the working classes is counteracted by a socially engineered arrest of consciousness, and by the development and satisfaction of needs which perpetuate the servitude of the exploited' and hence the proletariat 'by virtue of its sharing the stabilizing needs of the system, has become a conservative, even counter-revolutionary force'.[80] Quite simply, 'the coordinated masses do not crave a new order but a larger share in the prevailing one'.[81] Second, all classes are now within the enlarged universe of exploitation including hitherto untrammelled elements of the middle class. Now the salaried employees in the tertiary sector of the economy and the functional intelligentsia are organised in the interest and image of capitalism, and all wage and salary earners are in the common condition of exploitation behind the facade of consumer society.[82] The result is that all opposition to the (materially comfortable) system is highly diffused. To the degree to which the production of 'luxuries which are necessities for occupying a labour force sufficient to reproduce the established economic and political institutions' appears as 'superfluous, senseless, and unnecessary while necessary for earning a living, frustration is built into the very productivity of this society and aggressiveness is activated'.[83] But this is no more a threat to the ruling elite, those who especially benefit from the manipulative character of the apparatus,[84] than democratic institutions are a curb; for government is now exercised by 'a network of pressure groups and "machines", vested interests represented by and working on and through the democratic institutions . . . The representation is representative of the will shaped by the ruling minorities'.[85]

The oppressive system of advanced capitalism that Marcuse describes is underpinned by an ideology of technical rationality. The rationality associated with the progress of science and the development of bureaucratic administration cannot, it appears, be rationally opposed: 'the apparatus to which the individual is to adjust and adapt himself is so rational that individual protest and liberation appears not only as hopeless but as utterly irrational'.[86] Again, 'the bureaucracy . . . emerges on an apparently objective and impersonal ground provided by the rational specialization of functions and this rationality in turn serves to increase the rationality of submission'. Thus 'the objective and impersonal character of technological rationality bestows upon the bureaucratic groups the universal dignity of reason'.[87]

Although in these quotations Marcuse appears to suggest that technological rationality has its own necessity, and elsewhere to confirm this by writing that 'specific purpose and interests of domination are not foisted upon technology "subsequently" and from the outside; they enter the very construction of the technical apparatus',[88] he does in fact distinguish technical reason from the reason of domination. Weber, he argues, confused these two so that he believed bourgeois capitalist reason to be technical reason and both neutral and dominant; whereas it was dominant alone. In fact, contends Marcuse, 'technology is always a historical-social project' and 'technical reason is the social reason ruling a given society and can be changed in its very structure'. Hence 'the consummation of technical reason can well become the instrument for the *liberation* of man'.[89] Thus technology has a necessity that varies with the historical and social context and is determined by the ruling interests in society. It is not neutral, as the positivist tradition would have it, but it is not necessarily oppressive.

Finally we come to Marcuse's thoughts about the prospects for change in advanced capitalist societies: the need for it; how, despite the prevailing manipulative power of the apparatus, it may yet be possible to bring about; and how it may be achieved.

Marcuse, given his pessimistic view of capitalist society and its oppressive and degrading qualities, has to be an advocate of change; equally inevitably, in view of the apparatus' grip on the peoples' consciousness, he calls not for piecemeal social engineering but for the total transformation of the social system. The oppressive character of capitalist society restricts the scope of criticism and falsifies the individual's sense of his potentiality for freedom. On the one hand 'rationality is being transformed from a critical force into one of adjustment and compliance'; on the other, 'the prevailing type of individual is no longer capable of seizing the fateful moment which constitutes his freedom'.[90] Man must be allowed to discover that he has new needs every bit as vital as the old;[91] to permit this the aim must be 'to transform the will itself, so that people no longer want what they now want'[92] and to bring about 'a truly free civilization' in which 'all laws are self-given by the individual'.[93] We note how far Marcuse has moved from a Marxist analysis and how solidly he has grounded his argument on liberal humanitarian values and on psychological needs.

How, though, can change occur in so powerfully repressive a system in which individuals cannot even perceive a need for change? How indeed can the need for change be perceived? Marcuse did not directly address himself to these questions but answers to them are implicit in his writings. First, he assumed for philosophers such as himself the traditional function of criticism from a standpoint that transcends the limitations of particular structures of thought and, by implication, particular structures of social reality.[94] The philosophic mind could still maintain the critical rationality that was being stifled by the apparatus of capitalist society, though only just, and still espouse the 'transcending aims and values'[95] being cut off by techno-logical rationality.[96]

Second, although under advanced capitalism 'society has to insure a more effective mental co-ordination of individuals', so far this has not been achieved and only *objective tendencies* towards the achievement are observable. As it is, 'the particular interest is not simply determined by the universal: the former has its own range of freedom, and contributes, in accordance with its social position, to the shaping of the general interest'.[97] The implication must be that it is only the prevailing norm not to be able to perceive the small scope for real freedom and to combat the oppressive character of the system, and therefore many individuals can see through the surface gloss of the consumer society to its demeaning quality. It then follows that if the tendencies toward the system's determination of the individual's interest can be frustrated, then change is possible.

Third, the possibility of opposition to the tendencies of the system is offered by the Great Refusal, 'the protest against that which is'[98] of those who 'resist and deny the massive exploitative power of corporate capitalism even in its most comfortable and liberal realizations'.[99] The protesters offered in different contexts by Marcuse are the *Untermenschen* of the system — 'the substratum of the outcasts and outsiders, the exploited and the persecuted of other races and other colours, the unemployed and the unemployable';[100] déraciné intellectuals, especially students;[101] and what seems to be comparable to Bell's knowledge elite — in Marcuse's words 'the organised refusal to co-operate of the scientists, mathematicians, technicians, industrial psychologists, and public opinion pollsters'.[102]

Given the need for societal transformation and the ability and inclination of some individuals and groups to perceive the need, how may the transformation come about, and what will it look like? In sum, Marcuse gives no very clear answers to either question, despite the pressure he was under in the last years of his life to provide them, but he gave some indications. First, he was clear that the normal democratic process will not bring the needed transformation: this 'works of necessity against radical change because it produces and sustains a popular majority whose opinion is generated by the dominant interests in the *status quo*'.[103] Therefore, he urged 'the necessity of direct action and uncivil disobedience' which is legitimate whenever the liberal system of law and order is seen to betray, compromise or deny the underlying standards and values (such as those of liberty, equality and fraternity) upon which it was founded; for then 'the existing society . . . has invalidated its own law'.[104] Yet, beyond this, how any significant uprising against the established order is triggered remains vague. Marcuse merely urges self-liberation through self-education, which presupposes education by others (by the intellectual elite) and includes political education; decentralised organisation in face of the concentration of the Establishment; and leadership 'to translate immediate needs and aspirations towards the radical reconstruction of society'.[105] This programme Kettler has aptly termed the 'politics of hope', which depends upon the function of a prophetic order as a source of education and which precedes the 'politics of transcendence'.[106]

Marcuse is also unspecific about the state of liberation to come with the transcendence of capitalist society. He does, however, promise both a new harmony and a new individuality. 'The administered and enforced harmony' of the present time, writes Marcuse, will be replaced by '*solidarity* in work and purpose, expressive of a true harmony between social and individual needs and goals, between recognised necessity and free development'.[107] In yet more visionary vein, he states:

> When the associated individuals themselves have taken over the direction of the life process and have made the totality of social relations the work of their reason and freedom, what man is in himself will be related to his existence in a new way . . . Man will

then have to be 'defined' not as a free rational being in opposition
to contingent conditions of life but as the free and rational creator
of his conditions of life, as the creator of a better and happier
life.[108]

Of all the contemporary thinkers we have considered Marcuse has
most to say about the possibility of revolutionary change in advanced
industrial societies and this accounts for the attention given to this
aspect of his thought. These ideas will be returned to in Chapter 9.

Questions of Theoretical Concern

Although the exposition of theoretical ideas in this chapter has been
guided by the wish to do justice and give coherence to the thoughts of
each theorist in turn, it will have been apparent that there are a
number of areas of common concern.

The Issue of Social Dominance

First among these is what we may term the dominance issue: who
(what group) holds a position of dominance in society?; what is the
basis of their dominance?; how is their dominance maintained and
justified?[109] This issue was at the centre of all Marx's analysis. He
concluded that social power was determined by a group's relation to
the means of economic production, that the social class structure
embodied these power relationships and that the bourgeoisie held
the dominant position in nineteenth century capitalist society.
Further, the bourgeoisie held and justified its power by controlling
the organs of the state and the prevailing ideas in society while giving
these the appearance of class neutrality and objectivity. Thus all
citizens tended to accept the *status quo*, not realising that their
perception and interpretation of it were under manipulation.
However, the inevitably increasing exploitation of the industrially
subordinate class, the proletariat, would in due course forge the
revolutionary consciousness needed to overthrow the class system
and all the social arrangements of capitalism, and to bring in the new,
communist society.

Although the prophetic aspects of Marx's thinking have not been
realised by twentieth century revolutions,[110] his leading ideas remain
in good currency. Habermas retains Marx's class analysis even
though believing that class conflict is now latent and submerged in

advanced capitalist societies. The technological determinism of Bell and Galbraith has clear affinities with Marx's economic determinism. Aron recognised the role of ideology in resolving the contradictions of the power differentials of industrial society. Galbraith observes the sinister interdependence of economic power and government and the use of ideology by the technostructure in the psychological control of the consumer.

Elements of Marx's analysis have thus been retained by non-Marxist scholars even though the overall package is no longer accepted as valid or sufficiently comprehensive. Today not all social group mobilisation — the activities of what are described as interest groups or pressure groups — can be seen as having a traditional class basis. Bell points to the pre-eminence of a new professional and technical class, and Bell, Habermas and Mandel all document the rise of a range of pressure groups and associate with it the loss of legitimacy of the social order and the workings of government. Marcuse emphasises the emergence of intellectuals, and especially students, as a political force coincident with the 'incorporation' of the working class. Aron also notes the loss of legitimacy in industrial societies which promise egalitarianism but in which the individual is dominated by the emergence of ever-larger organisations. Such concerns echo Durkheim's worry over the loss of moral consensus in industrial society.

What is noteworthy about this development is that the legitimacy of the capitalist order, effectively secured by the liberal ideology which prevailed in Marx's own day, has broken down without the occurrence of social revolution. The economically dominant class would appear at least to have lost its former control of the ideology of society. With the increasingly pervasive and interventionist role of government and the ever more widespread decision-taking by administrative officers, by executive action and by regulative processes, the periodic substitution of overt decision-takers via the electoral process no longer suffices to confer legitimacy on all governmental activity. Citizens now mobilise themselves to seize the social initiative and to apply pressures upon government and upon dominant social groups. Yet they too lack legitimacy, that is, any justification for their own social and political efficacy which is inevitably achieved and exercised at the expense of more apathetic or acquiescent sections of the population. Those without legitimacy according to inherited norms apply pressure upon those whose historical legitimacy is now at best threadbare.

The Nature of Work

The second area of concern shared by Marx and Durkheim is the nature of work in the (capitalist) societies of their day. For both theorists it was the unnatural division of labour that was responsible for the worker's unsatisfactory experience of work. To Marx, what should have been a source of creative fulfilment was a source of *alienation*; to Durkheim, what should have given a sense of purpose and of solidarity created *anomie*. But, in both instances, it is essential to note, what is at fault is not the task itself or the technology determining the task, but the social organisation within which work and production take place.[111] Here Weber too concurs: for him it is bureaucratic *organisation* that, together with the machine, 'is engaged in building the houses of bondage of the future'.[112]

The Process of Rationalisation

The third theme is that of the continuing effects of the process of rationalisation first identified by Weber. Bell sees the importance of *theoretical knowledge*, as science continues its inexorable advance, as one of the principal features of post-industrial society. To Bell, information is the new basis of social power. For Habermas, the sciences as the leading productive and rationalising force, the scientisation of society and the technocratic approach to decision-taking are constant preoccupations. The common element is the belief that the control, and the use made, of knowledge and information is now a determining factor in shaping the future society. Galbraith sees the new power of 'men of technical knowledge', the technostructure, as already being exercised to manipulate the consumer, the corporation and the state and to define the public interest.

Marcuse concludes that the rationalisation process has gone so far that 'individual protest and liberation appear not only as hopeless but as utterly irrational'.[113] This issue, important as it was to Weber, has now become yet more salient in contemporary social analysis.

The Development of Bureaucratic Organisation

Weber observed the development of administration by bureaus that we now term bureaucracy, and he did so, as we noted above, with some misgiving; for while bureaucracy means administration on the basis of the most technically relevant knowledge, and therefore the most rational and efficient form of administration, which is also in its denial of favour and privilege the fairest, it also tends to establish its officials beyond the democratic reach and its processes beyond the lay understanding of ordinary citizens. It is indeed this tendency that has given 'bureaucracy' its bad name and worried social commentators about the continual growth of large-scale organisations. Aron is concerned over the increasing absorption of the individual within larger organisations and Bell notes the increase of state bureaucracy and the rise of political technocrats. Galbraith sees the imperatives of modern technology leading to the new industrial state that is dominated by giant corporations, even to the extent of governments being forced into finding interdependent accommodation with such organisations. For Mandel it is the centralisation of political decision-making in the State apparatus of late capitalism that brings about the union of top government and the largest corporations. Their focus is on the size and oppressive influence of bureaucratic organisations. That of Habermas has moved even beyond that of Weber himself, to the irresponsibility of bureaucratic administration and therefore its lack of legitimacy.

Solidarity and Moral Consensus

The final major theme of the various social theorists that we have considered is that which centrally concerned Durkheim, the breakdown and recovery of social solidarity and moral consensus. Durkheim himself foresaw the division of labour of modern industry leading to a new form of interdependence and solidarity which, with the development of new occupational groups, would lead to new bases for moral consensus. It has not happened; and although it has equally not happened, in Yeats' famous phrase, that 'things fall apart; the centre cannot hold', the fear of anarchy and social disintegration remains.

Bell finds tension between the oppositional culture being generated (especially among youth) by capitalist society and the technocratic social structure, a spiritual crisis as well as a lack of consensus. Both he and Habermas are concerned at the crisis of motivation, especially as exemplified by radical youth in the 1960s. Mandel notes the 'reprivatisation' of working class recreational life and the consequent loss of opportunities for the growth of solidarity, while Marcuse laments the substitution of 'administered and confused harmony' for the true harmony and free development that the transcendence of capitalist society would allow.

But the remedy is no longer, as by Durkheim, seen as likely to evolve spontaneously from the social fabric. Now the call is for extensive public debate. Habermas puts his faith in the essential rationality of man, in the power of critical reflection and unrestricted discussion brought to bear on a sufficient provision of relevant information. Galbraith has more limited trust, in the educational and scientific estate to respond to the intellectual demands of the modern state and to set for it new priorities. Bell believes that the newly developing 'sociologising' mode of thought will energise the drive for greater political participation. Marcuse envisions the liberation of man and the transcendence of capitalist society being inaugurated by the uncivil disobedience of radical students.

Conceptualisations of Society

Last of all among shared concerns, but common only to the thinkers of the contemporary period, is how to conceptualise the nature of advanced societies of today and the trends of their development. The approaches are wholly different. Among the non-Marxists, Aron is concerned with industrial society, Galbraith with the new industrial state, Bell with post-industrial society and Habermas with advanced capitalism. These conceptions, of course, reflect varying interests. None the less, it is noteworthy to find so little agreement about the salient determinants of the future of the advanced societies.

Aron sees no convergence of societies which differ fundamentally in their systems of ownership of the means of production and of economic regulation. The others happen to be concerned only with capitalist societies,[114] but each has a different principal interest: Galbraith in the large corporation, Bell in the changing occupational structure and Habermas in the working, and legitimacy, of government administration. They do indeed share concerns for the advance of science and for the increasing role of government, but these factors also they place in different conceptual frameworks.

For Galbraith the advance of science and the growth of government go hand in hand in increasing government expenditure on research and development. This produces in turn both the power of the technostructure within and outside the corporation and the interdependence of the major corporations and government; and also, with its potentiality for opposition, the development of the educational and scientific estate. For Bell, the advance of science leads to the growing importance of the universities and research institutions, the sites of the new knowledge resources, and to the new dominance of scientists, research personnel and a new professional and technical stratum. Government intervention underwrites the development of science and technology, as with Galbraith, but it also makes possible the trend to a new sphere of economic management, the 'public household', in which state revenues and expenditure become used for the satisfaction of public needs and wants. What is shared is a belief in a new knowledge elite and a recognition that scientific advance is now dependent on the funding provided by government.

For Habermas, however, the advance of science has on the one hand led to the development of the technology of decision-making and to an almost complete reliance on experts, which seems almost to oust the layman from any decision-making role, and on the other, through the secularisation of knowledge, to the collapse of traditional world-views and sources of motivation. The growth of government intervention has caused the submergence of traditional class conflict, and, in default of any theory or ideology of intervention, has involved government in efforts at crisis management which continually reduce the rationality and legitimacy of its actions.

The two neo-Marxists, Mandel and Marcuse, are expressly concerned with late capitalist or monopoly capitalist society, and both, in the Marxist tradition, foretell its doom. Both attach great importance to the development of an ideology of technological rationality and to the diminution of the prospects of revolutionary change as a result of the increasing commercialisation of life. But whereas Mandel soberly assesses the extension of the power and influence of the bourgeoisie as the expanding role of the State is brought under its control, Marcuse searches for the forces that will take over from the now incorporated working class the new revolutionary role of demystifying the consciousness of all who are in thrall to capitalism's affluent society. We may conclude by noting that while the aims and conclusions of the non-Marxist and neo-Marxist thinkers are different, none the less there are many points of agreement in their analyses. We shall further examine their views in the concluding chapter.

Having provided a framework of theoretical ideas, we now turn in the chapters that follow to an examination of major problems in advanced capitalist systems and to description and evaluation of the industrial systems of the Soviet Union and Japan.

Notes

1. The exposition of Marx's thought which follows is a distillation of many readings. Among the best selections of Marx's writings is still Bottomore and Rubel (1963); a commentary of especial value is Kolakowski (1978).

2. Throughout this study the term insight is used in preference to theory. There are no proven theories about societies and their development; there are, however, insights into ways of conceptualising societies and how they change.

3. See, especially, Karl Marx, *The Economic and Philosophic Manuscripts of 1844*, D.J. Struik (ed.) (Lawrence and Wishart, London, 1970).

4. Weber continued, 'acquisition is no longer a means to the end of satisfying his material needs'. Weber (1976), p. 53.

5. Charismatic domination is neither traditional nor modern nor part of any trend. Since it is based on the individual's extraordinary and exceptional powers, it may occur at any time.

6. Weber (1964), p. 337.

7. Ibid.

8. An ideal type has characteristics which no actual entity exemplifies in the fullest degree. But the more an actual organisation exemplifies the characteristics noted by Weber, the more bureaucratic it is.

9. 'Generally speaking', noted Weber, 'the trained permanent official is more likely to get his way in the long run than his nominal superior, the Cabinet minister, who is not a specialist'. Weber (1964), p. 338.

10. Quoted in Herbert Marcuse, 'Industrialization and Capitalism', *New Left Review*, no. 3 (March-April 1965), p. 15.

11. Weber (1964), p. 338.

12. Durkheim (1933), p. 79.

13. Ibid, p. 129. Durkheim called the first form of solidarity 'mechanical' 'by analogy to the cohesion which unites the elements of an inanimate body, as opposed to that which makes a unity out of the elements of a living body'. The second form of solidarity was 'organic' because 'the unity of the organism is as great as the individuation of the parts is more marked'. Durkheim was relating the emergence of this new form of solidarity to the simultaneous growth of individualism. See ibid., pp. 130–1.

14. Ibid., pp. 371–3.

15. Durkheim proposed a modern version of the medieval corporation, which he thought had failed to endure owing to its localism and hence inability to change.

16. Durkheim (1933), p. 24–5.

17. Ibid., p. 28.

18. Aron (1967a), pp. 47–8.

19. Ibid., p. 14.

20. Aron (1976b), Ch. II.

21. As Marx did.

22. Aron (1967a), p. 10.

23. Aron (1967b), Ch. III.

24. Aron (1967a), p. 232.

25. See Clifford Geertz, 'Ideology as a Cultural System', in David Apter (ed.) *Ideology and Discontent* (Free Press, London, 1964).

26. Aron (1967a), p. 234.

27. Galbraith (1967), p. 405. He comments, 'to deal with the complex of change is to deal with the world as it is. A change in one place alerts one to likely changes elsewhere'.

28. Ibid., p. 12.

29. Ibid., p. 59.

30. Galbraith accepts that shareholders have no power. He also judges banks to have little control because large firms tend to use retained earnings for their capital needs in preference to the equity market. Galbraith (1967), Ch. 7.

31. Ibid., p. 163.

32. Galbraith (1974), p. 162.

33. Ibid., p. 172.

34. Planning for Galbraith is evidently the equivalent of 'total administration' for Marcuse, which he asserts to be 'necessary' for the developed 'bourgeois society'. See Marcuse (1968a), p. xiii.

35. The ideal is a cold war, since 'a war without fighting neatly obviates the danger that fighting will stop'. Galbraith (1967), p. 330.

36. Galbraith points out that the planning system is reckless in causing inflation through its indifference to price rises and heedless of its remedies (reduction in public spending, reduction in private borrowing and increases in taxation), being insulated from their main effects. Galbraith (1974), Ch. 19.

37. Galbraith (1967), p. 398.

38. Ibid., p. 398.

39. Ibid., p. 318. He means here by the industrial system the system of large firms linked with government — the planning system.

40. Ibid., p. 399.

41. Bell does not perpetrate the term 'post-industrialism'. He describes industrialism as 'the application of energy and machinery for the mass production of goods'. Bell (1976), p. 14.

42. Bell (1974). Intellectual technology is distinguished from machine or organisational technology: for example, the use of computers for rational decision-making and the substitution of decision rules for intuitive judgement.

43. Bell (1974), Ch. II.

44. Bell (1980), p. 545.

45. Bell (1974), Ch. III.

46. The references are to Gilbert Burck, Fritz Machlup and Jacob Marschak. See Bell (1980).

47. Bell (1974), Ch. III.

48. Bell's category is at different times a stratum, an elite and a class; its qualifying specification varies between technical, professional and scientific. The variation appears to be related to whether his reference is to census categories or wider. See Bell (1974) and Bell (1980).

49. Bell (1980), p. 542. It is not unlikely that Bell, in Bell (1974), contributed to the exaggeration that he here repudiates.

50. Bell (1974), Chs. II and VI; Bell (1976), Ch. 5.

51. Bell (1976), Introduction and Ch. 6.

52. Bell (1974), Ch. IV.

53. Bell (1976), Ch. 6.

54. The three contradictions are: (1) within the polity (state bureaucracy vs. participatory politics); (2) in the ideological sphere (economising vs. sociologising); and (3) between the social structure and the culture. It is not self-evident that they are separate, but Bell treats them apart.

55. Bell (1976) is an exploration of this area of contradiction. See the Introduction for a summary statement of Bell's thesis.

56. Bell (1980), pp. 504–505 and 515.

57. Bell's account of the 'information society' leans heavily on the analysis of Marc Porat which is discussed in Chapter 5 below. For Porat's full analysis see Marc Uri Porat, *The Information Economy* (Stanford University Press, Stanford, Calif., 1976).

58. Habermas (1976a), p. 69.

59. Habermas is arguably the major European sociological theorist since World War II. The corpus of his work is large and complex. This section is based upon relatively few sources: Habermas (1971), Chs. 4–6; (1976a); (1976b); (1979), Ch. 5. For wider discussions of his work the reader is referred to Anthony Giddens, *Profiles and Critiques in Social Theory* (Macmillan, London, 1982), Chs. 7–8; David Held, *Introduction to Critical Theory: Horkheimer to Habermas* (Hutchinson, London, 1980); McCarthy (1978); and Thompson and Held (1982).

60. David Held, 'Crisis Tendencies, Legitimation and the State', Ch. 10 in Thompson and Held (1982), p. 184.

61. Habermas gives a critique of the creed of the specially privileged technological rationality prevalent in the West. To Habermas the worship of science and technology is itself irrational and a matter of value judgement; thus the scientific endeavour does not occur in a value-free realm. The facade of the objective necessity of technological development masks the social interests that actually determine it. See Jurgen Habermas, *Theory and Practice* (Heinemann, London, 1974), 254–76.

62. Habermas (1971), Ch. 5, p. 63.

63. Ibid., pp. 63–4.

64. Habermas calls this the decisionistic model.

65. Habermas (1971), p. 67.

66. Ibid., Ch. 4, p. 61.

67. We use the term neo-Marxist to denote those thinkers who have applied a Marxist perspective to subject matter that Marx himself could not have examined, for example, to forms of capitalism that had not developed in Marx's lifetime.

68. This section draws solely on Mandel's major study, Mandel (1975), but upon his social and political as against his economic analysis, upon Chs. 12–18.

69. This term, used by Mandel, covers government and administration, politicians and civil servants.

70. The quotations are from Mandel (1975), pp. 501 and 487.

71. Ibid., p. 569.

72. Ibid., pp. 567–8.

73. Because of Marcuse's emergence as a guru of the New Left in the late 1960s and early 1970s and because of the criticism of him (from all directions) that this attracted, readers may have firm views as to his standing and as to which of his ideas are important. As with the other theorists, only the ideas judged relevant to this study will be discussed.

74. Marcuse (1968a), 'The Concept of Essence', p. 73.

75. Marcuse (1968b), p. 26. Compare this with Galbraith's statement that 'many of the desires of the individual are no longer even evident to him. They become so only as they are synthesized, elaborated, and nurtured by advertising and salesmanship'. John Kenneth Galbraith, *The Affluent Society* (Penguin Books, Harmondsworth, 1962), p. 14.

76. Marcuse (1972), p. 14.

77. Marcuse (1941), p. 143.

78. Marcuse (1968b), p. 22.

79. Marcuse vividly writes 'the slaves of developed industrial civilization are sublimated slaves, but they are slaves'. Ibid., p. 41.

80. Marcuse (1969), p. 25.

81. Marcuse (1941), p. 151.

82. Marcuse (1972), Ch. 1.

83. Marcuse (1968a), p. 262.

84. The question may be raised, as by Berki, whether under a system in which all are oppressed there are oppressors who 'benefit'. See R.N. Berki, 'Marcuse and the Crisis of the New Radicalism: From Politics to Religion?', *The Journal of Politics*, vol. 34, no. 1 (1972), pp. 56–92.

85. Marcuse (1969), p. 74.
86. Marcuse (1941), p. 145.
87. Ibid., p. 154.
88. Marcuse (1968a), Ch. VI, p. 224.
89. Ibid., Ch. VI, pp. 223–5.
90. Marcuse (1941), pp. 146 and 152.
91. These needs are principally moral, aesthetic and erotic. See Marcuse (1972), Ch. 1 and David Kettler, 'Herbert Marcuse: The Critique of Bourgeois Civilization and its Transcendence' in Anthony de Crespigny and Kenneth Minogue (eds.) *Contemporary Political Philosophers* (Methuen, London, 1976).
92. Herbert Marcuse, *Five Lectures* (Allen Lane: The Penguin Press, London, 1970), p. 77.
93. Herbert Marcuse, *Eros and Civilization: A Philosophical Inquiry into Freud* (Sphere Books, London, 1969), p. 190. Marcuse continues, 'order is freedom only if it is founded on and sustained by the free gratification of the individual'.
94. Alasdair MacIntyre, *Marcuse* (Fontana, London, 1970), Chs. 1 and 3.
95. The phrase is from Marcuse (1941), p. 149.
96. Freud was certainly for Marcuse an example of an intelligence transcending the limitations imposed by internal repression. Marcuse set out to reconcile the insights of Marx and Freud, with only indifferent success; but his attempts in this direction are peripheral to the focus of this study. See MacIntyre, *Marcuse*, Ch. 4.
97. Marcuse (1968b), Ch. VIII, p. 252.
98. Ibid., p. 63. The phrase 'the Great Refusal' was originated by the philosopher Whitehead.
99. Marcuse (1969), p. 9.
100. Marcuse (1968b), p. 256.
101. He calls the student body 'the ferment of hope in the overpowering and stifling capitalist metropoles: it testifies to the truth of the alternative — the real need, and the real posibility of a free society'. Marcuse (1969), p. 60.
102. Marcuse, *Eros and Civilization*, p. 20.
103. Marcuse (1969), p. 69.
104. Ibid., pp. 72 and 81.
105. Marcuse (1972), p. 47.
106. Kettler, 'Herbert Marcuse'.
107. Marcuse (1969), p. 90.
108. Marcuse (1968a), pp. 80–1.
109. The issue is broader than what Jones calls the who/whom? question, itself based on Lenin's 'who does what to whom?'. See Jones (1982), Ch. 8. It is narrower than the consideration of stratification systems.
110. This is firmly brought out by Marcuse and acknowledged by Mandel.
111. The same point is made by Aron, as noted above.
112. See above, p. 11.
113. See note 86 above.
114. Bell is not necessarily so, since socialist societies can (and presumably will), following Bell, become 'post-industrial societies'; none has yet reached the point of becoming so.

Select Bibliography

Aron, Raymond (1967a) *18 Lectures on Industrial Society* (Weidenfeld and Nicolson, London)
_____ (1967b) *The Industrial Society: Three Essays on Ideology and Development* (Weidenfeld and Nicolson, London)
Bell, Daniel (1974) *The Coming of Post-Industrial Society* (Heinemann, London)
_____ (1976) *The Cultural Contradictions of Capitalism* (Heinemann, London)
_____ (1980) 'The Social Framework of the Information Society' in Tom Forester (ed.), *The Microelectronic Revolution* (Basil Blackwell, Oxford)
Bottomore, Thomas B. and Rubel, Maximilien (eds.) (1963) *Karl Marx: Selected Writings in Sociology and Social Philosophy* (Penguin Books, Harmondsworth and London)
Durkheim, Emile (1963) *The Division of Labour in Society* (Free Press, Glencoe, Illinois)
Galbraith, John Kenneth (1967) *The New Industrial State* (Hamish Hamilton, London)
_____ (1974), *Economics and the Public Purpose* (Andre Deutsch, London)
Habermas, Jurgen (1971) *Towards a Rational Society* (Heinemann, London)
_____ (1976a) *Legitimation Crisis* (Heinemann, London)
_____ (1976b) 'Problems of legitimation in late capitalism', in Paul Connerton (ed.), *Critical Sociology* (Penguin Books, Harmondsworth and London)
_____ (1979) 'Legitimation problems in the Modern State', Chapter 5 of *Communication and the Evolution of Society* (Heinemann, London)
Kolakowski, Leszek (1978) *Main Currents of Marxism: Its Rise, Growth and Dissolution*, Vol. I (Clarendon Press, Oxford)
McCarthy, Thomas (1978) *The Critical Theory of Jurgen Habermas* (Hutchinson, London)
Mandel, Ernest (1975) *Late Capitalism* (New Left Books, London)
Marcuse, Herbert (1941) 'Some Social Implications of Modern Technology', *Studies in Philosophy and Social Science*, Vol. IX (1941), 414–39. Reprinted in Arato, Andrew and Gebhardt, Eike (eds.), *The Essential Frankfurt School Reader* (Basil Blackwell, Oxford, 1978). Page references are to the 1978 reprint.
_____ (1968a) *Negations: Essays in Critical Theory* (Penguin London)
_____ (1968b) *One-Dimensional Man* (Sphere Books, London)
_____ (1969) *An Essay on Liberation* (Pelican Books, Harmondsworth)
_____ (1972) *Counterrevolution and Revolt* (Beacon Press, Boston)
Thompson, John B. and Held, David (eds.) (1982) *Habermas: Critical Debates* (Macmillan, London)
Weber, Max (1964) *Theories of Social and Economic Organisation* (Free Press, Glencoe, Illinois)
_____ (1976) *The Protestant Ethic and the Spirit of Capitalism* (George Allen and Unwin, London)

PART TWO

ISSUES FOR ADVANCED CAPITALIST SYSTEMS

3 THE CONTROL OF CORPORATE POWER

It does not seem to be useful or necessary to give a description of the most familiar and best documented industrial system, that of West European and North American capitalist societies. In place of this we turn immediately to three issues of principal importance for the current development of capitalist industrial systems: in this chapter to the control of corporate power, and in the following chapter to the impact of automation and the shift to services.

The Significance of Large Companies

What is significant about the growth of very large companies[1] in the advanced capitalist countries is their dominance over the economies of these countries. This development both changes the economic life of these societies and even challenges the supremacy of government. In the case of the multinational company the sovereignty of other governments (in 'host' countries) and the character of the economic and social development of other societies are also influenced and even threatened.

The concentration of economic resources and achievement among large companies is spectacular. In 1973 in the United States 50 companies accounted for 34.8 per cent of the sales of the 1500 companies quoted on the New York Stock Exchange (and 20.9 per cent of all US companies); 40.8 per cent of the assets (17 per cent of all companies); 38.9 per cent of total net profits (34.5 per cent of all companies); and 47 per cent of the market value of the 1500 companies (34.4 per cent of all US companies). The largest ten companies accounted for 48 per cent of the sales of the largest 50; 46 per cent of the assets; 61 per cent of the profits and 52 per cent of the market value (which was 24 per cent of the market value of all New York quoted companies).[2]

Also in 1973 among US industrial companies alone the largest 500 (by sales) accounted for 65 per cent of the sales of all industrial companies, 83 per cent of the assets and 79 per cent of net profits; in 1955 they had accounted for 58 per cent, 64 per cent and 77 per cent respectively. The largest 1,000 industrials in 1973 accounted for 72

51

per cent of the sales and 85 per cent of net profits; and the largest 200 accounted for 72 per cent of the sales of the largest 1000 and 77 per cent of net profits. The largest 100 industrials accounted in 1972 for 41 per cent of the sales of all US industrial companies, for 47 per cent of the assets and for 51.5 per cent of net profits. Another indication of growth is that in 1941 the largest 1000 industrials accounted for 61 per cent of the total assets of all industrial companies, a share held in 1970 by the largest 207; and the 38 per cent share of total assets accounted for in 1941 by the largest 100 industrials was held in 1970 by the largest 53.[3]

In the British case, even if the documentation is less full, the concentration is equally evident. In 1969 the 100 largest companies accounted for 60 per cent of the total market value of the 2765 companies quoted on the London Stock Exchange, as against 50 per cent in 1963; and the largest 40 for 45 per cent of the total market value.[4] In 1970 the 100 largest manufacturing companies accounted for 41 per cent of manufacturing net output, as against 37 per cent in 1963. While 50 per cent of manufacturing output was accounted for by the largest 240 manufacturing companies in 1963, this share was produced by 140 companies in 1970.[5] In the mid-1970s, according to Scott, the largest 100 British industrial companies accounted for 62 per cent of the sales of all industrial companies, 64 per cent of the assets and 69 per cent of the profits; the largest 50 accounted for 48 per cent, 49 per cent and 56 per cent of the sales, assets and profits respectively of all industrial companies; and the largest 10 accounted for 24 per cent of the sales of the largest 1000 industrial companies.[6]

It would be hard to gainsay the commanding position achieved by very large companies in Britain and the USA, one that dominates their economies regardless of the sheer number of small companies that remain in business.[7] Similar evidence could be produced in relation to other capitalist countries, but it will suffice to refer to other countries solely in relation to the sub-set of the largest companies of all, the multinationals.

The Separation of Ownership and Control

The most vexed issue among social scientists in relation to industrial companies is the question of the separation of ownership and control: in essence, how the development of the joint-stock company, to take the place of companies wholly managed and controlled by their owners, led to a divorce of ownership and control and to a divergence of interests between owners (that is, shareholders) and controllers. There have proved to be a number of subsidiary issues related to, confused with and subsumed under this main question, and several of them have been well treated in the literature. Yet a comprehensive view of them all has not yet been taken.

The Conventional Wisdom

The conventional wisdom on the main issue, all commentators are agreed, was enunciated in the pioneering work of Berle and Means published first in 1932.[8] Berle and Means's principal contentions were that among the 200 largest non-financial corporations in the US in 1930 there was a variety of types of control in accordance with different patterns of shareholding and that control was in the hands of non-owners in the majority of companies. The cause of these developments was the dispersion of share ownership: the larger the company, the greater the multitude of shareholders and the less their share in, and thence control over, the company. The consequences were the dissolution of the traditional unity of property into control on the one hand and beneficial ownership on the other and the emergence of a new group of controllers, the directors and managers of the companies, with interests different from those of shareholders. In the long term, management control of companies and the divergence of interests of owners and management were both likely to grow.

Berle and Means's method was to classify the 106 largest industrial companies, the 52 largest public utility companies and the 42 largest railroad companies into five categories of control, meaning by 'control' the power to select the board of directors or a majority of its members by exercising a legal right of selection or by exerting influential pressure. If they could identify a shareholding group owning 80 per cent or more of a company's stock, the company was classed as private. If an individual or a shareholding group held from 50 per cent to less than 80 per cent of a company's stock, it was classed as controlled by a majority of the shareholders; while if a group held from 20 per cent to under 50 per cent of the stock, the company was classed as minority-controlled.[9] If no group or groups held as much as 20 per cent of the stock, the company was deemed to be management-controlled. Their final category was 'control by a legal device', in such situations as pyramiding or where there was a

Table 3.1: Percentage Distribution of Control of 200 Largest US Non-financial Companies, 1930[10]

	Private controlled	Majority controlled	Minority controlled	Controlled by legal device	Management controlled
No. of companies	6	5	23	21	44
Company wealth	4	2	14	22	58

large element of non-voting stock or when a voting trust held the majority of stock.

On the basis of this classification Berle and Means found the distribution of control among the 200 companies that is set out in Table 3.1. In sum, 65 per cent of the companies they found to be under control of management or a legal device and not owner-controlled; and in terms of wealth the companies were 80 per cent not owner-controlled.

They characterised management control as a situation in which small shareholders hand over their votes in the selection of directors to individuals who are beyond their control and in whose election they do not participate. They noted that 'the proxy machinery has . . . become one of the principal instruments not by which a stockholder exercises power over the management of the enterprise, but by which his power is separated from him',[11] and Berle, a lawyer, later commented that directors 'are not agents of the stockholders and are not obliged to follow their instructions'.[12]

Beyond the shift in control is the divergence of interests. The shareholder's principal wants are that the company should make the maximum profit compatible with a reasonable degree of risk and that as large a proportion of the profits should be distributed as the company's best interests permit. Under management control, however, the controlling individual is likely to want personal profit, power, prestige and the gratification of professional zeal; and the less his shareholding, the more opportunities to profit at the company's expense will appear directly to his benefit. And Berle and Means quote Adam Smith's comment on joint-stock companies in their support: 'Negligence and profusion . . . must always prevail, more or less, in the management of the affairs of such a company'.[13] Managers, it would seem, were taking over control of the giant corporations and going their own sweet, divergent way.[14]

Berle and Means's study, despite its deficiencies, influenced the nature of investigations of the ownership and control issue for many years because directly or indirectly it raised so many questions in a critically interesting area. The only dispute at first was over what proportion of stock gave a shareholder or group of shareholders effective control of a company. In 1937 the US Securities and Exchange Commission, taking 10 per cent of stock as giving effective control, considered 70 per cent of the 200 largest non-financial companies to be owner-controlled — in sharp contrast to Berle and Means's 34 per cent; and among the remaining 30 per cent it could find no centre of control.[15] But in 1963 Larner, also taking 10 per cent as a controlling share of stock, found 84 per cent of the largest 200 non-financial companies to be management-controlled and 75 per cent of the largest 500.[16] Larner also found none of the largest 200 companies to be privately owned (using Berle and Means's 80 per cent stock-ownership definition) and only 5 among the largest 500. He concluded that, while in 1929 the managerial revolution had been caught by Berle and Means in process, by 1963 the revolution was complete.

In the period from 1930 to 1963 the actual size of the largest US corporations had of course increased. By 1930, in Larner's view, not all the largest 200 had yet reached an absolute size at which all shareholding individuals must lose control, but by 1963 all of the largest 500 had done so.

Larner's work did, however, differ severely from Berle and Means's on the question of divergence of interests. On the one hand he found that although management-controlled companies were less profitable than owner-controlled, the difference was only marginal, and that there was no difference between types of control in the readiness to take risks.[17] On the other hand he noted, for the group of companies in which he studied managerial compensation (that is, remuneration, dividends, stock options and average annual capital gains), that only the rate of company profit (and not, for example, sales) was significantly related to managerial income.[18] Larner concluded, 'it would appear that the nature of financial incentives and the structure of pecuniary rewards in management-controlled corporations are such that executive compensation and income have been tied to the diligence of managers in pursuing the interest and welfare of stock-holders'.[19] Thus, while the separation of ownership and control is complete by 1963, the effect upon company profits and shareholders' welfare is evidently of little significance.

Berle and Means's study was wholly an armchair exercise, which exposed them to the criticism of having taken plausible assumptions to be true without troubling to subject them to empirical test. Yet Larner made a less excusable error in confusing armchair analysis and empirical test: he tested for the effects of different forms of control without having checked against reality his arbitrary classification of companies in relation to types of control. Burch, the next analyst in this tradition, was more careful. First, he widened his data base by supplementing information from *Fortune* with data from many business journals and other published sources. Second, he broadened his concept of family control to comprise not only a holding of 4.5 per cent or more of the voting stock of a company but also family representation on the board of directors over an extended period of time (ten or more years). In fact Burch classified this situation as one of 'probable family control', while cases showing signs of family influence but with shortcomings in the data he deemed 'possible family control'. Burch's analysis of the largest 300 US industrial companies (on a sales basis) in 1965 is shown in Table 3.2.

Table 3.2: Percentage Distribution of Control among 300 Largest US Industrial Companies, 1965

	Largest 300	Largest 200	Largest 100	Largest 50
Probable family control	45	40	36	20
Possible family control	15	18	20	22
Probable management control	40	42	44	58

Burch concluded that there was enduring family influence among the largest industrial companies and that the case for the managerial revolution had been greatly overstated. Put another way, Burch's findings show that while the shareholders in general may be distinct from the directors and managers of the leading industrial companies and while the *majority* of shareholders may have little or no influence over the conduct of senior management, none the less in 1965 *some shareholders* may have exercised a controlling influence over the majority of the 100 largest US industrial companies and almost certainly did do so over more than a third of them.[20] Burch's work helps to show the danger of leaping from the fact of the dispersion of ownership among a multitude of shareholders to the plausible idea that no shareholders have any control. In fact the dispersion of share-ownership may itself allow a shareholder or group of shareholders who hold what is absolutely a small proportion of stock to exercise controlling influence over the management of a very large company.[21] Whether a shareholder or group of shareholders actually has this influence is an empirical question in each company's case.[22] There is then no necessary association between a stockholding of 5 per cent or 10 per cent and a certain type of control (minority control or management control). Obviously, increasing size of stockholding indicates an increasing *potential capacity* for control,[23] but whether a specified share of stock in two or a few hands leads in a particular company to the wielding of controlling influence is a matter for empirical determination.

The British Experience

The principal follower of Berle and Means in Britain has been Florence, who in 1951–2 studied the 1,700 largest public companies quoted on the London Stock Exchange. Florence found that the 20 largest shareholders in these companies held, on average, 30 per cent of the voting stock and often as much as 50 per cent. Among the very largest companies (with issued share capital in 1951 of £3 million or more) the 20 largest shareholders held only 19 per cent of the stock (although the 20 largest had held 30 per cent in 1936); while in companies of smaller size — still large and medium large — they held correspondingly more.[24] In the 268 companies of varying size that he studied more intensively Florence pointed out that 20 shareholders from each company represented one-sixth of 1 per cent of all shareholders.[25] The *potential* for shareholder control was clearly in evidence despite the wide dispersion of ownership.

Nyman and Silberston, studying the largest 250 UK firms in 1975, cast doubt on the idea that most large companies are controlled by managements with little proprietary interest in them. They suggest that a 5 per cent holding gives ground for *potential* control, and scope for the exercise of discretion in, for example, effecting change of management. On this basis they calculated that 56 per cent of the 250 companies were potentially owner-controlled and 55 per cent even of the largest 50.[26]

Thus in Britain also the evidence suggests that while ownership and management are distinct and the majority of shareholders can have little influence over the companies whose stock they hold, some few shareholders *may* wield considerable influence. But do they? And if they do, are their interests different from those of the management of the company or of other shareholders? Who are those few potentially powerful shareholders? And who are the directors and managers, and have they a variety of interests that they pursue? It is to these questions that we now turn.

The Role of Company Directors

If control of a company is to be defined as the power to select the board of directors, then it may be assumed that the strategic decisions are taken by the directors and, in addition, that the external part-time directors exercise an important influence over the decision of issues put forward by the full-time management of the company. While the appearance of these propositions is maintained, neither assumption is true.

In the American case the definitive research is that of Mace.[27] It would appear that boards of directors have three generally accepted roles: those of 'establishing basic objectives, corporate strategies and broad policies'; of 'asking key questions' that will keep management under some discipline; and of 'selecting the president'. But even these accepted roles are seldom fulfilled. The board rarely decides; it merely advises and approves, the issues and the proposed decisions being put forward by management. External directors cannot easily ask discerning questions because they lack sufficient knowledge of the company or information about each issue; only management has this information. And the president normally selects the next president. What emerges is that *when directors hold little voting stock* they have no power, since such directors are appointed by management — and not in order to rock the boat. They also lack a high degree of interest: they are likely to be too busy to get to know the business thoroughly and to recognise that their role is to increase their own prestige in exchange for the stature and reputation which they and the institution they represent bring to the board. Large stockholders, however, potentially have some control. They may be family members (of the company's founding family) or trustees or representatives of large institutions, and all of them chosen *because of their influence or from necessity*. These directors may well ask searching questions and wield a degree of control, for only they have the interest to demand the information upon which any significant decision could be based.[28]

In the British case these conclusions are confirmed by Pahl and

Winkler. They found directors on what they called 'pro forma boards' to be largely irrelevant and all board meetings to be carefully prepared for so that 95–99 per cent of all items were simply nodded through. An issue taken to a vote was seen to constitute a failure for management: 'pre-emption is the normal state of affairs'. They emphasise the importance of information control in keeping external directors in the appropriate, undisturbing, degree of ignorance.[29]

Research on directors, then, points to their weakness in the role of scrutinising and monitoring management and to management power to manipulate directors. This implies that control of large companies lies with those who control either information or substantial shareholdings, with management or an elite among shareholders. It is confirmed that control does not lie with shareholders at large.[30]

The Power and Interests of Managers

We have by now established that in the large companies the management (that is, senior executives among whom are the internal directors) has effective control — even if control is defined as the power to select the board of directors by whom the major strategic decisions are taken. The management controls the board of directors through control of the issues and information brought before the board and through choosing candidates for election to the board. It controls the majority, if not all, of the stockholders through the dispersion of ownership, the inactivity of large institutional stockholders and the proxy machinery.[31] As Berle and Means put it, 'The proxy machinery has . . . become one of the principal instruments not by which a stockholder exercises power over the management of the enterprise, but by which his power is separated from him'.[32] Thus the board of directors is a self-perpetuating oligarchy, served by a hierarchy of managers whose self-interest is achieved by pleasing their superiors[33] and who are, for the most part, effectively insulated from external pressures.

But if managers do control the majority of giant corporations, how do they use this power? Do they pursue interests that diverge from those of shareholders? According to the psychological premises of classical economic theory whereby each man pursues his own economic self-interest, the interests of managers (who do not own) and owners (who do not control) must diverge; and managerial theories of the firm have been developed to encompass this view.[34] While shareholders wish to maximise their economic gains, runs the argument, by balancing steady dividend income against appreciation of the market value of their shares, professional managers simply wish to maximise their lifetime incomes. Since income-maximisation is not directly related to company profit-making, in contrast to the owner-entrepreneur's profit-taking, managers will pursue interests that are different from, and wider than, those of shareholders.[35] They will be interested in growth, working capital requirements and internal cash flows, investment opportunities, the record of competitive companies, comfortable industrial relations, market confidence, the company's public image, environmental issues and other matters besides.[36] From the viewpoint of company profits they may be content to 'satisfice'.[37]

Thus runs the argument for divergence of interests. Yet it must be challenged in relation to its two principal assumptions. First, is it the case that the self-interest of managers differs from the self-interest of shareholders? In other words, do managers seek to maximise their lifetime incomes? Second, if the interests of managers are more diffuse than those of owner-managers (at least of yesteryear) are they in fact different from those of shareholders? The evidence indicates that the differences do not exist.

Lewellen's research into the remuneration of top executives of 50 large US manufacturing companies in the period 1940–63 shows clearly that high company profits led to increments to their personal incomes more directly and consistently than any other factor.[38] The 552 senior executives in his study had typically held portfolios of shares in their own companies in the early 1940s worth $400,000–600,000; in the early 1960s their portfolios were typically worth $2 million to $3 million. These men's stock-related remuneration included stock bonuses, stock options, profit-sharing schemes, dividends and capital gains. For the top five executives in each company stock-related returns in the 1940s amounted on average to two-thirds of their total annual compensation; in the 1960s they contributed four-fifths. It does not seem to be incautious of Lewellen to suggest that these men's gains in wealth 'should at least begin to sensitize even the most callous professional manager to the shareholder viewpoint';[39] and to conclude that it is very much in the self-interest of senior executives to perform their duties with paramount regard for the welfare of shareholders. Thus the self-interest of senior executives, assuming it to be the maximisation of their lifetime remuneration, coincides with that of the shareholders.

But then there is no evidence from empirical research that there is any divergence of interest, and a more proper null hypothesis would be that the fortunes of managers are coincident with the fortunes of their companies on the ground that it is by the harsh test of the market place that both managers and companies are assessed.[40] Certainly it is in the market that company performance is continually appraised. The appraisal, which assumes the good faith of management, would be undermined, with consequences for the company, should it appear that managers were making excessive gains for themselves. There is no well attested difference in performance between owner-controlled and professional-manager-controlled companies.[41] The threat of mergers and, in Manne's phrase, 'the market for corporate control' whips all less profitable companies equally into line.[42] Seider, in an unusual study of publicly expressed attitudes, found no differences between company executives in accord with different types of control.[43] Pahl and Winkler found among financially oriented managers 'a new ethic of hard capitalism' and 'rigorous and exclusive dedication to financial values'. In comparing professional managers with family owner-managers they concluded: 'not only were they more oriented to profit, they were more capable of obtaining it'.[44]

If we summarise the argument thus far, we may suppose it established that the interests of managers do not in general differ from the interests of owner-managers or owners (that is, shareholders), and many commentators have reached that conclusion.[45] But the conclusion assumes the equivalence of owner-managers (with their aura of traditional entrepreneurship) with shareholders, although we know the latter to be a very varied group. If this cannot be justified, the conclusion may not hold.

The Role of Investors

It may be helpful at the outset to employ a new word in place of shareholder or stockholder, with its emphasis on legal ownership. It is doubtful that shareholders think of themselves as part-*owners* of giant corporations; they are much more likely to think of themselves as *investors*.

Individual Investors. The average individual investor has no aspirations for either ownership or control. He and his fellows no longer provide most of the company's 'risk capital'. He knows that the shareholders' meeting is 'a kind of ancient meaningless ritual'.[46] He merely estimates the chances of steady dividend income or of the company's shares increasing in value. If his interest is in income, he is likely to spread his investments across several companies. If it is in capital gain, he may take more risks. In any event a disappointing outcome merely leads him to switch his investments with a freedom denied to a true owner.[47]

The great majority of individual shareholders hold small numbers of shares. Thus in 1970 individuals were 95 per cent of the shareholders on the London Stock Exchange but they held only 46.2 per cent of the total market value of the shares and the average value of their holdings was £1,320. In contrast, institutions were 5 per cent of the shareholders and held 53.8 per cent of the total market value of shares; among them the average value of holdings was £27,172 for banks and nominee companies, £30,000 for investment trusts, £31,655 for pension funds and £75,925 for insurance companies.[48]

Among the individuals, however, are some with very large holdings. In Britain in 1976, while 80 per cent of all individually owned shares were held by 5 per cent of the population, 54 per cent were held by the wealthiest 1 per cent.[49] In the US in 1970 just over 1 per cent of the population held 58 per cent of all individually owned shares.[50] This suggests again that, despite the distinction between ownership and control and despite the weakness and disinterest in ownership of the majority of investors there remains a residual small number of very wealthy shareholders with sufficient influence to affect the control even of the largest companies.

Institutional Investors. Even so, it is clearly the institutional investors who signify most. The trend in their favour is clear. In Britain they held in 1959 34 per cent of the total market value of shares on the London Stock Exchange, in 1963 46 per cent, in 1969 54 per cent and in 1975 62.5 per cent.[51] In the US in 1968 institutional investors owned 33 per cent of the value of stocks listed on the New York Stock Exchange;[52] in 1972 they held over 45 per cent.[53] Their share in the total volume of trading rose from 29 per cent in 1961 to 52 per cent in 1971.[54] Thus, while the share of institutional holdings may be less in the US than in Britain, the trend is equally clear. Also evident is the preference among the institutional investors for large companies.[55]

The secular trend is due to the massive growth of pension and welfare funds and specialist investment companies, to the accumulation of individual savings stimulated by tax incentives,[56] and to the shift of trust investments, as the result of inflation, from fixed-income securities to common stocks. As a result, institutional investors now dominate the stock markets of the world, with financial institutions pre-eminent among them, to an extent that warrants separate consideration below.

Their potential influence is obviously great even if seldom wielded. Their interest in general we may hypothesise to be in steady returns and stable performance over time and their normal policy to vote in support of management. Large corporations have reciprocal business dealings with each other to sustain and a mutual desire to preserve their relationships. They may be supposed to be reluctant to offend each other for fear of losing access to inside information, but the sheer difficulty of selling a very large holding in a company also encourages institutional investors to secure management performance consonant with their interests. Little is known of what behind-the-scenes influence is exercised but in Blumberg's words, 'although evidence is lacking, it taxes credulity to believe that such activity never takes place'.[57]

We are here, admittedly, in the sphere of surmise, where research into potential influence has to suffice in the absence of studies of the actual exercise of power. It is within this context that an investigation of institutional linkages through the device of interlocking directorships must fall.

The Significance of Interlocking Directorships

If we now bring together two intermediate conclusions of our argument thus far, that a few massive shareholdings in the hands of individuals or families remain significant for the control of some large companies and that institutional investors, rather than managers, are the newly influential agents in the arena of corporate control, we arrive at the hypothesis that all these agents will manifest their potential influence on the boards of directors of the dominant companies. Further, if we suppose that these agents have a joint interest, beyond their several, localised interests in the security of their own institutions, in the maintenance of the system[58] within which their institutions flourish, then we may hypothesise the existence of a structure of interrelationships manifested in the interlinking of boards of directors. This is exactly what the evidence reveals.

In the US the most substantial study is that of Warner and Unwalla carried out in 1961. They studied 500 of the largest representative corporations which had, between them, 5,776 directors (of whom 4,376 were company executives).[59] These directors held more than

20,000 directorships between them, interlinking the 500 firms with 8,372 others. Among the executives 9 per cent were directors of 10 or more companies and the 3,696 who were managers in the largest firms held over 10,000 directorships between them, 60 per cent of these in other large firms. This study certainly revealed a system of interlocking directorships.

In 1962 the US Federal Trade Commission found the 200 largest industrial companies to have 476 interlocks with each other and 974 with other companies among the 1,000 largest industrials.[60] Dooley, in his study of the 200 largest non-financial and the 50 largest financial corporations in 1965, found that 3,165 directors held 4,007 directorships and that the 200 non-financial companies had 616 interlocks with the 50 financial companies.[61] The larger the company, the more interlocks it had. Dooley identified tightly knit geographically based groups of companies with banks and insurance companies at the core of each group. He concluded, 'the institution of the interlocking directorate is extensive and enduring'.[62] The key role of financial institutions is further emphasised by Barber's report for 1968 that 324 out of the 373 board members of the 15 largest commercial banks held over 1,500 directorships.[63]

Finally, in their study of directors from the *Fortune* 500 in 1969, Sonquist and Koenig found 8,623 holding 11,290 directorships in a total of 797 companies. They also found 401 of the 500 companies to be interconnected and to form 32 cliques of companies with from 3 to 15 in each clique. In looking at the cliques they found four-fifths to have at the centre one bank or more and about half to be dominated by a single bank.[64]

In Britain there is less evidence but what there is is consistent with that for the US. Among 40 leading industrial companies Whitley found 36 links between boards of directors and 21 interlocks. When he added to the 40 companies 27 leading financial institutions he found 62 interlinks and 56 interlocks among the 67 companies.[65] Among the 50 major companies that they studied in 1970 Stanworth and Giddens found 29 interlinks; also 22 of the 50 accounted for 37 links with clearing banks, 15 accounted for 24 links with 10 merchant banks and 18 had 27 links with 7 insurance companies. Overall they identified a network of 73 companies with 193 interlinks.[66]

Thus a system of interlocking directorships exists just as clearly as it did (at least in the US) in 1914 when Justice Brandeis attacked it as a suppression of competition, a tendency to disloyalty, a source of inefficiency and undemocratic, 'substituting the pull of privilege for the push of manhood'.[67] But the system has changed. The interconnections between powerful corporations may involve some wealthy individuals and families but the massive concentrations of wealth and consequential influence are now in the hands of faceless institutions and pre-eminently in those of the major financial institutions. The web of influence is scarcely visible, even less any tightening of its threads. But it deserves consideration on its own.

The Web of Influence of Financial Institutions

Although the growing importance of institutional investors has already been brought out, that of financial institutions has not yet been sufficiently emphasised. The shareholdings of financial institutions, in the US and in Britain, now suffice to give them the capacity to influence the commanding heights of the economy in each society.

We may first demonstrate the concentration of influence within the financial world itself. In the US the Patman Committee found that in 1964 the 100 largest US commercial banks held 46 per cent of all deposits held by all 13,775 commercial banks, and the largest 14 held 24 per cent of all deposits. The Committee also found that of the 210 largest commercial banks 120 held more than 5 per cent of their own shares and 61 held more than 10 per cent.[68]

The holdings of financial institutions in the stocks of industrial companies are massive. In the US in 1968, according to Barber, banks held 60 per cent of all institutional investors' assets (that is, stock worth $600 billion) and managed a further $125 billion held in private trust accounts. Just 49 banks held over half of total bank trust assets, and thus effectively held control of 150 out of the largest 500 industrial companies. The 49 banks also had representatives on 300 of the 500 boards of directors.[69] In 1973 the 13 largest banks' trust departments held more than 5 per cent of the shares in 9 out of the 10 largest industrial companies in the US, in 47 out of the 100 largest and in 80 out of the 200 largest companies; they held more than 10 per cent of the shares in 6 of the 10 largest companies and in 30 out of the 100 largest companies.[70] Allen reports the 7 largest New York banks as holding 11 per cent of the shares of 25 of the 99 largest industrial companies.[71]

The banks are also most heavily represented in the network of linked directorships. Warner and Unwalla, in 1961, found bank executives to hold proportionately more external directorships than other executives.[72] Smith and Desfosses, in 1968, found bankers to constitute 21 per cent of all external directors of the 500 largest industrial companies and that 11 per cent of the commercial bankers among the directors and 15 per cent of the investment bankers among them sat on three or more boards of the 500 companies, while only 6 per cent of the industrial directors did so.[73] Allen, in 1970, found that bank chairmen held disproportionately more interlocking directorships among the 800 largest US companies than any other category of director.[74]

In Britain the shareholdings of financial institutions grew in value from £12,240 million in 1952 to £23,970 million in 1962 and £43,310 million in 1972. In 1957 the financial institutions held 18 per cent of all shares quoted on the London Stock Exchange. In 1973 they held 40 per cent.[75] We have already noted the part played by these institutions in the British network of interlocking directorships. There is no reason to suppose a lesser concentration of influence of financial institutions in Britain than in the USA.

If, then, there is a web of influence linking the major financial institutions (within each of the two societies) with each other and with the largest and the dominant industrial corporations, through cross-shareholding and interlocking directorships, what is its significance? The truth is, we cannot estimate it. We have identified a web of inter-connections and can claim this as evidence of a community of interest and of a capacity for common action. But we cannot catalogue instances of common action, which, if it occurs, we would expect normally to be veiled; and we cannot estimate the effects of a potentiality which may for the most part not need to be realised.

Despite this necessary caution, we can still assert the existence of a community of interest shared by the very largest and dominant corporations of capitalist societies and, by sociological inference, acknowledge a normative set of perceptions, interests and values.[76] It does not seem imprudent for Zeitlin to suggest that in the US the largest banks and corporations follow 'the *general* proprietary interests of the owners of capital',[77] nor for Blumberg to refer to 'the control of the economy by a relatively small unrepresentative, self-selected group, with like background, experience and values, inclined to have a common view on the underlying problems of business and the nation, who comprise an elite which dominates the centers of power'.[78] But to repeat these conclusions is not simply to affirm traditional class theory, because that would require evidence that the small group of wealthy men, who head the major corporations or have substantial stockholdings in them, form a social class or recognisably represent the interests of a defined class and are conscious of so doing; and that remains unproven. We merely assert the concentration of potential control in the hands of a small elite. The legitimacy of this is an issue that we discuss below.

The Challenge of Multinational Companies

There is at present no sociology of multinational companies,[79] but it is not the purpose of this section to fill the gap. Our limited objective is to establish that questions relating to the control of corporate power have international significance, beyond the frontiers of the nation state. Large multinational companies pose threats to the sovereignty of states. This very fact places the debate about the locus of control of giant companies firmly in the national political arena, where not only the rights of shareholders but the rights of all citizens can be considered.

The Scale of the Issue

A company is properly described as multinational when it manufactures outside its home country. The measure of multinational growth is thus direct foreign investment. Since World War II this growth has been massive.

Between 1946 and 1969 the book value of direct US foreign investment rose from $7,200 million to $70,763 million[80] (a value equivalent to one-fifth of the total assets of the 500 largest US companies). At that time the US exported approximately $43,000 million worth of goods and services but produced overseas to the value of $110,000 million. Of the 100 largest US industrial companies 62 had production facilities in six or more overseas countries, while 71 of the largest 126 companies on average employed one-third of their labour force overseas.[81] In 1971 the value of direct US foreign investment had risen to $86,000 million.[82]

By 1974 the 179 largest US multinationals made 40 per cent of their total sales (worth $500,000 million) through foreign subsidiary companies,[83] the 298 largest US multinationals made 40 per cent of their entire net profits outside the USA and the 7 largest US banks earned 40 per cent of their profits abroad.[84] One-third of the assets of the US chemical industry, one-third of the US pharmaceutical industry's, 40 per cent of US consumer goods industries' and three-quarters of the assets of the US electrical industry were then located outside the USA.[85] By 1976 the yearly sales of US foreign affiliates had risen to $515 billion. By 1978 US private assets overseas amounted to $377 billion and net earnings on overseas investments reached $21 billion.[86]

The scale of operations of multinationals based outside the US is harder to document. In 1971, when US direct foreign investments totalled $86,000 million, those of Europe amounted to $74,500 million (of which the British share was $24,000 million).[87] In 1977 Vernon established a world total of multinational companies of 490, with 250 based in the US, 150 in Europe, 70 in Japan and 20 in other countries (including such Third World countries as Brazil, India, Mexico and South Korea).[88]

In a more detailed examination of 391 multinational companies based in the USA, Europe and Japan, Vernon found the group as a whole to have 10,950 subsidiary companies, 63 per cent in other industrialised countries and 37 per cent in developing countries. He found that the 180 US-based multinationals in his study had 5,727 subsidiary companies (on average 32 subsidiaries each), distributed 63:37 between industrialised and developing countries; the 135 European companies had 4,661 subsidiaries (on average 34.5 each), distributed 69:31; and the 61 Japanese companies had 562 subsidiaries (on average 9 each), distributed 8:92 between industrialised and developing countries.[89] Another way of expressing these data is to state that the 391 multinational companies in Vernon's sample had 6,856 subsidiaries operating in industrialised countries and 4,094 in developing countries. There can be little doubt of the world-wide influence of these giant companies.

Finally, the scale of operations of the very largest multinationals may be noted. In 1978, the 10 largest companies in the world (in terms of sales) which earned more than 50 per cent of their earnings outside the countries of their headquarters[90] earned a total of $295,900 million, approximately 61 per cent or $181,100 million from overseas subsidiaries. In 1979, this same group earned $384,600 million, so that if the balance of earnings was maintained their subsidiaries' earnings may be estimated at approximately $230,760 million.[91] It can be of little surprise that even governments are in some awe of companies operating on this scale.[92]

The Causes of Multinational Development[93]

The basis of all multinational development has been technological innovation or technological advantage. Broadly, US companies have pursued technological innovation for labour-saving reasons while European companies have looked for savings in costs of raw materials and for process innovation. The attraction of multinational development has been the opportunity of growth in new markets free of the cost disadvantages of home markets and of the restrictive legislation of home governments (for example, anti-trust and anti-cartel legislation). US companies have looked for local markets as large as possible where their advanced marketing skills can be brought fully into play.[94] European companies have sought production in lower-income countries with low raw material costs. The growth of multinational companies started in the 1950s, gathering momentum during the 1960s as more industries reached a critical threshold of size, technology and domestic market saturation and as the technology of communications made more manageable the centralisation of control within the wide dispersal of operations.

Once multinationalism has been achieved, the advantages have been real. Negatively, entropy is avoided[95] through the shift, diversification and growth of a company's activities, and especially by the expansion of marketing opportunities. Positively, new freedoms are won: to vary dividends of subsidiary companies at will, to manipulate transfer prices in sales between subsidiaries, to arrange the flow of goods and services so that the highest tax liabilities are incurred in the countries with the lowest tax rates and, worldwide, to maximise profits. With no agency or agencies to limit their endeavours, to date the multinationals' freedom has been little challenged.

The Dilemma of Governments

There is no ignoring the genuine gains that accrue to governments from the activities of foreign-based multinational companies producing within their borders.

Industrialised countries benefit from injections of capital investment and from imported know-how, from increased employment and in-company training opportunities, from increased exports, with benefits to the balance of payments, from increased production adding to the GNP. They collect customs duties and taxes from the companies; the companies purchase local goods and services. US companies are likely to bring the host country into contact with advanced research, new production techniques and new management methods.[96]

For developing countries those benefits also accrue but the position of governments in relation to the multinationals is relatively weak. Frail policies concerning currency exchange rates, the balance of payments or the availability of credit may be threatened by the self-interest of multinational companies moving funds internationally. Governments that, for example, tighten exchange control procedures or closely monitor tax avoidance run the risk of weakening confidence in their currency or undermining multi-national investment. Governments indeed know that multinational companies classify countries according to their 'premium for risk', and hence a policy of nationalisation in order to assert control may simply cause a flight of the assets and resources that it was designed to gear to the support of national interests.[97]

For it is by no means certain that multinational activity brings to developing countries the kind of development that they require. Local investment required to launch local enterprise may be attracted into secure, multinational companies and its profits repatriated overseas. Local talent (including scientists) may be similarly attracted away from local endeavours and exploited for alien gain. Local wealth depletion may keep local consumption levels low and reduce the capacity to develop the local knowledge and ability to create wealth. Funds for R and D may be devoted to technologies suited to advanced economies (short on labour, long on capital) and designed to reduce labour. The multinational companies, in short, for all the new opportunities that they bring, may well squelch local enterprise, introduce 'inappropriate' technology, and interfere with local economic development and growth objectives.[98]

Vernon has pointed out that in all countries industrialisation has led to increases of the visible rich, corruption, shoddy production and pollution. Multinational companies may both stimulate this concentration of wealth and favour a stable environment friendly to business and hence rightist regimes.[99] Thus the companies may retard not only economic development but also the social revolutions required for modernisation.[100] In such circumstances multinational companies, whatever benefits they bring, pose a challenge to government and a threat to sovereignty. In all countries they represent a major concentration of power without responsibility and without legitimacy.[101]

The Question of Legitimacy

The development of very large companies and the concentration of power which they embody and which is in many respects unaccountable has outstripped changes in the legal framework within which they operate. In the United States in the early nineteenth century lawyers viewed corporations as performing public functions in the public interest, but gradually the power to form and control corporations passed from the state into the private hands of promoters and entrepreneurs until by 1870 corporations were thought of as entirely private organisations.[102] It is hard to recognise today that the public interest in the activities of corporations was ever held to be superordinate, yet in 1905 the US Supreme Court affirmed: 'the corporation, insofar as it is a legal entity, is a creation of the state. It is presumed to be incorporated for the benefit of the public . . . Its rights to act as a corporation are only preserved to it as long as it obeys the laws of its creation'.[103]

Today the large corporations impose so powerfully upon the economic and social life of society that it might appear obtuse not to recognise a legitimate public interest in their activities and in their wealth, originating as social property.[104] Beyond this, in Dahl's words, 'every large corporation should be thought of as a political system, that is, an entity whose leaders exercise great power, influence, and control over other human beings', and, Dahl further comments, as 'an entity whose existence and decisions can be justified only insofar as they serve public or social purposes'.[105]

Yet it is not so. The ideology of capitalism continues to assert the sacred privacy of business enterprise, and the powers-that-be continue to fend off challenges to this stance with anti-trust and anti-monopoly legislation. The record suggests, however, that regulatory agencies and procedures have developed laggardly, far more slowly than the growth of corporate power, and have become dominated by the very industries they seek to control[106] to the point where regulation declines into protection and, in Adams's phrase, '. . . instruments of countervailing power degenerate into handmaidens of coalescing power'.[107] Galbraith likewise dismisses anti-trust laws with the comment 'they sustain the hope, and thus perpetuate the myth, of the all-powerful market. Consequently, they keep alive the illusion that business is private'.[108]

We find ourselves sliding into the area of values, of subjective perceptions and judgements, but not wholly so. For the growth and dominance of giant companies is real and thus the power of corporate managers without public accountability is also real. Further, expectations have moved ahead of the law. It is expected and accepted that company executives will act in any legal way for the benefit of their business and will take into account the interests not of the shareholders alone (as the law would require) but also of employers, consumers and the community at large. The law has not changed to take account of new business norms and does not define the permissible limits of executive action.[109] The giant corporations have enormous power (and they are centralised, hierarchical and secretive); they operate within a weak legal framework and often apparently arbitrarily; they are political institutions but only infrequently and often ineffectively regulated; and they cannot be said to be under democratic control. In Berle's words, 'these instrumentalities of tremendous power have the slenderest claim of legitimacy'.[110]

The Weberian Dilemma

We are firmly back with the dilemma recognised by Weber, but it no longer needs his prescience to see it. All organisations are consciously devised by groups of men for the pursuit of specifiable goals and, in Bower's words, 'a large firm is one of the most sophisticated institutions for the conduct of organised purposive behaviour ever invented'.[111] Multinational companies are merely the largest and most powerful of such devices. They have carried the pursuit of efficiency and effectiveness across 'the barriers at the political frontiers of states'.[112] They are much more adaptable than the nation-states 'because their goals are simpler, their bureaucracies are often more authoritarian, their planning cycle is shorter, and fewer conflicting interests need be heard'.[113] Sovereign states, according to Eells, can no longer meet the demands and aspirations of their citizens. As global expectations mount, only the multinational company can overcome the handicaps of balkanisation in the international system of states. The multinational company is 'a partial response to the need for larger geographical reach, for more flexibility in organisational experimentation, for greater latitude in corporate procedure, and, above all, for more imaginative innovation in the design of corporate goals', while the system of fixedly sovereign states is hopelessly anachronistic.[114] In short, the inexorable drive for rationality and efficiency is being impeded, just as Weber foresaw, by an attachment, however weakened, to the values of democracy, to which at least some nation-states remain beholden. It is of the nature of democracy to be inefficient, shambling, fitful and slow, and so at the time when organisations devoted to rationality and efficiency had grown to a size enabling them to match the power and influence of states, potentialities for tension and conflict were inevitable. That time is now. But although the political and social problem is perceived, no theories or policies exist for its solution.

Eells, perhaps taking Galbraith's prediction for prescription, states that a symbiotic relationship of private and public polities is an essential characteristic of contemporary capitalism.[115] He looks forward to new international agencies to regulate the activities of multinational companies and their interactions with nation-states. Adams prefers to put the clock back, by reversing the concentration of power. He quotes Justice Douglas's judgement: 'power that controls the economy should be decentralised. It should be scattered into many hands so that the fortunes of the people will not be dependent on the whim or caprice, the political prejudices, the emotional stability of a few self-appointed men'.[116] Heilbroner just wrings his hands. 'It is only', he writes, 'because we do not know how else to organise large masses of people to perform those tasks essential for society that we have to depend on the nation state with its vicious face and shameful irrationality, and the corporation with its bureaucratic hierarchies and its reliance on greed and carefully inculcated dissatisfaction'.[117]

The issues raised by the challenge of corporate power have now been posed, and it is timely to relate our assessment of it to the ideas set out in Chapter 2. Marx is widely held to have been wrong to suppose that the development of the joint stock company would lead to a divorce of ownership and control that would reduce the exploitative character of capitalism.[118] Yet, even if the divorce is more in form than in substance, the rough edge of the manifestly exploitative stage of capitalism has been blunted and it is still the individual's relationship to the means of production and the control of capital that determines his social and economic power. Weber was entirely right to predict the continuing growth of bureaucracy and its threat to democratic norms of legitimacy, while Durkheim was right to expect the emergence of new occupational structures to provide new bases for organic solidarity and loyalty.

The giant corporations were before the eyes of the contemporary theorists. Our analysis has perhaps provided reasons for the partial dependence of governments upon the largest corporations and underlined the power of these corporations to which both Galbraith and Mandel have drawn attention; it has supported Habermas and Mandel's claims as to the loss of legitimacy of advanced capitalist systems; and it has surely made plausible Marcuse's contention that living under a system in which such vast accretions of corporate power exist, under controls that are veiled if not hidden, strongly induces a sense of mystification.

Notes

1. The terms company, corporation, firm and enterprise are throughout used interchangeably as synonyms for the legal entities in industry.
2. These figures are drawn from Blumberg (1975), by far the most useful source on large US companies. The total number of US corporations in 1973 was of the order of 1.7 million.
3. Blumberg (1975), Ch. 2.
4. Moyle (1971), Chs. 1 and 3.
5. S.J. Prais, *The Evolution of Giant Firms in Britain* (Cambridge University Press, 1976), Ch. 1.
6. Scott (1979), Ch. 1.
7. The argument is not that small companies are crushed out of existence by the giants or are of no significance, nor that the market economy is eliminated by oligopoly; it is simply that a relatively small number of companies have enormous and dominant economic power.
8. Berle and Means (1967). All references will be to the revised edition published in 1967. Berle and Means were exercised about the concentration of corporate wealth, noting that in 1930 the 200 largest non-financial companies controlled 49 per cent of all non-financial corporate wealth and received 43 per cent of the income.
9. Later critics have considered a much smaller proportion of stock than 20 per cent to suffice for minority control. It would appear that John D. Rockefeller's difficulty in mobilising fellow-stockholders of Standard Oil of New Jersey, when he held just under 15 per cent of the stock, behind his much publicised and eventually successful attempt to sack Colonel Stewart, the managing director, convinced them that 20 per cent would normally be necessary.
10. Berle and Means (1967), Ch. V.
11. Ibid., p. 129.
12. Ibid., Preface, p. ix.
13. Ibid., p. 304.
14. We should note that the major debate, following Berle and Means's work, has concerned whether the separation of ownership and control has invalidated Marx's focus on the conflict between the property-owners and the propertyless. The Marxist view is that the exploitative nature of capitalism is made more stark now that owners (shareholders) are so manifestly remote from the labour process. See Michel De Vroey, 'The Separation of Ownership and Control in Large Corporations', *Review of Radical Political Economics*, vol. 7, no. 2 (1975), pp. 1–10. The argument here goes beyond this narrow debate.
15. Quoted in Larner (1970), Ch. 1.
16. Ibid., Ch. 2.

17. Larner tested 187 companies for variations in profitability and 179 for variations in risk-taking over the period 1956–62. Ibid., Ch. 3.

18. Larner's conclusions are based on a study of 94 companies during 1962–3. Ibid., Ch. 4.

19. Ibid., p. 61.

20. Burch (1972). His data sources included SEC reports, *Moody's* manual, Standard and Poor's *Corporation Records, Business Week, Forbes* and the *New York Times*, all over the period 1950–71.

21. See J.R. Wildsmith, *Managerial Theories of the Firm* (Martin Robertson, London, 1973), Ch. 1. Scott writes of 'effective possession' being possibly dissociated from shareholding but possibly in the hands of a sub-set of shareholders, whatever the legalities of ownership. Scott (1979), Ch. 2.

22. In a case-study of the Anaconda Company's activities in Chile in 1971, Zeitlin concluded that, whoever controlled the company, management did not. Zeitlin (1974).

23. Even this statement is too strong for some sceptical critics. See Louis de Alessi, 'Private Property and Dispersion of Ownership in Large Corporations', *Journal of Finance*, vol. xxviii, no. 4 (1973), pp. 839–51.

24. Florence (1961), Ch. VIII.

25. Ibid., Ch. III.

26. Nyman and Silberston believe these figures to be underestimates in view of there being some large private firms excluded altogether and others included in which there were large nominee holdings whose controllers were not identified. Nyman and Silberston (1978).

27. Mace (1971).

28. Before Mace's more empirical research the principal study of this area was that of Gordon. Gordon's work at no point conflicts with Mace's conclusions. See R.A. Gordon, *Business Leadership in the Large Corporation* (University of California Press, Berkeley, 1961).

29. Pahl and Winkler (1974) closely studied the directors of 19 assorted companies. The quotation is from p. 110.

30. Eells confirms this conclusion. He writes, 'the shareowners own only paper claims on the directors of a corporation who, collectively, are the true holders of corporate property.' Eells (1972), p. 87.

31. Blumberg (1975), Ch. 7.

32. Berle and Means (1967), p. 129.

33. Monsen and Downs argue that top management is weakened by self-seeking layers of management below (another instance of the effects of information control) but control still remains within the management hierarchy as a whole. R. Monsen and A. Downs, 'A Theory of Large Managerial Firms', *Journal of Political Economy*, vol. 73 (1965), pp. 221–36.

34. See, for example, W.J. Baumol, *Business Behaviour, Value and Growth* (Macmillan, New York, 1959); R. Marris, *The Economic Theory of Managerial Capitalism* (Macmillan, London, 1964); and O.E. Williamson, *The Economics of Discretionary Behavior: Managerial Objectives in a Theory of the Firm* (Prentice-Hall, Englewood Cliffs, New Jersey, 1964).

35. See Gordon, *Business Leadership in the Large Corporation*, Ch. 14; Monsen and Downes, 'A Theory of Large Managerial Firms'.

36. Wildsmith, *Managerial Theories of the Firm*, Ch. 1.

37. See C. Kaysen, 'The Corporation, How Much Power? What Scope?' in E.S. Mason (ed.), *The Corporation in Modern Society* (Harvard University Press, 1960). The word 'satisfice', now widely used, was originated by Simon. H.A. Simon, *Administrative Behaviour* (Macmillan, New York, 1950).

38. Lewellen (1971). He included in his study of 950 senior executives of 80

companies the 552 highest paid executives in 50 very large manufacturing companies.
39.   Ibid., pp. 86–7.
40.   Blumberg (1975), Ch. 1. Manne agrees with the coincidence except for the fact that managers 'have no incentive, as managers, to buy management services for the company at the lowest possible price'. H. Manne, 'Mergers and the Market for Corporate Control', *Journal of Political Economy*, vol. 73 (1965), pp. 110–21.
41.   Larner's research was inconclusive, as others' has been. In Britain Brown found management-controlled companies more profitable and owner-controlled companies more successful in growth, the opposite of what managerial theorists have predicted. See Michael Barratt Brown, 'The Controllers of British Industry', Ch. 7 in John Urry and John Wakefield (eds.), *Power in Britain: Sociological Readings* (Heinemann, London, 1973). But the research is, overall, inconclusive and contradictory, as might be expected from its simplifying assumptions and naïvety.
42.   Manne, 'Mergers and the Market for Corporate Control'.
43.   He found differences according to sector of industry. Maynard S. Seider, 'Corporate Ownership, Control and Ideology: Support for Behavioral Similarity', *Sociology and Social Research*, vol. 62, no. 1 (1977), pp. 113–28.
44.   Pahl and Winkler (1974), p. 118.
45.   That is certainly the Marxist view. See De Vroey, 'The Separation of Ownership and Control in Large Corporations'.
46.   A.A. Berle, 'Economic Power and the Free Society', Ch. 5 of Andrew Hacker (ed.), *The Corporation Take-Over* (Harper and Row, New York, 1964), p. 95.
47.   A London Stock Exchange survey of 1966 found 43 per cent of shareholders interested in capital appreciation, 40 per cent in income and the remainder in short-term speculation. Quoted in R.J. Briston, 'The Fisons Stockholder Survey: An Experiment in Company-Shareholder Relations', *Journal of Business Policy*, vol. 1, no. 1. (1970), pp. 38–46.
48.   Moyle (1971), Ch. 7.
49.   Royal Commission on the Distribution of Income and Wealth, *An A–Z of Income and Wealth* (HMSO, London, 1980).
50.   Blumberg (1975), Ch. 5.
51.   Moyle (1971), Table 4.2 and M.J. Erritt and J.C.D. Alexander, 'Ownership of Company Shares: a New Survey', Central Statistical Office, *Economic Trends*, no. 287 (HMSO, London, 1970).
52.   Barber (1970), Ch. 4.
53.   Blumberg (1975), Ch. 5.
54.   Ibid.
55.   Ibid., for the US; for Britain, see Prais, *The Evolution of Giant Firms*, Ch. 5.
56.   In the US the number of individual stockholders grew from 6.49 million in 1952 to 17.01 million in 1962, and to 31.7 million in 1972. Blumberg (1975), Ch. 5.
57.   Ibid., p. 134.
58.   By 'system' here is meant no more than a set of connected variables. If companies are in any way interconnected, therefore, they form a system in at least this modest sense.
59.   The 500 included 265 industrial companies, 100 in merchandising, 65 financial, 10 in services and 20 each in transportation, utilities and life insurance. Warner and Unwalla (1967).
60.   Quoted in Blumberg (1975), Ch. 8.
61.   The term 'interlock' signifies that each of two companies has a representative on the other's board. An 'interlink' need not be reciprocal.
62.   Dooley (1969). His companies, drawn from *Fortune* magazine's listing for 1965, comprised 115 industrial companies, 10 in merchandising, 25 in transportation, 50 in public utilities, 32 banks and 18 life insurance companies.
63.   Barber (1970), Ch. 4.

64. John A. Sonquist and Tom Koenig, 'Examining Corporate Interconnections through Interlocking Directorates', Ch. 3 in Tom R. Burns and Walter Buckley (eds.), *Power and Control: Social Structures and Their Transformation* (Sage Studies in International Sociology 6, Sage Publications Ltd., London, 1976).

65. Richard Whitley, 'The City and Industry: The Directors of Large Companies, Their Characteristics and Connections', Ch. 4 of Philip Stanworth and Anthony Giddens (eds.), *Elites and Power in British Society* (Cambridge University Press, 1974). See also note 59.

66. Philip Stanworth and Anthony Giddens, 'The Modern Corporate Economy: Interlocking Directorships in Britain, 1906–1970', *Sociological Review*, vol. 23, no. 1 (1975), pp. 5–28.

67. Louis D. Brandeis, *Other People's Money and How the Bankers Use It* (Frederick A. Stokes, New York, 1914), p. 51.

68. Quoted in Zeitlin (1974).

69. Barber (1970), Ch. 4.

70. Blumberg (1975), Ch. 5.

71. Allen quotes from a US Congressional Inquiry for 1973. M.P. Allen, 'Management Control in the Large Corporation: Comment on Zeitlin', *American Journal of Sociology*, vol. 81, no. 4 (1976), pp. 885–94.

72. Warner and Unwalla (1967).

73. Quoted in Zeitlin (1974).

74. Allen, 'Management Control in the Large Corporation'.

75. Prais, *The Evolution of Giant Firms*, Ch. 5; Drucker, also for 1973, quotes a comparable figure for the US of 35–40 per cent. Peter F. Drucker, 'The New Capitalism', *Dialogue*, vol. 4, no. 3 (1971).

76. Blumberg (1975), Ch. 5.

77. M. Zeitlin, 'On Class Theory of the Large Corporation: Response to Allen', *American Journal of Sociology*, vol. 81, no. 4 (1976), pp. 894–903.

78. Blumberg (1975), p. 176. The conclusion is much the same as Kolko's, now over 20 years old. See 'The Concentration of Corporate Power' in Gabriel Kolko, *Wealth and Power in America* (Thames and Hudson, London, 1962), Ch. 4.

79. The term 'multinational corporation' appears to have been first used in 1960, reputedly by David Lilienthal.

80. Tugendhat (1971), Ch. 2.

81. Heilbroner (1971).

82. Franko (1976), Ch. 1.

83. Vernon (1977), Ch. 2.

84. Barnet and Muller (1974), Ch. 1.

85. Ibid.

86. Eli Ginzberg and George J. Vojta, 'The Service Sector of the US Economy', *Scientifc American*, vol. 244, no. 3 (1981), pp. 32–9.

87. Franko (1976), Ch. 1.

88. Vernon (1977), Ch. 1.

89. Ibid., Table 4. Vernon's data are for 1975 for US-based companies, for 1970 for all others.

90. Thus General Motors, the world's largest company, is excluded, earning only 22 per cent of its revenue outside the US. In 1969 the sales of GM exceeded the GNP of Belgium (Tugendhat (1971), p. 2). The 100 human collectivities, excluding Communist countries, earning the largest incomes in 1970 comprised 46 states and 54 companies. General Motors came 15th in rank order. See Thomas Kempner, Keith Macmillan and Kevin Hawkins, *Business and Society: Tradition and Change* (Penguin Books, Harmondsworth, 1976), Ch. 6.

91. These calculations are based on figures given in Madsen. Madsen's sources were the US Securities and Exchange Commission and *Forbes*. Axel Madsen, *Private*

Power (Abacus, Sphere Books, London, 1980).

92. The GNP of the six EEC countries in 1968 totalled $380,000 million. Tugendhat (1971), Ch. 3.

93. For this section and that following see Barnet and Muller (1974); Franko (1976); Heilbroner (1971); Tugendhat (1971).

94. Barnet and Muller note that in 1972 the 30 leading US advertising agencies obtained a third of their work from overseas. In 1971 J. Walter Thompson and McCann Erickson respectively earned 52 per cent and 61 per cent of their profits from outside the US. Barnet and Muller (1974), Ch. 6.

95. Vernon evidently sees this as of paramount importance. Vernon (1977), Ch. 5.

96. John H. Dunning, 'The multinational enterprise and UK economic interest', *Journal of Business Policy*, vol. 1, no. 4 (1971), pp. 17–29; Tugendhat (1971), Ch. 3.

97. Jack N. Behrman, 'Government Policy Alternatives and the Problem of International Sharing' in John H. Dunning (ed.), *The Multinational Enterprise* (Allen and Unwin, London, 1971); Tugendhat (1971), Ch. 12.

98. Barnet and Muller (1974), Chs. 6 and 7; Robert D. Keohane and Van Doorn Oms, 'The Multinational Enterprise and World Political Economy', *International Organization*, vol. 26, no. 1 (1972), pp. 84–120; Vernon (1977), Ch. 7.

99. Vernon (1977), Ch. 7.

100. Heilbroner (1971).

101. Behrman, 'Government Policy Alternatives and the Problem of International Sharing'. In this section the threat to trades unions posed by multinational companies has been deliberately ignored. That important topic falls outside the scope of this study.

102. Ralph Nader, 'The Case for Federal Chartering' in Nader and Green (1973).

103. Ibid., p. 81.

104. Barnet and Muller (1974), Ch. 13.

105. Robert A. Dahl, 'Governing the Giant Corporation' in Nader and Green (1973), pp. 10–11.

106. Barnet and Muller (1974), Ch. 9.

107. Walter Adams, 'The Anti-Trust Alternative' in Nader and Green (1973), p. 133.

108. John Kenneth Galbraith, 'On the Economic Image of Corporate Enterprise' in Nader and Green (1973), p. 7.

109. Blumberg (1975), Ch. 1.

110. Berle in Hacker, *The Corporation Take-Over*, p. 103.

111. Joseph L. Bower, 'Planning Within the Firm', *American Economic Review*, vol. lx, no. 2 (1970), pp. 186–94.

112. The phrase is Eells'. Eells (1972), p. 42.

113. Barnet and Muller (1974), p. 366.

114. Eells (1972), *passim*. The global demands referred to are the production and distribution of goods and services. The quoted passage is from pp. 15–16.

115. Ibid., Ch. VIII.

116. Justice Douglas's 1948 judgement is quoted by Adams. See Adams in Nader and Green (1973), p. 147.

117. Heilbroner (1971), p. 25.

118. For a discussion of Marx's views on joint-stock companies see Ralf Dahrendorf, *Class and Class Conflict in Industrial Society* (Stanford University Press, Stanford, California, 1959), pp. 41–8.

Select Bibliography

Barber, Richard J. (1970) *The American Corporation: Its Power, Its Money, Its Politics* (MacGibbon and Kee, London)

Barnet, Richard J. and Muller, Ronald E. (1974) *Global Reach: The Power of the Multinational Corporations* (Simon and Schuster, New York)

Berle, Adolf A. and Means, Gardiner C. (1967) *The Modern Corporation and Private Property* (Harcourt Brace and World Inc., New York)

Blumberg, Phillip I. (1975) *The Megacorporation in American Society: The Scope of Corporate Power* (Prentice Hall, Englewood Cliffs, New Jersey)

Burch, Philip H. Jr. (1972) *The Managerial Revolution Reassessed: Family Control in America's Large Corporations* (Lexington Books: D.C. Heath and Co, Lexington, Massachusetts)

Dooley, Peter C. (1969) 'The Interlocking Directorate', *American Economic Review*, vol. lix, no. 3, pp. 314–23.

Eells, Richard (1976) *Global Corporations: The Emerging System of World Economic Power* (Free Press, New York)

Florence, P. Sargant (1961) *Ownership, Control and Success of Large Companies* (Sweet and Maxwell, London)

Franko, Lawrence G. (1976) *The European Multinationals* (Harper and Row, London)

Heilbroner, Robert L. (1971) 'The Multinational Corporation and the Nation-State', *New York Review of Books*, vol. xvi, no. 2

Larner, Robert J. (1970) *Management Control and the Large Corporation* (Dunellen Publishing Co. Inc., New York)

Lewellen, Wilbur G. (1971) *The Ownership Income of Management* (National Bureau of Economic Research, New York)

Mace, Myles L. (1971) *Directors: Myth and Reality* (Division of Research, Graduate School of Business Administration, Harvard University, Boston)

Moyle, John (1971) *The Pattern of Ordinary Share Ownership 1957–1970* (Cambridge University Press)

Nader, Ralph and Green, Mark J. (eds.) (1973) *Corporate Power in America* (Grossman Publishers, New York)

Nyman, Steve and Silberston, Aubrey (1978) 'The Ownership and Control of Industry', *Oxford Economic Papers* (New Series), vol. 30, no. 1, pp. 74–101.

Pahl, R.E. and Winkler, J.T. (1974) 'The Economic Elite: Theory and Practice' in Stanworth, Philip and Giddens, Anthony (eds.) *Elites and Power in British Society* (Cambridge University Press)

Scott, John (1979) *Corporations, Classes and Capitalism* (Hutchinson, London)

Tugendhat, Christopher (1971) *The Multinationals* (Eyre and Spottiswoode, London)

Vernon, Raymond (1977) *Storm over the Multinationals: The Real Issues* (Macmillan, London)

Warner, W. Lloyd and Unwalla, Darab B. (1967) 'The System of Interlocking Directorates' in Warner (ed.) *The Emergent American Society, Vol. I: Large Scale Organisations* (Yale University Press, New Haven, Conn.)

Zeitlin, Maurice (1974) 'Corporate Ownership and Control: The Large Corporation and the Capitalist Class', *American Journal of Sociology*, vol. 79, no. 5, pp. 1073–119.

4 THE WORLD OF WORK: THE IMPACT OF AUTOMATION AND THE SHIFT TO SERVICES

In this chapter our concern moves away from questions of power and control in relation to the typical structures of advanced industrialism to issues relating to work and employment. Continuing industrialisation has produced two major effects in the advanced economies: an expansion of the areas of work affected by the progressive introduction of mechanisation and automation and a shift in employment away from (the secondary sector of) manufacturing industry into the tertiary, service sector. We examine each of these developments in turn.

The Impact of Automation

Introduction

Discussions of automation are bedevilled with difficulties of definition. No agreed definition of automation exists, either of what counts as automated machinery or of the process of its achievement, but some classification of terms is necessary to save the reader from confusion. For this purpose we shall distinguish between rationalisation, mechanisation and automation.[1]

Rationalisation is the most suitable term to apply to those changes in the work process that can be put into effect even when machines and machine power are in no way involved. That type of division of labour and specialisation based upon the breakdown of the operations of manufacture into simple constituent motions is then an instance of rationalisation. This was vigorously pursued by F.W. Taylor and by the proponents of organisation and methods procedures whose object was to treat the human hands of the labour force *as if* they were parts of a machine. This approach, mechanistic though it is, is separable from the use of any actual man-made machine.[2]

Likewise the orderly and pre-planned layout of the shop floor that allows the product in process of manufacture to progress systematically from station to station in the shop and be subjected to a series of planned operations is also an achievement of rationalisation.

In principle at least every operation and every transfer could be carried out by hand. Mere rationalisation, therefore, can bring about the detailed fragmentation and standardisation of a process of production, the separation of planning and execution (of brain and hand), the reliance upon unskilled workers and the subjective ill-effects of trivial work activity. Thus, extreme division of labour and the experience of alienation can exist independently of the use of machines and have no necessary connection with their use.

In historical fact the 'scientific management' approach does not predate the widespread use of machinery in production although more rudimentary forms of the division of labour in manufacture naturally enough have done so. Advanced forms of the division of labour, associated with mass production, have relied upon extensive mechanisation, the substitution of machines for men in aspects of production previously undertaken by men alone. As is apparent from this last phrase mechanisation could be used to describe a process which starts with the use of the most elementary mechanical device driven by man and continues all the way to the fully automatic factory. There are, however, two significant break points in this long continuum. The first is the development of power-driven equipment and ushers in what we shall call mechanisation. The second is the emergence of advanced automatic control systems and brings in what we shall call automation.

Mechanisation makes possible mass production on the basis of the assembly line. Transfer operations between work stations become mechanised and the speed of movement of the whole production line, although set by man, is now experienced as determined by machine. This advance in technology also allows the combination of work processes and units previously only casually linked. It was, famously, developed by Henry Ford in the production, in the first instance, of magnetos. What had been a 20-minute job for one man was split into 29 operations carried out by 14 men working at a continuously moving assembly line. In eight hours these men produced 1,335 magnetos, taking 5 minutes over each unit; whereas in the same time 14 men working singly could have produced a mere 336. Furthermore the men on the assembly line needed to be much less skilled than men capable of 29 separate operations. By 1914 Ford had extended this process to the building of a complete car chassis, in 84 minutes.[3]

It will be apparent that mechanisation is an evolutionary process with continual possibilities for its further extension. Bright identifies certain of the common steps in its development. First, machines are introduced to take over workers' manually performed operations. Second, machinery is arranged in a sequence of production operations so as to achieve a continuous flow. Third, compound machines are devised, combining several production functions into a single machine base. Fourth, the machines involved in the production process are integrated into a system with automatic work feeding, work removal and materials-handling devices so as to create a continuous mechanical movement of work. Fifth, changes are introduced into product design so as to allow for mechanical operations of manipulation, assembly, etc. Sixth, changes in materials occur so as to allow for automatic production techniques or a more easily mechanised design form.[4] Bright draws attention to the fact that changes are cumulative and take place in spheres ancillary to production: for example, in the materials used and in design.

Automation has to be seen as an especially significant part of the overall process of mechanisation. A power-driven assembly line 'controls' the process of production in an unquestionably meaningful sense. But it seems preferable to reserve the word automation,[5] which in all the writing about it is a word commonly associated with an advanced state of mechanisation, for control systems that programme the operations of given equipment in advance or which employ feedback mechanisms for the automatic self-control and self-regulation of the equipment. Automation is thus a vital and analytically distinguishable stage on the way to realising what Bright calls 'a conscious effort to synthesize a total mechanised production system'.[6] The control devices associated with automation serve to direct and integrate a production system more fully and more perfectly.[7]

The first example of automation is normally considered to have been the 'Detroit automation' (as it became known) introduced in Cleveland in the period 1948–51 by the Ford Motor Company. The new production process automated the preparation of the cylinder block, crankshaft production, the production of various small parts and all material handling into a vast engine assembly operation: 71 previously separate machines were linked together into an automatic line 1600 feet long within which more than 500 distinct operations were performed.[8]

Automation, like mechanisation, is a relative concept, a matter of degree. Systems may be more or less automated in at least four respects: in triggering, in response, in support, and in content. They may be triggered by man, by pre-programming or by an environmental variable; they may respond in a fixed manner or be programmed for variable response; they may be reliant on human service or be self-reliant for certain support services (aspects of maintenance); they may be freestanding 'islands of automation' or be part of a fully integrated system of automatic machines. Thus automation, like mechanisation, is not an end-state but an evolutionary process with no predictable end.[9]

The use of micro-electronic technology is a development of the machinery employed in a mechanised or automated system. The technology allows the substitution of machines for men to be carried much further than ever before because now more mental processes, even those of judgement and intuition, may be replaced. And because this process promotes the rapid, reliable, cheap and pervasive substitution of electronic for mechanical or electro-mechanical control elements, it is overwhelmingly in the sphere of automation that the 'micro-electronic revolution' is having its effect.[10] Although Maddock states that the qualities of the technology add up to 'the advent of the most remarkable new technology ever to confront mankind',[11] it is properly to be regarded as an evolutionary development and seen in the context of the historical extension of the mechanisation process. Its aims are exactly those of earlier advances in mechanisation: to expand output, to increase the quality of output, to save labour, to save on· stocks and materials, and to improve working conditions.[12]

The Effects of Mechanisation on Factory Work

Modern research on mechanised work is much concerned with its effects upon the work force. At earlier stages the rationality of vigorously extending the division of labour to permit the greatest possible substitution of machines for men in the performance of what were simply manual operations and of machine-minders for craftsmen was clearly seen and eagerly pursued. The mechanical linking of the machinery into assembly line production was but a logical extension of this process. But it had a human cost, clearly evidenced by sociological research since World War II.

Workers have been found to vehemently dislike the repetitiveness of their tasks and the relentless machine pacing of their work. They have also disliked the fatigue and monotony, the atrophy of work groups, the lack of scope for advancement, the low level of skill required, the lack of interest of the atomised work, the absence of challenge. They have expressed feelings of powerlessness, meaninglessness, normlessness and low self-involvement.[13] Only utility men among production workers, polyvalent specialists who substitute for those who are temporarily or in the longer term absent, find varied and satisfying work.

The compensation for the work is an above-average rate of pay. This is popular, and is attractive to those who seek purely instrumental rewards from their work or those who may once have had higher aspirations but decide, with experience, to settle for such rewards. These workers may well be satisfied with their work (though this is not to say that they might not prefer other work with equivalent earnings) as may those who do not seek variety or the exercise of skill or the possibility of promotion in their work. They may look for greater satisfactions — as may all who work in mechanised factories — outside their work, in their families, their houses, their possessions, their leisure pursuits. In Western culture, cash reward and material benefits are both ends in themselves and means to other ends. But there is none the less no gainsaying the fact that in the situation of a mechanised factory where the work provides no intrinsic satisfactions the monetary reward is a compensation, a recompense for an experience that is neither satisfying nor fulfilling in itself.[14]

The Effects of Factory Automation

When a degree of automation has been introduced into a previously mechanised factory there are invariably beneficial effects. There are always some improvements in the work situation and in addition higher earnings, so that, while there may be some accompanying deficits, automation has been greeted as the harbinger of significantly more agreeable and more satisfying factory work. Blauner even suggests that the process of mechanisation produces a U-curve of satisfaction: satisfaction declines with the development of assembly line mechanisation but then rises again with the introduction of automation.

What automation generally means in the context of factory production is that the worker is relieved of constant, repetitive and strenuous involvement in machine control or machine feeding or machine tending and becomes an (often white-coated) overseer of the machine. In continuous process technology, in, for example, a chemical factory, the worker sees neither product nor process but merely monitors the automatic machinery. The likelihood is that the need for labour is substantially reduced and there are fewer real work groups.

The benefits of such change are universally commented upon. The working conditions are greatly improved: they are cleaner and safer. The work is physically easier. The pay is invariably higher than in the pre-automated factory. In most instances the work is more interesting and the responsibility greater. There is less expression of alienation than among assembly line workers.[15] Relationships with supervisors are generally reported to be better.

Of more neutral character are other changes. There are inevitably new job classifications in the new factory and fewer hierarchical levels. This means on the one hand a reduction in distance between categories of workers but on the other hand there may be fewer promotion opportunities. More senior posts in supervision may be reserved now for the better educated and qualified, even for graduates.[16]

The greater capital investment involved in automated plant may give security to those employed, because it is likely that the work force will at the opening of the plant be at a minimum, irreducible, but it also brings about the most disliked aspect, shift-work. Shift-work seems to be almost universally disliked although not always for the same reasons. It certainly has adverse effects upon eating and sleeping habits; beyond that it is reported as disturbing either family life or outside social and community life. The other criticisms voiced by workers are of isolation, mental strain, and boredom. The work itself is less involving but more mentally testing than merely mechanised work. The individual worker is more on his own and, more often than not, has a lesser sense of teamwork.[17]

The interest of the majority of the classic studies of work in newly automated factories lay in a comparative examination in relation to assembly line and pre-automated mechanised work. The researchers seem to have devoutly wished to find a relatively improved work situation and to have been well satisfied. This focus of the studies is now their weakness, since the more workers become accustomed to automated factories and the more distant from assembly line work, the more that basis of comparison will fade. One may well wonder how long what was once seen as preferable to other work circumstances can remain a source of satisfaction in itself when the less palatable alternative has receded into the past. Gallie has clearly made the point that workers' reactions to work conditions depend to a great degree on the cultural values and the institutional setting that provide a context for perception and judgement. One aspect of the judgemental context is the alternative work situation with which a worker compares his present job.

The Effects of Automation in the Office

Whereas automation in the factory has been welcomed, at least in contrast to the experience of assembly line work, the reaction to office automation has been more equivocal. Given that office automation means the introduction of computers, the process involves the creation of entirely new jobs, certainly those of computer operators and software specialists (programmers and systems analysts) and therefore often the employment of new personnel. There may then be three groups to be considered: former employees employed in new work, supervisors and new personnel. Thus the creation of new jobs may provide new work for former employees or it may involve recruitment. Because of this, new job creation does not necessarily balance the number of redundancies. While often, initially, new jobs outnumber those lost, the normal pattern is for this to be only a temporary phenomenon.

Shephard carefully distinguished the reactions of computer operators from those of software specialists. The latter he found to be much more satisfied with their work than the former.[18] Mumford and Banks found clear differences between men and women. The men in their bank study had greater interest in their work generally and greater investment in promotion possibilities; they thus had greater expectations than their female colleagues of job changes upon computerisation and became the more open to disappointment. The women in this study had lower expectations of their jobs and were the less disappointed.[19] Again the importance of relative judgement is stressed.

Some personnel have benefitted from upgrading and being given greater responsibility. Whisler found supervisors to benefit from job enlargement and less isolation than before computerisation.[20] On the other hand some personnel also found their work less interesting and less flexible (now more machine-dependent); some found less responsibility than formerly; and Mumford and Banks's male bank employees were less satisfied with both work and prospects of promotion.[21] As with factory automation, the introduction of shift work to achieve best use of expensive capital equipment was unequivocally disliked.[22]

Rhee notes that the amount of upheaval following office

automation depends upon the prior level of rationalisation,[23] whether, for example, punched card systems and Hollerith machines had previously been introduced into the office; and all commentators emphasise the need for careful preparation before major innovation. But however computerisation is introduced, it is not easy to see why it should be welcomed by office staff. The fear of redundancies has proved to be well grounded; in the medium to long term at least jobs are lost.[24] Job levels are compressed and promotion opportunities are reduced. Interesting new posts are certainly created but they are filled for the most part by new, better educated and better qualified people than those (large numbers of) people who become displaced.

The Effects on Management

The broad effect of computerisation on management is to centralise decision-making, pushing its locus up the management hierarchy and at the same time flattening the hierarchical pyramid and giving the managers who survive the process increased spans of control. The decision-making process itself is served with an increase of information; it is more objective, more quantified and rationalised. The process tends to make middle management redundant or have feelings of redundancy and to reveal the decisions to be made to be more interdependent than was previously realised. This in turn puts a greater premium on collaboration, effective communication and mutual goodwill.[25] The sequence of change necessarily involves functional realignments and structural reorganisation.[26]

At management level the results of computerisation would seem to be wholly beneficial to the firm as a whole and to those managers unthreatened with displacement. The process of innovation may still not be without its pains. As Whisler comments, 'those in authority, once able to turn a deaf ear to the protests from below when change was planned, may find their hearing strongly affected by their own self-interest'.[27]

In the longer term computerisation comes to place far greater emphasis than hitherto on the need for better market analysis, technical forecasting and long-range planning. It also promotes organisational integration.[28]

The Effects of Automation on Employment

The point has been made many times, and it is indeed obviously true, that it is hard to isolate the effects of the increasing use of automation upon employment from the effects of numerous other interrelated factors that also influence employment. The displacement by new products owing to changes in taste, foreign competition, increases in productivity, slackening of demand, rationalisation of production may all cause unemployment; and these factors may themselves be the result of, and give rise to, the introduction of automation. If import penetration is achieved by less developed countries with the advantage of lower labour costs, the only defence may be to cut labour costs by the introduction of labour-saving technology. If, as is now more likely, the foreign competition is from developed countries which have already introduced such technology, then again the only defence is to adopt the same technology. In short, rich countries can only compete with poor countries in cutting labour costs by bringing in new technology, and the robots of other rich countries can only be fought with robots. The point is reached where technology that may cause unemployment has to be introduced to prevent an increasing loss of world market shares that will inexorably lead to yet greater unemployment. To automate is a lesser evil than not to automate.

This argument may seem to yield the conclusion that the introduction is benevolent; but the cost cannot be gainsaid, for the unemployment that results is structural. Where a process of production is superseded (as with the displacement of mechanical watches by electronic watches) the workers concerned with the old technology lack the skills and the educational and vocational preparation required by the new. There is a mismatch of what is needed and what is available, with dire results for those too old to acquire new skills and those among the young who lack the educational foundation for their acquisition.

This kind of dislocation of employment is of course not new, and it may be said that it is the inevitable price to be paid by the few for the benefit of the many or even by one generation for the benefit of those to come. Or is it the case that the dislocations of today, resulting from an increasing rate of technological change, especially owing to the introduction of micro-electronic technology, are of a different nature and of direr consequence than those experienced before? Is this a more significant watershed in the history of employment than others gone through in this century by the advanced industrial countries, because it heralds a long-term decline of employment in manufacturing industry?

The traditional response to the Cassandras who foresaw spreading unemployment and social distress was that the visible and immediate unemployment was transitional and that the displacing technology itself was triggering a series of compensatory mechanisms that would alleviate this unemployment. The argument was as follows. The new technology will lead to higher productivity, reduced unit costs and higher profits which in turn will lead to higher levels of investment. At the same time the higher productivity will bring about decreases in relative prices and higher real earnings and hence an increase in consumers' real incomes and higher overall demand. The long-term result, then, of the new technology is higher investment and higher demand which give rise to new products and new services with new employment opportunities. It is recognised that the new employment opportunities may be elsewhere, geographically far off from the loss of the old and, as already noted, that the new needs may not match the old skills, yet overall, it is held, employment opportunities are either maintained or enhanced.[29]

Before this argument is accepted and before the questions raised earlier are examined, the micro-effects of automation on employment need to be examined.

The Displacement of Labour. The victims of labour-saving technology are above all the unskilled and the semi-skilled.[30] As Killingsworth comments, low-skilled jobs are eliminated faster than low-skilled workers:[31] natural wastage and 'silent firing' (the non-employment of those who but for the newly introduced technology would have been employed) do not keep pace with the elimination of work, and the silently fired are of course other non-skilled men and women. The losers are the less-educated and the socially disadvantaged: the old and women, who may have missed earlier skill-learning and training opportunities, and ethnic minorities and blacks, who are likely to be at a disadvantage in profiting from any social opportunity at all. These findings hold true for office automation as well as factory automation although unemployment may be more masked in the office situation in which there is anyhow a high turnover of female clerical workers and other accompanying elements of rationalisation.[32] Everywhere there may be a degree of masking of real or developing unemployment because of under-employment, short-time working and temporary lay-offs.[33]

The New Demand for Labour. In the factory situation automation is likely to lead to demands for more skilled men, or men with a wider range of skills (utility men, maintenance men, technicians) and for more skilled, versatile and responsible supervisors, who may now be engineers, even graduates: for white coat, and some white collar, workers. This means that the new opportunities are for the better-educated and those with polyvalent skills; in areas affected by micro-electronic technology they are for those with software skills, control theorists and electronic engineers.[34]

The Overall Results.[35] Some authors have believed that the effects of automation on employment can be demonstrated by sets of figures. This is obviously not true of the qualitative and individual experience of being declared redundant and lacking the skills or the opportunity for re-training or the educational preparation needed for the alternative employment available. It is also not true for the long-term where figures lend spurious exactitude in a context in which macro-social factors make accurate forecasting impossible.[36] They have their place in recording, in a narrow compass, short-term changes in employment.

Rothwell and Zegveld have documented the decline of employment in specific industries owing to the introduction of labour-saving technology: for example, in British coal-mining, in the Canadian railway system, in textile machinery manufacture, in metal working and in the machine tools industry.[37] There is no room for doubt that factory automation reduces employment in the immediate industry concerned. In the case of office automation it has been said that computerisation often has unintended and unexpected consequences among which is the creation of new jobs to deal with the increase of information, the enlarged overall work load, the development of new administrative systems, and the opportunities for more comprehensive decision-making and long-term planning now made possible. However, while this may be the immediate result, it is not sustained; an increase in jobs as a result of the introduction of computers is followed by a secular decline.[38]

The loss of jobs in the innovative industry is thus not in serious question nor is the increase in the level of jobs (in terms of qualifications and skills) in doubt. But this latter process, we should note, is not a simple matter of upgrading or the total elimination of unskilled work. The increment of skill required for the new higher level jobs is beyond the reach of the displaced unskilled worker. Yet many unskilled jobs continue to exist because it is simply not economically worthwhile to automate them (they are not, in short, related to productivity). The danger, therefore, in the automated industries themselves is of a polarised labour force, divided between the more highly skilled than before and the most unskilled. A structural embodiment of such polarisation is the development of subcontracting of unskilled work.[39]

The trend is also clear, however it is regarded. The use of automation is increasing. In Britain the most recent and dramatic innovation in manufacturing, the use of robots, increased in the period 1978–83 by more than 1,600 per cent; the number rose from 100 to 1,753. The rate was in excess of that of Britain's competitors but the competitors' advantage shows how necessary this was: Japan's robots increased in this period from 3,500 to 16,500 and the United States' from 2,500 to 8,000.[40] Some commentators are untroubled by the trend, lulled by what Killingsworth terms the three myths of automation: that more jobs are created than are lost, that automation leads to the upgrading of the labour force, and that automation comes slowly.[41] The reader may agree that the first two myths have been exploded; the third has been proved false by the advent of micro-electronic technology that has caused costs to plummet, according to Maddock 100,000-fold, in the period 1960–80.[42] Others find the structural displacement of labour merely the continuance of an inevitable process and comment reassuringly.

Sleigh and his colleagues write: 'the process of penetration of new technology in industry is generally an evolutionary rather than a revolutionary one, and micro-electronic technology is unlikely to prove an exception'.[43] Those who reflect that the evolutionary process throws up survivors and losers as inexorably as any 'revolution' will not be greatly soothed by such statements.

What seems likely is that employment in the secondary sector of manufacturing will continue to decline no less dramatically than did employment in agriculture at an earlier stage of industrial development. Employment in the service sector may expand in some degree in compensation. But labour-saving technology will inevitably lead to a new wave of unemployment, or at least insufficient new employment, in that sector also in the near future. This issue is discussed in the next section of this chapter. The advanced industrial societies are fast reaching a watershed that recession, however severe, should not disguise. Man's dream of less work and of machines being devised to take over man's work is on the point of realisation, and lower levels of employment than those expected, known and valued in the processes of advanced industrialisation are the inevitable result.

The Significance of Social Organisation

The use that is made of technology and the experience of its use are matters of social organisation and social relations. They are not determined by the technology itself, although the technology unquestionably influences social choice, because it can be differently employed in different social contexts. Cherns has stated the essential nature of technological determinism: 'Technological determinism entwines two strands of belief: that technology has its own "logic"; and that what can be done will inevitably be done'.[44] But neither belief is true, at least in its first meaning: technology does not have its own 'logic' causing events to unfold in a manner dictated by the technology alone, *regardless of social factors*; nor is what can (in terms of technological possibility) be done necessarily done, *unless social factors are congenial*, and then not necessarily at a predetermined time and in a predetermined manner.

Two classic sociological studies have proved the shortcomings of naive technological determinism beyond doubt. Woodward's study of 100 British manufacturing firms employing 100 or more employees, back in the 1950s, conclusively established that technological change is always coincident with organisational change and that the technological change is only one among several elements (that include economic and social factors) that together determine the nature of the organisational change(s).[45] Gallie's study of automation in two oil companies, one British, one French, established just as clearly that the results of automation vary significantly according to the social and cultural context: in particular, according to different norms (of collective bargaining, of participation, of legitimacy in industrial relations practices) and expectations (for example, of industrial conflict), and as a result of different historical development (especially of management-union relations). With the same automation, structure, processes, norms and practices all differed.[46]

The importance of these research findings is that technology as such (mechanisation, automation, micro-electronics, robots) cannot be blamed for any unfavourable experience of working with particular machinery, at least not wholly so. For management who bring in new technology it cannot be the scapegoat for consequent workers' dislike of it. For workers suffering from working with the technology the mute machine cannot be made to answer for their frustration.[47] Thus the alienation or apathy or harmony variously experienced by workers is not the product of technology alone.

The point harks back to the earlier distinction between rationalisation and mechanisation which approached the same issue in a different way. It is the rationalisation, the modification of social organisation, that is significant, for this is the motive behind the division of labour and the various forms of specialisation which so surely affect work experience and perceptions. A change of technology may accompany a change in social organisation or may encourage it, but it may not be involved at all.

Thus alienation as variously understood is only indirectly related to machinery. Marx did not think otherwise in commenting on the lot of his contemporary industrial worker. His concept of alienation has proved difficult to define for social scientific purposes, to operationalise, for the simple reason that it is a metaphysical concept, encapsulating a statement about man's nature. To Marx the proletarian factory worker was estranged or alienated from his product (which was not his own), from the process of manufacture (which was not his own), and from himself (who was not free). Such a worker was no longer a self-sufficient craftsman converting an idea for a product into the product itself by mixing his labour with his chosen materials. To Marx the craft worker embodied in his work man's creative potential and thus to him factory work was a denial of a part of man's essential nature that could be fulfilled in work, his creativity.[48]

Machines are not a necessary part of this conception and it may be thought mistaken of Blauner to associate alienation with mechanisation in its various stages of development. Blauner found 'alienation' to be least evident among craft workers and most evident among assembly line (highly mechanised) workers; in between came machine-minders (moderately mechanised) and workers in automated plants. He was thus able to argue that the secular trend after being one of increasing mechanisation (as distinct, in Blauner's terminology, from automation) and increasing alienation was now one of increasing automation and (overall) declining alienation. By focusing on the machinery Blauner by-passed the central issue.

Blauner operationalised alienation into four elements: feelings of powerlessness, normlessness, isolation and self-estrangement. He contrasted these feelings with those of control, purpose, social integration and self-involvement.[49] The first three elements can be seen to be social and to relate to social organisation. The fourth seems to attempt to do so but fails to reach man's sense of his creativity. Yet it is not difficult to see that where machinery is involved what matters for this sense is the workman's degree of control over, or mastery of, the machine. This too is a question of social arrangement. Thus all Blauner's facets of alienation may properly be seen as contingent directly upon social organisation and only indirectly on the nature or type of machinery. It is not technology that has brought about increasing division of labour, monotony of work, close supervision, a low degree of control and fragmentation of work into severally meaningless operations. Division of labour has brought the disagreeable consequences, and machinery has been invented to make even more extreme divisions of labour possible.[50]

Friedmann's discussion of alienation is not so tied to machinery. For him alienation means a sense of depersonalisation, lack of interest in work, low self-esteem and little sense of participation; all are social products. He therefore asks, what are the social conditions for the humanisation of work? If the work of a modern factory cannot be made interesting and fulfilling, the answer, he suggests, must lie in a fundamental remodelling of social institutions.[51]

One further worker disposition is sometimes attributed to machinery, namely, an instrumental orientation to work. It is suggested that although some workers come to work with an instrumental approach others have it induced by the experience of mechanised work. It is clear however that this orientation is pre-existent to work experience, and confirmed or reinforced by it. The orientation, suggests Cotgrove, is a product of a culture in which market relations prevail — in the formation of social relations;[52] it is, as Marx expressed it, a product of the social relations of production; it follows also, in Durkheim's phrase, from the forced division of labour.

Conclusion

This survey of the effects of automation upon work and upon employment in Western advanced industrial societies leads to two conclusions. First, the substitution of machinery for man is a secular trend, bringing with it regular structural displacement of employment, which there is no warrant for supposing will not be sustained. Second, the disagreeable experiences of work that are prevalent in these societies and which also look likely to be sustained are the product not of the technological trend itself but of prevailing modes of social organisation. Modes of social organisation differ in other societies, as is brought out in Parts Three and Four, and therefore advocates of change must focus on social organisation and societal arrangements which determine the use made of, and the human experience of, changing technology. Changes in these would result in changes in the meaning attached to work and in the sense of identity that may accrue from experiences of jobs, employment[53] and occupation. It may turn out that no existing or realistically imaginable society could offer the satisfactions in employment associated with creative craft work. In that case the fulfilment of man's creative urges must be looked for elsewhere. They should not, however, be forgone in employment until every attempt to create congenial social relations in employment has been found wanting.

One final comment is in place here. It has been hinted that there are two principal forms of work specialisation: that usually called the division of labour in which work is broken down in Taylorian style, into smaller and smaller tasks that the low skilled can undertake and that which leads to the high levels of expertise (and self-esteem) associated with professional work. The professional has a large measure of control over his work and over the resources required for it. The issue of the control of organisations was the subject of the previous chapter. That of the individual's control of his work will be returned to in the final chapter of the book.

The Shift to Services

The Growth of Service Employment

It is conventionally known that the ..dvanced industrial countries of the world have been characterised for a number of years by an increase in the proportion of the labour force in service employment, and to some commentators this increase is evidence of a society moving into a post-industrial phase of development.[54] The shift implies that the movement of labour off the land and out of agricultural employment, which provided the work force for manufacturing industry that initiated the process of industrialisation, has continued, with the newly available labour now moving into service industries. In addition, it is widely assumed that there has been a decline of employment in manufacturing industry. Labour from both sources is thought to have allowed the growth of the service sector.

Table 4.1: Percentage Distribution of Employment in Six Countries, 1950–70

		Agriculture	Industry	Services
France	1950	31.0	34.5	34.5
	1960	22.4	38.1	39.5
	1970	15.1	39.7	45.3
West Germany	1950	22.7	43.1	34.2
	1960	14.0	48.0	38.1
	1970	9.6	49.0	41.4
Japan	1950	43.1	23.5	33.4
	1960	29.5	28.5	41.9
	1970	16.9	35.6	47.5
UK	1950	5.4	46.5	48.1
	1960	4.2	47.3	48.5
	1970	2.9	44.8	52.3
USA	1950	12.3	33.7	54.0
	1960	8.5	33.4	58.1
	1970	4.5	33.2	62.3
USSR	1950	55.8	21.6	22.6
	1960	41.9	28.6	29.5
	1970	25.7	37.6	36.7

Sources: Sorrentino (1971) and ILO (1977)[55]

The actual broad trends are revealed in Table 4.1, for the period 1950–70, for six major industrial countries. The table shows in all countries a declining proportion of the labour force employed in agriculture and a rising proportion employed in services over the 20-year period. However in four countries the proportion employed in industry continued to rise in this period; only in the UK and USA was the labour force in industry stable with a suggestion of decline.

It is noteworthy that in five of the countries the agricultural labour force was more than halved in the 20-year period.[56] In the UK it was too small already in 1950 to allow this reduction. The most spectacular rates of decline, over 60 per cent, occurred in Japan and the USA. The largest absolute decline (30 percentage points) occurred in the USSR but the Soviet Union still has easily the largest agricultural sector and is therefore, by this criterion, the least advanced of the six economies.

The movement of labour into the service sector would seem to be an inexorable trend. If 50 per cent employment in services may be said to mark a significant stage of development, the USA and the UK had reached this stage in the 1940s and 1960s respectively and France, Germany and Japan did so in the 1970s.[57] We may note that the USA is 'ahead' of all other countries in the shift to services and in the proportion of service employment; thus it is the front candidate to reach whatever stage of development is next to come. Japan also is noteworthy for being the only one of the six never to have had industry as the largest employment sector; in the Japanese case there have always been more employees in services than in industry from the very start of the process of industrialisation.[58]

The Several Service Sectors. But this crude analysis cannot suffice. While all extractive and goods-producing industries can be clearly identified and distinguished, 'services' in any analysis like that above is simply a residual category.[59] To record the fact that workers are moving out of extractive and manufacturing industries into 'other' work is to record real occupational change but its crudeness buries its significance. Sorrentino's analysis groups under 'services' employment in transportation, communication, public utilities, trade, finance, public administration, private household services and miscellaneous services.[60] This employment is indeed not goods-producing but it is not (as often seems to be thought) all not-for-profit and non-contributory to GNP.[61] And it is extremely diverse.

The principal attempt to differentiate service employment is that of Singelmann who distinguished distributive services, producer services, social services and personal services. His analysis of the five leading capitalist countries is given in Table 4.2.

The table shows the patterns of development in the five countries to be broadly similar. Employment in distributive services (transportation, communication and the wholesale and retail trades) and in personal services (hotels and catering, entertainment, laundry and dry cleaning, barber and beauty shops, repair services, domestic services and miscellaneous personal services) has been steady during the 40-year period, although employment in the distributive services has risen somewhat higher in the USA and Japan. Employment in producer services (banking, insurance, real estate, engineering, accountancy, legal services and miscellaneous business services) has risen from a low base (especially low in Japan). It has risen conspicuously higher in the USA than elsewhere. Employment in social services (health, education, religious and welfare services, the postal service, government service and

Table 4.2: Percentage Distribution of Service Employment in Five Countries, 1930-70

		Distributive Services	Producer Services	Social Services	Personal Services	Other Employment[62]
England	1930	21.6	3.1	9.7	14.5	51.1
	1950	19.2	3.2	12.1	11.3	54.3
	1960	19.7	4.5	14.1	9.0	52.6
	1970	17.9	5.6	19.4	9.0	48.0
France	1930	13.3	2.1	6.1	7.2	71.1
	1950	14.4	2.7	9.4	7.4	67.1
	1960	16.4	3.2	12.3	7.4	60.7
	1970	15.5	5.5	14.8	7.9	56.3
West Germany	1930	12.8	2.7	6.8	7.8	67.8
	1950	15.7	2.5	11.5	6.8	63.4
	1960	16.4	4.2	12.9	6.4	60.3
	1970	16.9	5.1	17.4	6.5	54.1
Japan	1930	15.6	0.9	5.5	7.3	70.7
	1950	14.6	1.5	7.2	5.3	71.3
	1960	18.6	2.9	8.3	7.6	62.6
	1970	22.7	5.1	10.2	7.6	54.3
USA	1930	19.6	3.2	9.2	11.2	56.9
	1950	22.4	4.8	12.4	12.1	48.3
	1960	21.9	6.6	16.3	11.3	44.0
	1970	22.1	9.3	21.5	8.6	38.4

Source: Singelmann (1978)

miscellaneous social services) has risen substantially in all countries; on average the rise was 124 per cent. A comparison of service employment profiles for 1970 shows Japan to have a significantly low proportion of the labour force (10.2 per cent) in social services while the USA had a significantly high proportion (21.5 per cent).

Overall, except in the case of Japan where it has been in distributive services, the expansion of service employment has been in social services. In the case of the USA there has also been noteworthy expansion in producer services.

Singelmann's analysis is a marked improvement on the single primary-secondary-tertiary division and it discriminates between different categories of service employment but it still does not go far enough. In the cases of the USA and Britain we can refine the analysis.

For the USA the first trend to note is the increase in government service. Fuchs's analysis categorises employment differently to Singelmann's but it allows him to show that the growth of service employment up to 1965 was overwhelmingly in government (including the armed forces). Between 1929 and 1947 employment in government rose from 6.0 per cent of the labour force to 10.6 per cent, and by 1965 to 15.5 per cent; the share of all other service employment rose from 34.4 per cent to 35.2 per cent and 39.3 per cent. Thus over the full 36-year period the government share increased by 158 per cent while the share of other services rose by just over 14 per cent.[63]

Ginzberg and Vojta record that in the period 1962–78 the number of people employed by government or in direct employment in the private sector occasioned by government purchases rose by 16.2 million, which confirms the continuing increase of those in government service.[64]

The second and more recent trend evident in the USA is the growth in what may be termed low-status service employment. In the period 1973–83 employment in services[65] increased by 14 million jobs (while non-service employment declined by 1.2 million) of which 84 per cent were in the private economy. Of these, 48 per cent or approximately 5.7 million, were at eating and drinking places,[66] in health services and in business services[67] (personnel supply services, data processing, reproduction and mailing). Over the decade the increases in these three spheres of employment were 64, 65 and 80 per cent respectively.[68]

If, with Personick, we peer into the future, we may estimate by 1990 a further increase in jobs in these three spheres ranging from 4.3 million, on pessimistic employment assumptions, to 5.6 million on optimistic assumptions; these forecasts imply an increase in jobs at eating and drinking places ranging from 22 to 38 per cent over the 1979–90 period, an increase in employment in health services ranging from 53 to 64 per cent and an increase in employment in business services ranging from 31 to 51 per cent.[69] In other words the importance of these employment spheres as continuing growth areas does not seem to be in doubt.

The significance of this second trend is that the increase is in the numbers of what Gorz calls unprotected workers:[70] on short hours or in temporary employment, on low pay, with few or no prospects, little unionised, disproportionately old and disproportionately female.[71] Rothschild notes that in 1979 when women constituted 41 per cent of the US labour force they were 56 per cent of workers at eating and drinking places and 81 per cent of health service workers.[72]

In the British case the two areas of growth in service employment in recent years have been 'professional and miscellaneous services' and 'social services and public administration'. In 1954 they employed, respectively, 12.5 and 17 per cent of the labour force, in 1975 16.9 and 21.6 per cent, and in 1982 21 and 22.6 per cent.[73] But while the increase in the share of the labour force employed in social services and public administration over the 28-year period (1954–82) was 32.9 per cent, the increase for professional and miscellaneous services was 68 per cent. And while over the shorter 7-year period (1975–82) the increase in the first group's share was real, at 4.6 per cent, in the case of the second group it was 24.3 per cent.[74] In fact there was zero growth in employment in public administration (central and local government and defence) in the period 1975–82, while there was a 25 per cent increase in employment in professional services.[75] Public administration accounted for 7.9 per cent of the British labour force in 1982 and professional services accounted for 8.5 per cent.

We may then conclude that the shift to services has had different significance in the two countries. In the USA it has meant a steady and substantial increase in employment in government service and in recent years in low-status services. In Britain it has meant a real increase in government service but a much longer and more significant increase in employment in professional services.[76] These trends are clearly distinguishable and they need to be identified and examined if the growth in service employment is to be understood. First, however, we may look at another analysis currently in vogue, that which focuses upon growth in the 'information' sector.

The Information Economy

The idea of the information economy, originated by Porat, has been widely popularised by Bell.[77] Porat's contention is that the major growth area in the US economy is the information sector. There are two components of this. First, there are the primary information industries, producing information machines and marketing information services; examples are the telephone and computer industries and the banking industry. Second, there is the secondary information sector made up of those working in information services, such as research, planning, programming and marketing, in private or government service, in sectors not themselves defined as

Table 4.3: Four-Sector Percentage Distribution of the U.S. Labour Force, 1950–80

	Agriculture	Industry	Service	Information
1950	11.9	38.3	19.0	30.8
1960	6.0	34.8	17.2	42.0
1970	3.1	28.6	21.9	46.4
1980	2.1	22.5	28.8	46.6

Source: Bell (1980) Table 9.2, p. 522.

producing information goods or services. In other words, there is a hidden information industry to be found spread through all sectors of the economy. According to Porat, by 1967 53 per cent of total compensation paid in the US was paid to information workers; 21 per cent of national income was accounted for by the primary information sector (and 42 per cent of corporate profits) and a further 21 per cent by the secondary information sector. 'In sum', writes Bell, 'nearly fifty per cent of GNP, and more than fifty per cent of wages and salaries, derives from the production, processing and distribution of information goods and services. It is in that sense that we have become an information economy'.[78]

Using a four-sector approach to analysis of the US labour force gives the distribution shown in Table 4.3.[79] The table shows that the information sector had taken the largest share of the labour force by 1960 but it also shows the rate of increase of this share to be slowing virtually to a halt. In the three decades shown the ten-year increase in the information sector's share of the labour force slows from 36.4 per cent to 10.5 per cent and (in the projected decade) 0.4 per cent. In contrast, the service sector's share first declines by 9.5 per cent, then rises by 27.3 per cent and is predicted to rise again by 31.5 per cent. These two trends seem to bear out those taken from Fuchs's and from Rothschild's data, and may well be explained by the greater vulnerability of information workers to the introduction of micro-electronic technology. This at least is the explanation put forward by Jones for the very similar findings of his own four-sector analysis of the Australian labour force.[80]

Bell has announced the discovery of the information sector with noteworthy éclat, and assuredly 'information workers' have come to be a considerable and significant share of the labour force. But their thrust to prominence may well have weakened already in the most advanced economies. In Australia during 1960–80, according to Jones, computers eliminated 244,000 jobs and created 77,000, with a net loss of 167,000 jobs. Computerisation seems certain, on present indications, to reduce employment in office work, in banking, insurance, social security and the postal service. After all, as Jones notes, 'computers are *intended* to displace labour. Their manufacturers promise to reduce manpower, and there is no reason to doubt them'.[81] More importantly, the missionary zeal of the prophets of the information economy has led them to an analysis that in the end conceals more than it reveals. Porat's definition of information is 'data that have been organized and communicated. The information *activity* includes all the resources consumed in producing, processing and distributing information goods and services'.[82] If the concepts employed are as gross and undiscriminating as this suggests, not distinguishing between, for example, general office work, banking, the mass media and government, they are of little help in identifying detailed employment trends and establishing their significance. They may then safely be jettisoned.

What is important is that the information sector is also shedding labour while personal needs, many stimulated by education, continue to grow more complex and the demand is therefore sustained for increased diversity of services. The issue is where these needs will be met. Will it be by the generation of new employment in some part of the service sector, or will it be, either by choice or as a result of a lack of employment opportunities, within the household? Are we seeing the development of what Gershuny calls the 'self-service economy'? It is to this that we now turn.

The Self-Service Economy

Gershuny's insight is to distinguish, within tertiary industry, goods-related from service-related employment and to observe that the firm trend in the UK is for consumers to substitute goods for services.[83] The implication, of course, is that the provision of services, which has in recent years required more and more manpower, will not continue to do so. An increase in demand for 'services' is not the same as an increase in the need for service employment. In the UK in 1971 Gershuny found 21.8 per cent of the labour force to be in goods-related employment within tertiary industry[84] and 23.4 per cent to be in service-related employment.[85] By 1975 these proportions had both risen, to 22.7 and to 28 per cent respectively, the service-related workers increasing notably more than the goods-related. Gershuny's interest, however, is in the fact that goods-related workers make up almost half the tertiary sector labour force: 48 per cent in 1971 and 45 per cent in 1975.

But while in the twenty-year period, 1954–74, the proportion of consumption expenditure on services in the UK increased by 37 per cent, matching the 39 per cent increase in the proportion of the labour force in service employment, this conceals the fact that household expenditure on transport increased by 88.7 per cent while expenditure on other services remained exactly the same.[86] In fact expenditure on transport *services* declined from 3.5 per cent of the household budget in 1954 to 2.4 per cent in 1974, while expenditure on transport *goods* rose from 3.5 per cent to 11.1 per cent; put another way, expenditure on *goods* was 50 per cent of transport expenditure in 1954 and 82 per cent in 1974.[87] This change of course represents a shift from the use of transport services to the purchase of cars. Similarly in this period ownership of domestic appliances has been substituted for the use of laundries and the hiring of domestic help and the buying or renting of television sets has been substituted for cinema and theatre-going. Gershuny estimates that expenditure in these categories (transport, domestic help, laundry, cinema, theatre) in 1954 was split 70 per cent on services and 30 per cent on goods, while in 1974 the split was 20 per cent on services and 80 per cent on goods.[88]

The self-service economy, then, is the culmination of the consumer society. The demand for luxuries is universal, the willingness to work for others is severely reduced and more and more goods are individualised, personalised and open to individual choice. Thus *investment* is in the home rather than in manufacturing industry, and consumer *expenditure* is on household goods rather than on services.[89] The logic of increasingly refined production systems and the logic of persuading the consumer to be king both lead to the self-service, household economy.

The Household Economy

The importance of the household economy (that is, the sum of all goods and services produced in households) is further brought out by Burns's analysis of the United States. Burns calculates that by 1960 investment in single-family residence construction equalled that in business construction and that investment in major domestic consumer durables *exceeded* that in producer durables. Thus, after 1960, 'the household became the focus of capital formation'.[90] In addition, Burns estimated for 1969 that the value of household labour in the US was equivalent to roughly one-third of GNP and approximately 50 per cent of all after-tax labour income.

Jones also stresses the importance of household labour, making home-based work part of the quinary sector in his five-sector analysis of the Australian labour force.[91] As women have taken work in the conventionally recognised labour force, the proportion of household workers in the Australian economy has fallen, from 39.3 per cent in 1947 to 27.6 per cent in 1979. But the quinary sector remained the largest sector of the labour force throughout, and the vagaries of more conventional employment do not seem likely to undermine this dominant position.

The conclusions we wish to draw from this material are two. First, families increasingly invest in capital equipment to obtain goods and services that they would otherwise buy in the marketplace. The arrival of the video-recorder has underlined this trend; the home computer is assuredly extending it. Second, the quinary sector, of domestic labour and quasi-domestic services, providing a haven from inflation and progressive taxation,[92] is now likely to be the sector with greatest potential for development and for job creation.

Conclusion

The above analysis is but a first step toward the more refined investigation on which fuller understanding of the well-publicised trend to service employment must be based. We can at least say that in the leading industrialised nations the growth area is what Singelmann terms the social services: health, education, religious and welfare services, the postal service, government service and miscellaneous social services. In the USA recent employment growth has occurred in government service and in low status services — at eating and drinking places, in health services and business services — among 'unprotected' workers. In Britain it has occurred in professional and scientific services.

As far as consumers are concerned, the clear tendency is to buy, not services outside the home, but service-producing goods (such as cars, washing machines, TV sets or video-recorders) for final consumption within the household. This tendency seems already to be slowing the growth of some types of service employment.

The general tendency, therefore, for an overall increase in service employment to be generated as consumers' needs become more differentiated and personalised, would appear to be coming to an end in the most advanced industrial economies. It is no longer true that job displacement in one economic sector is followed by new employment in a complementary sector. New, lower levels of employment, as noted earlier in this chapter, are in the most advanced industrial societies here to stay.

What the wider social effects of these trends may be is at this stage speculative. From a Marxist viewpoint the extension of service employment, and especially the increase of 'unprotected' workers, is seen as part of the process of proletarianisation of white collar work, but it may not lead to a common sense of identity among white and blue collar workers. The development of the household economy and the self-service economy seems likely indeed to decrease opportunities for solidarity and possibly even to increase anomie. At the same time this development may make the victim of the affluent society — in terms of a Galbraithian or a Marcusean analysis — somewhat more independent, in the privacy of a more independent household, of the manipulative apparatus of public relations and advertising men. The time may be arriving, foreseen by Keynes, when man has to face the novel but long-term problem: 'how to use his freedom from pressing economic cares . . . to live wisely and agreeably and well'.[93] But if the abundance assumed by Keynes coincides with diminishing employment, a retreat into the household and a loss of opportunities for collective approaches to decision-making, we may have doubts as to how the society of the future will manage its new freedom. It is an issue to which we shall return in the concluding chapter.

Notes

1. Of the many discussions of this subject some of the most helpful are to be found in Bright (1958), *passim*; Robert Dubin, 'Automation: The Second Industrial Revolution', in Marcson (1970); Mann and Hoffman (1960), Ch. 1; Walker and Guest (1952), Ch. 1.

2. See F.W. Taylor, *The Principles of Scientific Management* (Harper and Bros., New York, 1911).

3. Bright (1958), Ch. 2.

4. Ibid., Ch.3.

5. The word was first coined by D.S. Harder of the Ford Motor Co. in 1946, in reference to automatic work-feeding and material-handling devices.

6. Bright (1958), p. 18.

7. The use of robots, therefore, is just another step in the development of automated systems of production.

8. Bright (1958), Ch. 5; Edward B. Shils, 'Automation: Technology or Concept' in Marcson (1970).

9. This note of variations draws again upon Bright's valuable work. Bright (1958), Chs. 1 and 4.

10. Sir Ieuan Maddock, 'The future of work' in *Technology Choice and the Future of Work* (British Association for the Advancement of Science symposium, 22 November 1978).

11. Ibid., p. 17.

12. John Bessant *et al.*, 'Microelectronics in Manufacturing Industry: The Rate of Diffusion' in Forester (1980). This is not to deny the evolutionary leap involved. As Jones comments, 'micro-electronics permits an exponential rise in output together with an exponential fall in total inputs — energy, labour, capital, space and time. In economic history there is no remote equivalent to this'. Jones (1982), p. 107.

13. Blauner (1964); Shephard (1971). These researchers both carried out comparative studies in which workers in mechanised situations scored more extremely on these scales than those in craft (non-mechanised) or automated work. These factors are taken to be the operational manifestations of Marx's concept of alienation.

14. For relevant case studies the reader is referred to Blauner (1964); Ely Chinoy, *Automobile Workers and the American Dream* (Doubleday and Co., New York, 1955); Shephard (1971); Walker and Guest (1952); and for informed discussion to Friedmann (1964).

15. Blauner (1964), Ch. 6; Stephen Cotgrove, 'Alienation and automation', *British Journal of Sociology*, vol. xxiii, no. 4 (1972), pp. 437–51; Shephard (1971), Ch. 2.

16. Chadwick-Jones found this in the steel mill that he studied. Chadwick-Jones (1969), Ch. 12.

17. This section draws upon a range of classic studies including those of Blauner (1964); Chadwick-Jones (1969); William A. Faunce, 'Automation in the Automobile Industry: Some Consequences for In-Plant Social Structure' in Marcson (1970); Gallie (1978); Mann and Hoffman (1960); Shephard (1971); Walker (1957). It also makes use of the commentaries of Beaumont and Helfgott (1964), Bright (1958) and Leonora Stettner, 'Survey of Literature on Social and Economic Effects of Technological Change' in Stieber (1966).

18. Shephard found computer operators to experience the alienation of a sense of powerlessness; software specialists tended to show little feeling of powerlessness or normlessness. Shephard (1971), Ch. 5.

19. Mumford and Banks (1967), Chs. 4–5.

20. Shephard (1971), Ch. 4; Thomas L. Whisler, *The Impact of Computers on Organizations* (Praeger Publishers, New York, 1970). Ch. 6.

21. Floyd C. Mann and Lawrence K. Williams, 'Organization Impact of Automation in White-Collar Industrial Units', in Marcson (1970); Claudine Marenco, 'The Effects of the Rationalization of Clerical Work on the Attitudes and Behavior of Employees' in Stieber (1966); Mumford and Banks (1967), Ch. 5; Rhee (1968), Ch. IV.

22. Mann and Williams, 'Organization Impact of Automation' in Marcson (1970); Rhee (1968), Ch. IV.

23. Rhee (1968), Ch. IV.

24. Jones records that in Australia in the period 1960–80 computerisation eliminated 244,000 jobs and created 77,000, a net job loss of 167,000. Jones (1982), Ch. 5.

25. This section draws upon William A. Faunce, 'Automation and the Division of Labor' in Marcson (1970); Stettner, 'Survey of Literature on Social and Economic Effects' in Stieber (1966); Thomas L. Whisler, 'The Impact of Advanced Technology on Managerial Decision-Making' in Stieber (1966); Andrzej Zalewski, 'The

Influence of Automation on Management' in Stieber (1966).

26. Mann and Williams, 'Organization Impact of Automation' in Marcson (1970).

27. Whisler, *The Impact of Computers . . .*, p. 41.

28. Bright (1958), Ch. 15.

29. Discussions drawn on in this section are those of Beaumont and Helfgott (1964); Rothwell and Zegveld (1979); Sleigh *et al.* (1979).

30. See Beaumont and Helfgott (1964), Ch. II; Rhee (1968), Ch. V; Rothwell and Zegveld (1979), Ch. 5; Sadler (1968), Ch. 2. Hitachi has forecast that by 1986 it will employ no shop floor workers, merely maintenance and administrative staff. Andre Gorz, *Farewell to the Working Class: An Essay in Post-Industrial Socialism* (Pluto Press, London, 1982), Appendix 1.

31. Charles C. Killingsworth, 'Structural Unemployment in the United States' in Stieber (1966).

32. Rhee (1968), Ch. V.

33. Stettner, 'Survey of Literature on Social and Economic Effects' in Stieber (1966).

34. See Beaumont and Helfgott (1964), Ch. II; Rothwell and Zegveld (1979), Chs. 5–6; Sadler (1968), Ch. 2; Sleigh *et al.* (1979), Ch. IV; Stettner, 'Survey of Literature' in Stieber (1966).

35. The discussion in this chapter leaves unemployment due to economic recession out of account. Unemployment due to automation must be distinguished from that.

36. In the author's view figures have no useful place in works of polemic such as Colin Hines and Graham Searle, *Automatic Unemployment* (Earth Resources Research Ltd., London, 1979) and Clive Jenkins and Barry Sherman, *The Collapse of Work* (Eyre Methuen Ltd., London, 1979).

37. Rothwell and Zegveld (1979), Ch. 5.

38. Rothwell and Zegveld (1979), Ch. 2. In the period 1970–77 the German office equipment and computer industry lost 27.5 per cent of its labour force while its output rose by 49 per cent. Gorz, *Farewell to the Working Class*.

39. Such as exists in Japan. See Chapter 8.

40. See Philip Beresford, 'At Last . . . the Robots Are on the March' (23 Sept. 84); Ricardo Zermeno *et al.*, 'The Robots are Coming—Slowly' in Forester (1980). Gorz notes that world robot production is rising by 33 per cent a year. Gorz, *Farewell to the Working Class*. Simon foretold, in 1960, that by 1985 man would be fraternising with robots as readily as in 1960 he did with cars. Herbert A. Simon, 'What Computers Mean for Man and Society' in Forester (1980). Like all forecasts by true believers in technology this was over-optimistic, but the inevitability of this day coming is not in doubt. For other examples of over-optimism see James Martin and A.R.D. Norman, *The Computerized Society* (Prentice-Hall, Englewood Cliffs, New Jersey, 1970).

41. Charles C. Killingsworth, 'Implications of Automation for Employment and Manpower Planning' in Marcson (1970).

42. Maddock, 'The Future of Work'.

43. Sleigh *et al.* (1979), p. 15.

44. Albert Cherns, 'How it may affect the quality of life', part of 'Automation – Friend or Foe', *New Scientist* (8 June 1978), pp. 648–66. The quotation is on p. 654. A wide-ranging discussion of the theories of the relationship of technology and society is that of Fleron. See Frederick J. Fleron, Jr., 'Afterword' in Fleron (ed.), *Technology and Communist Culture: The Socio-Cultural Impact of Technology under Socialism* (Praeger, New York, 1977).

45. Woodward (1965).

46. Gallie (1978).

47. As the Luddites well knew, who broke machines to hurt management, not to hurt machines.

48. Karl Marx, *The Economic and Philosophical Manuscripts of 1844* (ed. D.J.

Struik; Lawrence and Wishart, London, 1970).

49. Blauner (1964), Ch. 1.

50. Just as F.W. Taylor's ideas of scientific management preceded Henry Ford's assembly line.

51. Friedmann (1964), esp. Ch. 7.

52. Cotgrove, 'Alienation and Automation'.

53. The word 'employment' is used in express contrast to the word 'work', since the latter is independent of the former.

54. Bell is foremost among these. See Chapter 2.

55. All figures are from Sorrentino except those for the USSR and for France in 1950. The two sources differ, but insignificantly, and are therefore compatible. 'Agriculture' includes forestry and fishing, 'industry' covers mining, manufacturing and construction. *Labour Force Estimates and Projections: 1950–2000* (International Labour Office, Geneva, 1977), vol. i, Asia, Table 3; Sorrentino (1971).

56. This is due to what has been called the 'industrialisation of agriculture', the introduction of chemicals, the displacement of labour by machines and improvements in labour organisation. It is a twentieth-century phenomenon.

57. Jones (1982), Ch. 1.

58. Singelmann (1978). In 1872 10.2 per cent of Japan's labour force was in tertiary employment and 4.9 per cent in secondary. Secondary sector workers outnumbered primary sector workers for the first time in 1962. See Koichi Emi, 'Employment Structure in the Service Industries', *The Developing Economies*, vol. vii, no. 2 (1969), pp. 133–57.

59. This formulation whereby mining is classed with agriculture under 'extractive' industry is of course different from that used in Table 4.1. However, in both formulations 'services' is the residual category.

60. 'Miscellaneous services' includes hotel, repair, recreational, medical, legal, educational and personal services. Sorrentino (1971).

61. On the contrary, Ginzberg and Vojta estimate that the service sector in the US accounted in 1978 for 66 per cent of GNP. Eli Ginzberg and George J. Vojta, 'The Service Sector of the US Economy', *Scientific American*, vol. 244, no. 3 (1981), pp. 32–9.

62. 'Other employment' combines Singelmann's two categories of 'extractive' and 'transformative' industries. Transformative industry covers manufacturing, construction and public utilities.

63. Fuchs (1968), p. 19, Table 2. Emi, using Fuchs's figures for the USA, contrasted the Japanese situation in this period. Japan had only about 2.3 per cent of its labour force in government service in 1965 and this share was not evidently on the increase. Emi, 'Employment Structure in the Service Industries'.

64. Ginzberg and Vojta, 'The Service Sector of the US Economy'.

65. Using Singelmann's definition (see note 62).

66. Rothschild has pointed out that the increase in employment at eating and drinking establishments in the period 1973–1979 was greater than the total number of workers employed in the US automobile and steel industries combined in 1980. Rothschild (1981).

67. Many of these service jobs arise from the re-classification of jobs that formerly were classified within manufacturing industry. Firms now buy in services that were previously performed in-house.

68. The figures in this paragraph have as their source data on 'Employment and Earnings Statistics for the United States' published by the US Bureau of Labor Statistics. They have been obtained from 'Changing Employment Patterns: Where Will the New Jobs Be? (National Economic Development Council, 28 Nov. 1983, unpublished).

69. Valerie A. Personick, 'The Outlook for Industry Output and Employment

through 1990', *Monthly Labor Review*, vol. 104, no. 8 (1981), pp. 28–41. The figures are from Table 4, p. 37. The exact equivalence between Personick's classification and that used by the Bureau of Labor Statistics is uncertain, but the raw figures are close enough to guarantee that percentage errors are of little significance.

70. Andre Gorz, *Farewell to the Working Class*.

71. Approximately 10 of the 13 million new jobs went to women.

72. Rothschild (1981).

73. Institute of Employment Research, University of Warwick, *Review of the Economy and Employment* (Summer 1983), Table 2.7, p. 30.

74. And in its forecast for 1990 the Warwick Institute predicts increases from 1982 in the first group's share of the labour force of 0.4 per cent and in the second group's of 8 per cent. Ibid.

75. Ibid., Table 3.2. In the period 1979–81 there was a marked growth in self-employment, the greater part of it doubtless in the service category.

76. It is true that in both countries there have been increases in service *occupations*, whether in service or other *employment*. The two countries are alike in this respect.

77. This section closely follows Bell (1980).

78. By information Bell means 'data processing in the broadest sense: the storage, retrieval, and processing of data'. Bell (1980), p. 504.

79. The figures for 1980 were based on Bureau of Labor Statistics projections. Bell (1980), p. 504.

80. Jones (1982), Ch. 3. Jones found that Australia's information sector expanded rapidly in the period 1961–71, but its rate of increase (3.7 per cent) was only just over half the service sector's (7.2 per cent) in the period 1971–79.

81. Jones (1982), p. 114.

82. Jones (1982), p. 49.

83. Gershuny (1978). In general terms this observation was made in 1975 by Mandel, who wrote: '*The logic of late capitalism is . . . necessarily to convert idle capital into service capital and simultaneously to replace service capital with productive capital, in other words, services with commodities*: transport services with private cars; theatre and film services with private television sets; tomorrow, television programmes and educational instruction with video-cassettes' (italics in the original). See Mandel (1975), p. 406.

84. Gershuny used a primary, secondary, intermediate and tertiary division of employment. The intermediate sector comprised transport, communications, utilities and construction. Gershuny (1978), Table 6.7, p. 98.

85. Goods-related employment, according to Gershuny, comprises distribution, finance, some professional and scientific work, some public administration. Ibid., p. 97.

86. Expenditure on services rose from 16.4 per cent of expenditure to 22.5 per cent, while service employment rose from 34.5 per cent of total employment to 48.1 per cent. Household expenditure on transport rose from 7.1 per cent to 13.4 per cent of household budgets, while expenditure on other services varied from 9.5 per cent to 9.6 per cent. Ibid., Tables 5.1 and 5.11.

87. Ibid., Table 5.2.

88. Ibid., Table 5.5.

89. This tendency is confirmed by Linder. He makes the point that as income rises, activities with high goods intensity become more attractive. Staffan Burenstan Linder, *The Harried Leisure Class* (Columbia University Press, New York, 1970).

90. Burns (1975), p. 52.

91. Jones (1982), Ch. 3. Jones's quinary sector covers (1) unpaid word (family, voluntary and do-it-yourself), (2) home-based work with incidental remuneration, and (3) the professional provision of quasi-domestic services (such as hotels and restaurants, the care of children and the aged, domestic services, home repairs and

laundry). His tertiary sector is tangible economic services and his quaternary is information processing.

92. Gershuny and Pahl have pointed to the necessity also of an underground, hidden, black economy as the proportion of the labour force in manufacturing has declined and as the price of goods has fallen relative to the price of legitimate labour. The black economy can restore to workers personal autonomy and initiative, variety of work, and opportunities to use skills. J.I. Gershuny and R.A. Pahl, 'Work Outside Employment: Some Preliminary Speculations' in Stuart Henry (ed.) *Can I Have It In Cash?* (Astragal Books, London, 1981).

93. Quoted in Jones (1982), p. 8.

Select Bibliography

The Impact of Automation

Beaumont, Richard A. and Helfgott, Roy B. (1964) *Management, Automation and People* (Industrial Relations Counsellors, New York)

Blauner, Robert (1964) *Alienation and Freedom: The Factory Worker and his Industry* (University of Chicago Press)

Bright, James R. (1958) *Automation and Management* (Graduate School of Business Administration, Harvard University, Boston)

Chadwick-Jones, J.K. (1969) *Automation and Behaviour* (Wiley-Interscience, London)

Forester, Tom (ed.) (1980) *The Microelectronics Revolution* (Basil Blackwell, Oxford)

Friedmann, Georges (1964) *The Anatomy of Work* (Free Press, Glencoe, Illinois)

Gallie, Duncan (1978) *In Search of the New Working Class: Automation and Social Integration within the Capitalist Enterprise* (Cambridge University Press)

Jones, Barry (1982) *Sleepers, Wake! Technology and the Future of Work* (Wheatsheaf Press, Brighton)

Mann, Floyd C. and Hoffman, L. Richard (1960) *Automation and the Worker* (Henry Holt and Co., New York)

Marcson, Simon (ed.) (1970) *Automation, Alienation, and Anomie* (Harper and Row, New York)

Mumford, Enid and Banks, Olive (1967) *The Computer and the Clerk* (Routledge and Kegan Paul, London)

Rhee, H.A. (1968) *Office Automation in Social Perspective* (Basil Blackwell, Oxford)

Rothwell, Roy and Zegveld, Walter (1979) *Technical Change and Employment* (Frances Pinter, London)

Sadler, Philip (1968) *Social Research on Automation* (Heinemann, London)

Shephard, Jon M. (1971) *Automation and Alienation: A Study of Office and Factory Workers* (MIT Press, Cambridge, Mass.,)

Sleigh, Jonathan, *et al.*, (1979) *The Manpower Implications of Microelectronic Technology* (Her Majesty's Stationery Office, London)

Stieber, Jack (ed.) (1966) *Employment Problems of Automation and Advanced Technology* (Macmillan, London)

Walker, Charles R. (1957) *Toward the Automatic Factory* (Yale University Press, New Haven, Conn.)

_____and Guest, Robert H. (1952) *The Man on the Assembly Line* (Harvard University Press, Boston, Mass.)

Woodward, Joan (1965) *Industrial Organization: Theory and Practice* (Oxford University Press)

The Shift to Services

Bell, Daniel (1980) 'The Social Framework of the Information Society' in Forester, Tom (ed.) *The Microelectronic Revolution* (Basil Blackwell, Oxford)

Burns, Scott (1975) *The Household Economy: Its Shape, Origins and Future* (Beacon Press, Boston, Mass.)

Fuchs, Victor R. (1968) *The Service Economy* (National Bureau of Economic Research, New York)

Gershuny, Jonathan (1978) *After Industrial Society? The Emerging Self-Service Economy* (Macmillan, London)

Jones, Barry (1982) *Sleepers, Wake! Technology and the Future of Work* (Wheatsheaf Books, Brighton)

Rothschild, Emma (1981) 'Reagan and the Real America', *New York Review of Books*, vol. xxviii, no. 1, pp. 12–18.

Singelmann, Joachim (1978) 'The Sectoral Transformation of the Labour Force in Seven Industrialized Countries, 1920–1970', *American Journal of Sociology*, vol. 83, no. 5, pp. 1224–34.

Sorrentino, Constance (1971) 'Comparing Employment Shifts in 10 Countries', *Monthly Labor Review*, vol. 94, no. 10, pp. 3–11.

PART THREE

THE INDUSTRIAL SYSTEM OF THE USSR

5 THE PLANNING PROCESS AND THE CYCLE OF REFORM

The Soviet System of Government

Under the Soviet system of government the administration of the state is in the joint hands of the government and the Communist Party, and is constructed in accord with the principles of Marxism-Leninism of which the only true interpreter is the Party. The Party aggregates and articulates the interests of the working class and, given that this implies rule in the working class interest, the society remains transitional to the ultimate state of classless Communism. It is at present socialist, as the Soviet Government declared it to be in 1936. Further political and cultural development is required before the Communist stage is reached.

In this transitional socialist stage of development the state assumes all principal administrative functions and state power is needed and used to mobilise economic development and to introduce modernisation.

In this situation changes occur and must occur, but from the socialist stage of development onwards these changes arise from non-antagonistic contradictions. Social classes remain: collective farmers on the one hand and workers, manual and non-manual (mental), on the other. The latter are further divided between specialists and non-specialists and the specialists are distinguishable into engineering and technical workers and the intelligentsia. But with no class conflict arising from the system of property relations, antagonistic contradictions and conflicts disappear. Social differences and social strata there may be, based on income, education, status and social influence, but these lead not to social class subordination and conflict, merely to a prestige hierarchy.[1]

This description is one that would be recognised within the Soviet Union although, because it is in part interpretative and evaluative, it may be thought tendentious by Western critics. What matters, however, is not whether it is agreed or true but that it underlines that the Party is a primary and integral part of the administrative structure and not supplementary to it.[2] And what follows from this is that the system is first and last a political system and not one whose political structure is determined by its economic relations. Therefore, at least in theory, political decision-makers could reintroduce a form of capitalist economy, which is precisely what some critics contend that they have done in a form called 'State Capitalism' or a 'State Monopoly Capitalist Economy'.[3]

Thus the entire social system is guided and controlled from above, led and monitored by the Party that represents the interests of the working people. In such a system there is by definition a source of tension, a touch of paradox. The Party knows best the people's interest, it is said, and the ambiguity of this English sentence (is it description or assertion?) reveals the difficulty. The Party has to both lead and respond; it must mobilise grassroots energy, at the same time as it issues instructions from the centre; it must be centralised to govern but be decentralised to keep in touch with the opinions of the people and to tap their energies to carry out the programme of government.

Kassof describes the Soviet Union as an 'administered society' in which an entrenched and powerful ruling group claims exclusive and scientific knowledge of social and historical laws and has a belief in the practical desirability and moral necessity of planning, direction and co-ordination from above in the name of the welfare and progress of all citizens. The political elite of Party and government leaders is supreme; and while it makes use of scientific and technical cadres these remain subordinate to the elite's 'self-proclaimed ultimate knowledge about the proper use of science and technology in the larger socio-historical setting'.[4]

It is recognised that the achievement of the Soviet Government in promoting the economic growth of the Soviet Union has been outstanding. In 1928 the GNP of the Soviet Union was one-quarter that of the United States; in 1980 it was three-quarters.[5] In the period 1928–1953 the economic growth rate was 6 to 7 per cent *per annum* achieved by a rate of investment of nearly 20 per cent.[6] Maximum effort was put into developing producer goods industries — steel, coal, electric power and transport — at the expense of consumer goods, and the economy was constantly at full stretch with small reserves. Inevitably the huge and only partially co-ordinated system suffered from problems of scarcity and oversupply at one and the same time, and from differences of perspective and perceptions of interest and priority between the central planning authorities and the managers of industrial enterprises. The massive directive effort required to launch the Soviet economy into a state of advanced industrialisation gave rise to a complex planning system, the examination of which is the central concern of this part of the study of industrial systems.

Soviet Planning

It is important to examine economic planning in the Soviet Union in the recognition that it is like all other economic systems known to man. It is imperfect. It works, and there is ample testimony to that in the impressive achievement of the economy since the founding of the USSR. But it does not work as well as it might and in certain respects, such as responsiveness to the consumer, it works less well than capitalist economies which also, in other respects, such as the provision of public services, do not work as well as could be wished. It is an economic system knowingly adopted, and with all the risks that that implies: that its faults will be blamed on those who devised it, elaborated it, and have implemented it — whether those who blame are sympathetic or hostile to the system itself.

There is a second necessary caveat to note before the Soviet system is examined. The Soviet Union is a vast country[7] and thus the difficulties of managing the economy, however this last phrase is understood, are correspondingly large. It does then follow that if a centralised management system is adopted, the cumulative effect of any faults in it will also be large and conspicuous, and difficult to remedy. The mere gathering of information on the basis of which judgements about the system and its well-being may be made is a task involving thousands of people over long periods of time. Like a dinosaur, the body-economic senses fitfully and sluggishly what is going on and its reactions are correspondingly equivocal and slow.[8] The point is that this must be so; there is no way round the problem. Even the increased speeds of modern methods of information processing do not solve the difficulties. Indeed if they are put to work on data gathered too late for the timely making of decisions and on incorrect data, the planners' problems may be greatly worsened both by the larger amounts of data which can, at least in principle, be handled and by the higher expectations that men have of modern information systems.

The most important statement to be made in this section of the book, in which many of the imperfections of, and problems related to, the Soviet planning system are noted, is that the system is necessarily imperfect. It is this that must be understood. And it is no part of the purpose of this book to score simple points at the expense of Soviet economists, administrators, politicians, planners, computer specialists or managers, or to suggest that another economic system would work better. More important is to understand how it does work and what have been the effects of some of the changes made in the system in recent years.

The essence of administrative planning is that central authority determines the economic targets of the industrial system and also the means of achievement of those targets. Planning issues are thus manifestly political as well as economic — there is no disputing this.[9] Hence approval of plans by the highest authorities takes precedence over the achievement of detailed coherence; and the overall coherence of planning is derived from what must in the end be arbitrary decisions about growth rates. Plans in the Soviet Union are built around national output goals and decisions about which major sectors are due for an expansionary effort; they are stated principally in terms of physical output targets for key commodities and classified goods, together with specifications of financial and time limits; and relationships between economic units, down to enterprise level, are prescribed. Once choices are made by the topmost central authorities, there are no alternative plans available. Low level units have their part to play in the planning process because high level decisions can only be taken on the basis of the best information available about what is going on below. Given this need and the social fact that information and judgements are necessarily affected by perceptions and interests at all levels, then planning has to be based on an accumulation of largely unassessed and uncoordinated data and decisions which there is simply insufficient time to evaluate and which are affected (and presumably at times distorted) by exposure in the transmission process to the special interests of intermediate levels of the system. It cannot be surprising that plans are frequently too taut and poorly co-ordinated.[10]

There are other immediate consequences of the political nature of the planning process. Plans can be changed willfully and certain sections of the economy, dear to the interests of certain groups, can be disproportionately stimulated — with consequences that compromise the plan's coherence and also threaten inflationary pressures. The whole political apparatus of a highly centralised state can be brought to bear on economic activity; hence the role of the Party (and occasionally the police) is of great consequence in the Soviet system.[10]

Background

The directive planning system was born of the first Five Year Plan, in the years 1928–32.[11] It takes its place in the Soviet Union's threefold system of administration: the all-union government, the republican governments and the Communist Party. The Soviet 'parliament' is the Supreme Soviet which elects the praesidium and the Council of Ministers; this structure is duplicated in the 15 republics although subject to all-union government. This duplication produces a dual administration whereby union-republican ministries are subordinate both to all-union ministries and to the appropriate republic's council of ministers. The third element of administration is provided by the Party structure. Here it is the Party Congress that is nominally supreme and which elects the Central Committee to which the Politburo is accountable. Great complexity in responsibilities and accountability is thus a basic ingredient in the system of government.[12]

The direction of the economy within this overall framework is in the hands of 48 economic ministries, all of which originally contained divisions and chief administrations (*glavki*), and of various central agencies whose numbers and division of responsibilities have fluctuated over time. Of these agencies the principal is *Gosplan*, the State Planning Commission. *Gosplan*, however, is not a true central planning agency, the arbiter of the plan. It acts rather as an expert adviser, one among many interests represented on the Council of Ministers and inevitably restricted by the parallel administrative structures. At one time (1963–65) *Gosplan* was formally subordinated to the Supreme Council of the National Economy (*VSNKh*), and although it was freed in 1966 it remains under pressure from ministries, all-union and republican.[13]

Planning is in fact not unitary but divided into current planning and long-range planning. Long-range plans are for a five-year or longer period and are on an aggregate basis: they are not operational or specific. Their operational counterparts are investment plans. Short-term plans, for one year or less, are necessarily operational: they are invariably urgent, and therefore take precedence over longer-term plans.

How the Planning System Works[14]

How the Soviet planning system works, in what Gregory and Stuart call 'an idealised version',[15] is described in what follows, in an eight-stage sequence (see Figure 5.1).[16]

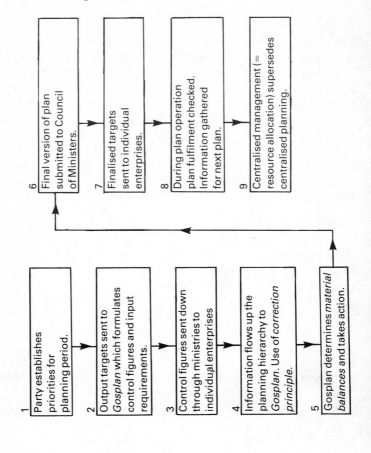

Figure 5.1: The Planning Process

1. Party establishes priorities for planning period.

2. Output targets sent to *Gosplan* which formulates control figures and input requirements.

3. Control figures sent down through ministries to individual enterprises

4. Information flows up the planning hierarchy to *Gosplan*. Use of *correction principle*.

5. *Gosplan* determines *material balances* and takes action.

6. Final version of plan submitted to Council of Ministers.

7. Finalised targets sent to individual enterprises.

8. During plan operation plan fulfilment checked. Information gathered for next plan.

9. Centralised management (= resource allocation) supersedes centralised planning.

In the first stage the Party (the Politburo or the Central Committee) makes the political decisions for the coming planning period by establishing its priorities. The Party expresses these priorities by setting output targets for certain crucial funded commodities.[17]

In the second stage these output targets descend through the state apparatus to *Gosplan*, which has been collecting data on past plan fulfilment[18] and bottlenecks. *Gosplan* formulates a set of control figures (tentative output targets) for some 200 or 300 product groups that will satisfy the Party's chosen priorities. *Gosplan* also estimates on the basis of past performance the inputs needed to achieve the control figures. The planning departments of the ministries assist *Gosplan* in formulating the full set of control figures and in projecting input requirements.

The third stage sees the control figures sent down through the ministries to industrial enterprises. As the control figures move through the planning hierarchy they are disaggregated into specific tasks until each enterprise receives its own control figures. At the same time the planning branch of each ministry prepares a list of input requirements, based on the ministry's control figures, for internal use by each enterprise.

While the first three stages have witnessed directives coming from the top downwards, at the fourth stage information from enterprise level begins to flow upwards through the planning hierarchy to *Gosplan*. Enterprises inform their superiors of their input requirements so that these may be aggregated as they are passed up the hierarchy. At each stage in this process the unit's actual request for inputs is compared with the estimate that has come down from above, and what is called the *correction principle* is used to adjust for differences between the two. There is considerable bargaining involved in this process.

It is at the fifth stage that the concept of *material balances* comes into the picture. In Gregory and Stuart's succinct sentence, 'A material balance is achieved when the planned supplies of each commodity equal its targeted material input requirements and final uses'.[19] It is *Gosplan*'s task to ensure that material balances exist.

The sixth stage, after *Gosplan* achieves material balance, is one in which the final version of the plan is submitted to the Council of Ministers for approval (and sometimes modification), and the seventh sees the final planning targets in the form of the *techpromfinplan* (the technical-industrial-financial plan) passed to industrial enterprises. The *techpromfinplan* gives output targets, input allocations, supply plans, delivery plans, financial plans, wages bills and other targets.

Finally, at the eighth stage, and in anticipation of the next planning cycle, *Gosplan* checks plan fulfilment at all levels of the system during the actual operation of the plan and gathers information upon which the forthcoming year's plan will be based.

Given that this is an idealised description of the system, actual experience is different. Unfortunately the scale of the operation seriously affects timing and may preclude the possibility of adequate information to serve as the basis of planning. An enterprise may have to estimate what its input requirements will be in the future planning period before it knows what its actual production plans will be, with the consequence that output plans when finally drawn up and issued from above are determined by previously estimated input needs.[20] But if the enterprise delayed its input bid until its production plan was drawn up, then the central plan would emerge only when the period to which it related was already under way — as indeed does happen. The result is that intermediate and final parts of a plan may be determined together. In such a system a high degree of coordination is vital, and it cannot be achieved. Different administrative bodies issue different parts of the plan; some contradiction is inevitable.[21] The difficulties of the system arise from its very nature, a central plan for a vast country: the centre must issue directions to units about the details of the plan when it may not know what needs to be done in disaggregated detail. Hence micro-economic instructions are often crude.

From the centre the answer to such difficulties is plan adjustment, a practice developed since the earliest five-year plans. Again it must be emphasised that adjustments are not evidence of incompetence on the part of planners who could have done their jobs better without any subsequent need for adjustment. Wilhelm says that a planning system is not working if it is continually adjusted during its fulfilment,[22] but it is essential to any planning process that first estimates and approximations are followed by later adjustments when information significant for the plan and not available at the time of its inception comes to hand.[23] In such circumstances, not to adjust is evidence of incompetence or delusion. It is also perhaps often forgotten that 'plans' are always adjusted in any economic system: in a market economy the adjustments are disaggregated and because privately effected, invisible.

As the years have gone by, the significance of the adjustment process has inevitably increased and the central administrative task in this whole planning process, in which directives flowing down the system meet information flowing up, has become that of reconciliation, the achievement of material balances. It must be normal for planned supplies of a commodity to be out of balance with estimated input needs, and then a balance must be achieved. There are five recognised ways of restoring equilibrium.

First, *Gosplan* can order an increase in the planned output of the commodity that will otherwise be in deficit. Unfortunately, this change is likely to have secondary effects, for example, to increase planned inputs in order to achieve the increase in output. More commonly the planners avoid any chain reaction by simply calling for increased production *without any increase in planned inputs*, thus forcing economies upon enterprises and increasing the tautness of plans.

As a second possibility, *Gosplan* can increase imports of the deficit commodity. This, however, is not a popular approach since it would make material balance dependent on foreign supplies and possibly use scarce foreign exchange reserves.

Third, *Gosplan* can reduce inter-industry demand for the commodity in question by directing enterprises to use substitute materials that are not in short supply or by reducing their inputs. The danger here is of a knock-on effect should the enterprises not be able to meet their output targets.

Fourth, *Gosplan* can reduce final demand for the commodity affected. This means reducing either exports or household demand or investment demand. The attraction of this alternative is that the buck stops with the consumer (the household) and there are no further effects on inter-industry balances.

Fifth and finally, *Gosplan* may occasionally draw upon stocks of the deficit commodity if these are adequate, but this has rarely been done.

Historically *Gosplan* has used the third or fourth approach to achieving material balance within a priority system which has tended to favour producer-goods industries. Thus the consumer has often borne the brunt of material balance crises, at least in the five-year plans up to 1950, and the consumer sector has at times been known as the 'buffer' section of the economy.

The View from the Enterprise

Having set out the system of planning as seen from the macro level, we should balance this with the viewpoint of the enterprise. The enterprise does, as noted, send vital information up through the hierarchical structure about its required inputs, its capabilities, and its past performance, and it takes part in bargaining in establishing the 'correction principle'. But of necessity the bargaining is not between equals and the enterprise is for the most part in the position of receiving and reacting to directives from above. The *techpromfinplan* sets the social goals for the enterprise and its plan targets — output levels (in quantity and value), output assortment, labour and other inputs, productivity norms, productivity indexes, etc. The central and over-riding aspect, however, is the production plan based on the estimated capacity of the enterprise, its expected resource utilisation and estimated productivity increases. The plan specifies also the ruble value of the output, the commodity assortment and the delivery schedule of output. In addition the *techpromfinplan* specifies for the enterprise the financial plan, the plan of material and technical supply, the delivery plan, the plan of plant and equipment utilisation, the plan for wages and labour, and indexes of labour productivity.

The enterprise management on the receiving end of these plans has multiple objectives, yet one over-riding one. This leads to some uncertainty: which plan targets should not be met if all cannot be and how should priorities be chosen?; but also to a position with a potentiality for bargaining, and a licence for informal resourcefulness and one in which the over-riding target is clear — output plan fulfilment.[24]

From the enterprise's viewpoint, therefore, plan adjustments are constantly sought in order to obtain the better performance that gains recognition from higher authority. For example, if an enterprise's targets are uneven, some too high and others too low, an overall scaling down of targets will lead to the previously too high being achieved and the previously too low being overfulfilled — which means overall overfulfilment and, as a consequence, recognition and reward. Enterprise managements learned early that a modest fulfilled plan is more advantageous than an ambitious but underfulfilled plan for which no bonus is given. The resources of management to cope with pressures from above and the informal practices that are employed are discussed more fully in Chapter 6.[25]

Criticism of the System

Economists have long noted the power of the Soviet system for achieving rapid growth of industrial output in selected priority sectors and, overall, the massive success of the Soviet Union's drive for industrialisation. Taut planning does indeed force enterprises to the limits of their production possibilities. Economists demur somewhat at some of the informal practices that the tautness of plans gives rise to, but they recognise that at least some informal and even illicit practices uncover resources of output potentiality that might otherwise have remained untapped.

But having recognised the achievement of the system in forcefully accelerating the process of industrialisation, economic critics in the West focus with evident relish on its disadvantages and on the unsuitability of its continuance.

To Zaleski the planning is arbitrary, overdetailed, not locally specific, inefficient, uncoordinated, inconsistent and unstable.[26] To Nove the system leads to errors, bottlenecks, amendments, mismatching, misallocation, disequilibrium and delay.[27] The system has outlived its usefulness, say other critics; it is not appropriate to a mature, developed economy with an increasingly sophisticated and well-educated labour force; it sufficed when the need was for the diffusion of known techniques (often borrowed from overseas) but it cannot manage fundamental research and development; it cannot adapt to the information society with its rising tide of data and its subtle and compendious methods of data storage, retrieval and analysis; and much more on the anachronistic nature of the system.

Levine, more subtly, has hypothesised that there are two elements in the Soviet system that can, if only with difficulty, be analytically distinguished: planning, which is a Soviet development, and pressure, which is an historical inheritance. In other words he wishes to separate the effects of the tautness of plans from those of the plans themselves.[28] The implication is of course that the planning system could be looser and more flexible, and perhaps, as a consequence, more efficient. Levine's distinction will be considered below.

An unorthodox, but possibly helpful, division of the criticisms is between, on the one hand, those of certain objective consequences of the system where values could in principle be calculated and, on the other, those of certain subjective or psychological consequences and their behavioural manifestations.

The objective problems of the planning system concern the

matching of multiple plans, the measurement of plan fulfilment, the costs of the system and the relationship of producers' and customers' needs. First is the issue of multiple plans. This arises from the need to match the overall plans of each unit in the economic system with the plans of each related unit whether above or below or on the same level in the system, and the need to match for each unit the different plans that go to make up that unit's overall plan. Each enterprise has, among other less important plans, plans for output,[29] supply, finance[30] and labour,[31] and these may not be consistent at the outset. If they are, it may be difficult to sustain consistency if any of the sub-plans was based on faulty information or if for any reason adjustments are subsequently made to the plans. Likewise two related enterprises may find that one's output plan is not matched as it needs to be with another's supply plan; or, again, that if they are at first, they may cease to be subsequently. The more aggregated indicators there are, the greater are the inconsistencies that may arise between them.

Second is the measurement of plan fulfilment. This also has two aspects: the choice of the appropriate unit of measurement and the verification of measurement. If units are measured by the ton, why should not a factory produce one large unit? If shoe manufacture is measured in numbers of pairs, what is to control the thickness of the leather? If lamp manufacture is measured in aggregate watt power, what ensures the production of low-powered lamps? For manufacturers of sheet steel or plate glass how is the appropriate mix of products by thickness to be achieved? For hauliers paid according to tons moved per kilometre, how is the necessity of their journeys assessed? These are just some of the detailed problems of output measurement that have been noted.[32]

But beyond this kind of problem is that of the choice of indicator to measure. Should gross output be the measure? It may simply lead to accumulation in an enterprise's warehouse rather than the alternative of products more readily sold or of materials allowing the manufacture of more saleable products. Should value-added be the measure, or will it encourage the addition of unnecessary value? If the measure is not output but expected sales, will no-one work to cheapen inputs? Overall, if overfulfilment of plans is always rewarded, will not waste be exacerbated?[33] All these problems are of course better known to Soviet planners than to gleeful western commentators whose knowledge of them is principally dependent on the Soviet press, and they have proved difficult to cure. The remedy has been to combine measures, but doing so generates more inconsistency and further complicates already difficult planning and management problems. Success is the satisfaction of manifold criteria simultaneously, with opinion shifting as to which of the criteria should be regarded as of principal importance and, as a consequence, further opportunities for manipulation.[34]

Third are the costs of the system. The criticism here is quite simply that enterprises need not bother with costs, and therefore with waste, hoarding, high cost materials, low sales, overmanning, and so forth, because the plan covers all costs; or, to be more exact, because each new plan assumes costs at the level of the last plan, so that there is no incentive to reduce costs. The most obvious reaction to this point is to suggest that reduction of costs might well increase the chances of overfulfilment of at least some part of an enterprise's plan and thus attract the rewards of overfulfilment but, as is more fully discussed below, the unacceptable consequence of such a policy is the raising of the thresholds of future plans.

Fourth is the relationship of producer and customer. In a planned production economy the customer, whether consumer or another producer, is manifestly in a weak position. Determination of needs and choice of goods for sale are both decided by planners and administrative superiors, not by customers; thus enterprises feel little responsibility to customers. Choice of supplier, for producers, is also determined by plan; the customer has no choice. Further, although obviously buyer and seller have direct contact on the occasion of actual transactions, in the management of dealings they are separated by a long line of offices and organisations; Zaleski records documents for the distribution of tires being processed through 32 stages.[35]

These 'objective' difficulties could all be solved or, in any case, mitigated, many Western commentators imply, by allowing the customer a role closer to that which he possesses in the capitalist market economy system. Give the consumer choice and most problems of lack of contact, wastefulness, planning contradictions and measurements of success will fall away. But this is a deliberately naive point, for no free market is possible in a system with centrally planned inputs, while centrally planned output is inconsistent with supply arrangements based on direct ties between enterprises,[36] and no principal-subcontractor relationships of the kind familiar under Western capitalism can be allowed if bankrupcies are to be avoided in a system in which all enterprises administer property owned by the state.[37] The criticisms are of course of the system as a whole, a further confirmation that the system must be judged as such.

The subjective consequences of the system are of at least equal importance to its understanding since its continued operation is so obviously dependent on the attitudes and behaviour of those who man the system. The fundamental characteristic of the system, from which others follow, is that self-interest, which Adam Smith believed to be the motor of every economy, has to be manifested within the confines of the system itself. Because it is a political system, in which power, and ultimately coercion, determines the limits of behaviour in obvious ways, the survival game has to be played within the system. There are broadly three results of this in relation to the planning system: tactical targeting, illicit practices and conservatism.

Tactical targeting would seem to be an appropriate term for the practice of seeking best advantage under the notorious tautness of the planning system. This means that an economic ministry will be inclined to adjust plans in order to maximise the ministry's credit for plan fulfilment or overfulfilment, even if this introduces lack of stability into plans, norms and bonus calculations. It will also go in for 'reserving' a portion of each month's material allotments to deal with bottlenecks.[38] Tactical targeting also means that enterprise management will adopt any means to avoid underfulfilment of plans: it will avoid high targets, and therefore a high output in the present which could lead to high targets in the future; it will understate its output possibilities and overstate its input claims and costs; it will neglect quality in favour of volume of output; it will eschew all innovation. This practice of course is known to the enterprise's administrative superiors and has the predictable result that the planners start to assume misinformation and allocate targets that will compensate for what they believe this may be, thus setting up a vicious circle of concealment and compensatory targeting,[39] and an unwillingness at higher levels to take the protests of enterprises seriously.[40]

Tactical targeting is no doubt a national practice but it is also dishonest. It is merely one among many informal and illicit strategies. Others are stockpiling, irregular production (including 'storming'[41]), unofficial barter, the use of *blat* and the employment of *tolkachi*. *Blat* is the use of personal influence to obtain illicit favours in procurement; most usually not so much by bribery as by offers of raw materials or products with alternative uses. *Tolkachi* are supply agents who may use bribery to obtain or expedite delivery of much needed supplies.[42]

Perhaps, however, the existence of such practices should not be seen as pathological. In any highly formal framework it is entirely to be expected that many informal practices will develop, some of which will be illicit. Not only will they develop, but they must do so if the system is to work — if flesh and blood humans are to operate a skeletal blueprint. Given this sociological fact, it follows that the more formal the system and the more comprehensive its procedures, the more informal practices will develop. Thus their presence, often witnessed gleefully by Western critics of the Soviet system, is not evidence that the system is not working but evidence that it *is*.

The final major consequence of the Soviet planning system is conservatism, which follows from two characteristics of the system. These are that planning is carried out 'on the achieved basis'[43] and that it is imposed from the top down. A system based on the precept 'steady as she goes' does not encourage innovation: research and development have an uncertain return while an increase in the resources given to them clearly reduces resources available elsewhere;[44] the procedure of periodic plan adjustment discourages systemic reform. At the same time a system in which inevitably somewhat arbitrary, and at times contradictory, calculations reach the plan implementers with obligatory force and in which subsequent intervention is commonplace presses enterprises toward the goal of self-sufficiency — the avoidance, where possible, of reliance on the vagaries of uncertain sources of supply — and stifles initiative and innovatory discretion.[45] To misappropriate a phrase of Joyce's, in the Soviet system 'one thing alone is needful — the fulfilment of the plan'.[46] In that circumstance, in which goals are external and given, fundamental new thinking is largely eliminated. Management plays safe.

This is by and large a pessimistic view of the Soviet economy: Leviathan-like, a cumbrous and clumsy giant. And it is not alleviated by recognition of the power to set priorities exercised in relation to defence. The command system, which allows, for example, the space industry to be given priority and massive resources, effectively underlines the basic inertia. The defence industry is necessarily treated as exceptional and it is wholly secure; other industries are doubly not so.

In addition, the consumer is the manifest victim of the inflexible economy which is able to serve whole industries all the time but individuals only some of the time. Thus goods go periodically into short supply and there has to be some effect of this upon personal incentives and labour productivity.

What then is left of the Soviet system when all these powerful criticisms have been made? The answer, perhaps unexpectedly, is 'all of it', for what have temporarily been allowed to appear as sober and objective criticisms are for the most part mere observations, or polemic. The sole legitimate ground for rational criticism of any system, economic or political, is *assessment in terms of its own objectives*. Judged in this manner, the Soviet system succeeds overall; only in relation to some of its sub-goals, such as the provision of a satisfactory system of incentives or openness to the introduction of new technology or sufficient accountability to customers, does it fail.

The first priority at issue here, a point made by Ellman, is a negative one. The Soviet planning system should not be compared with Western market systems *as if their goals were the same*. They are not. In Ellman's words

> Planning and the market are not alternative roads to the same destination. Planning is advocated by those who wish to achieve a very different distribution of goods among the population than would have been achieved by the market, and to allocate resources, in a dynamic economy, in a direction which the market, left to itself, would not have chosen.[47]

The planning system has unquestionably succeeded in achieving a distribution of goods that is different, owing to its relative neglect of consumer demand, from that which the unfettered market would provide and that is shaped by the planners' decisions. Plans are devised that are feasible, that is, capable of achievement, given available resources and technology, and that are more or less achieved. This measure of success is more important than the consistency of plans, or their optimality (that is, the achievement of the maximum level of output, yielding the greatest satisfaction to the planning authorities, for given input).

The second point is a positive one, and is the answer to Levine. The planning system cannot be distinguished from pressure because it is itself, and is designed to be, a system for applying pressure. It is, in sum, a political device, a system of central control. This is the overall importance of the planning system in the Soviet Union, and from it flow two significant corollaries. It does not, in the last analysis, matter if the system does not deliver all the economic goods that have been expected of it. It is not, in the last analysis, possible to introduce significant decentralisation measures. For everything is subsidiary to the maintenance of a system of centralised political power.

There is, however, one important corrective footnote to this impression of stagnation. Possibilities for innovation exist in every system and in the Soviet system as elsewhere. The simple point is that in a centralised and coercive system they exist exclusively in the centre. At the centre priorities for the entire system can be shifted and forced through at any time.[48] Most usually major shifts will occur at a time of change in political power, but they may occur at any time.

An Examination of Economic Reforms

Having taken a general overview of the Soviet economic system, it is now possible, against this background and with a view to greater depth of understanding, to look at some of the principal efforts at reform that have occurred in the post-Stalin era.[49] The intention is to examine the reforms and their aftermaths solely with the aim of throwing more light on the industrial system and how it changes; it is not to satisfy the detailed interests of an economic historian in the post-World War II Soviet economy.[50]

The Territorial Reorganisation of 1957

The major reform introduced by Khrushchev in 1957, namely a massive decentralisation of economic power to *sovnarkhozy* (regional economic councils controlling industry and construction, under the union republics) was in itself a culmination of earlier steps in reform of the system which had been subjected to criticism very similar to that made already in this chapter.

Stalin died in 1953, at a time when the ministerial control of the economy had already been found wanting in many respects. In 1954 the system itself was criticised for emphasising current at the expense of long-term planning, and industrial at the expense of regional planning; for too much centralisation, too much paperwork, too many staff, too many administrative links. A great many current practices were also attacked: the fabrication of reports; the reconciliation of resources and plans by command or by informal practices such as bargaining, simulation[51] and outright illegality; the inflation of supply requests while hoarding; the padding of overheads; the overstatement of capital needs and manpower and wage needs while establishing low material utilisation norms and easy plan targets for labour productivity; the manipulation of assortment mixes.[52]

In 1955 the criticism was led by Bulganin. It was alleged that bureaucratisation and routinisation were inhibiting economic efficiency and technological progress. As a result of the accumulation of criticism, measures of decentralisation and structural rationalisation were introduced. In 1954, 46 ministries and departments, 200 *glavki*, and 147 trusts were abolished, and a process of bringing enterprises under republic rather than union control was initiated.[53] In 1955 current planning was split from long-term planning,[54] and centrally planned items were reduced in number.

Then in 1957 Krushchev's major reform was introduced, the setting up of 105[55] *sovnarkhozy*, to establish a new relationship between centralised planning and decentralised plan execution, in place of 141 union, union-republic, and republic ministries. All planning now returned to *Gosplan* which absorbed the supply and sales administrations of the abolished ministries, and was enlarged in staff as well as function; it took on more than 30 commissions of planning officials and scientists from universities and research institutes to work on the 1959–65 plan.[56] The *sovnarkhozy* themselves had a role in plan-drafting on the basis of *Gosplan* targets, and pre-eminently the task of close regional co-ordination of enterprises in plan-implementation; the regions were encouraged to develop local interests and pursue self-sufficiency. It was intended to develop more national supply lines and better use of transport. At enterprise level new commissions, committees and standing conferences were introduced. At union-republic level other *Gosplans* were charged with adjusting lower-level plans, co-ordinating *sovnarkhoz* production programmes and preventing undesirable 'localistic' tendencies.[57]

The reform also greatly affected procedures as well as structures, now that the locus of control over about 75 per cent of gross industrial output was the *sovnarkhoz*.[58] Production came under *sovnarkhoz* control; profits were aggregated and taxed at *sovnarkhoz* level; the *sovnarkhoz* distributed retained profits to enterprises; without superior ministries many *sovnarkhozy* became *inter*-dependent. In surveying its subordinate enterprises a *sovnarkhoz* could deal with loss-makers by forcing mergers, transferring capacity, closing plants, continuing subsidies or requesting higher selling prices. It could reduce staff, transfer stocks, move idle equipment, redistribute capital grants. In short, at regional level, more responsive to grass-roots reality than ministries could ever be, the *sovnarkhozy* were powerful instruments for rationalisation, and for regional integration and self-sufficiency.[59]

And yet in a few years the changes were themselves abolished, the remedy was found to be more damaging than the original ailment. Empire-building was not halted: it merely became territorial rather than industrial.[60] Resources were diverted locally in pursuit of a self-sufficiency that most *sovnarkhozy* were simply not large enough to achieve. It became yet more difficult to introduce new technology. Planning with a regional focus ignored any consequences for other regions as well as losing the traditional emphasis on the national perspective. Common sectoral problems were simply not considered.[61] In short, partial decentralisation of a centralised system gave rise to local (regional) abuses that the weakened centre now lacked the power to control. The sociological fact is that a consciously controlled centralised system cannot operate with the power of centralised control weakened, and the renewed emphasis on power and control is a reminder that the Soviet system is essentially a political system — a system whose economic nature is determined by prior political choice.

From 1958 a conservative reaction to the *sovnarkhoz* reform set in. Bureaucratic and centralist controls were reimposed from 1959.[62] In 1960 republican (higher level) *sovnarkhozy* were formed and the number of centrally planned products was increased. In 1961 investment planning was centralised and central control over supply was increased.[63] Also in 1961 in recognition that *sovnarkhozy* were too small, 17 economic territories were set up with councils to co-ordinate several *sovnarkhozy* in relation to planning.[64] From 1958 to 1961 *Gosplan* was strengthened, taking back from *Gosekonom-komissila* current planning functions, but in 1961 long-range planning was placed under a new planning agency, *Gosekonomsovet*. In 1962 the massive USSR *Sovnarkhoz* was introduced, charged with management and administration and also with current planning at the same time that *Gosplan* received control of long-range planning. Then from 1963 to 1965 both USSR *Sovnarkhoz* and *Gosplan* were placed under the Supreme Council of National Economy (*VSNKh*).[65]

The detail of all these changes is not significant in the context of this discussion. What matters is the cumulative evidence of continuing uncertainty and vacillation, a product, unsurprisingly, of the shifting influence of various pressure groups, jockeying for position around Krushchev's controversial policies. With Krushchev's dismissal in 1964, the structural clock was finally and firmly put back: in 1965 *VSNKh* was abolished; *Gosplan* again became the sole planning agency; the all-union republic and regional *sovnarkhozy* were abolished; 17 all-union and 12 union republic ministries were re-established (as against the 16 and 11, respectively, of 1957) with direct administrative authority over enterprises and major industrial research institutes.[66] The political and economic debate was once more decisively settled.

Liberman's Reform Proposals

Many Soviet economists have been strongly critical of the planning system and debate has been continual whenever not expressly disallowed. The best-known proponent of reform in the early post-Stalin period was the economist Liberman, who put forward his ideas for change in the period 1956–65.[67] His proposals exemplify Soviet theorists' attempts to modify the system.

Liberman proposed three principal innovations: that enterprises should have greater autonomy in planning and management, provided that this was compatible with the overall system; that plan operation should be geared to 'profitability';[68] that planning at enterprise level should be entirely separated from planning in the government's economic apparatus so that each enterprise would form its own plan. Liberman suggested that while gross quantitative indicators concerning volume of output and assortment should be announced, the working out of details and specifications should be agreed between suppliers and customers; and that qualitative indexes should be developed as a composite of 'profitability', average wages, norms for expenditure on labour, and productivity indexes.[69]

These proposals, developed round the key ideas of autonomous planning, the use of profits as a prime measure of success, and greater accountability to the customer, aroused strong opposition and were defeated. However small these suggested changes may seem to be, they have implications that defenders of the system had to resist. First was the fear that the system would unravel like a ball of wool, that there would be no stopping the process of decentralisation once begun, leading to the end of the planning system itself. Perhaps more important here is recognising the fear rather than assessing the risk. Second was the argument to protect the knowledge and vision of the centre where national (social as against individual) needs were known and national plans (for long-term projects and high priority sectors such as the chemical industry or defence) could be identified and promoted. One critic, Zverev, noted, 'The enterprises are ignorant of the various economic interrelations, and even if they wanted to establish the balance of the economy they could not do it.'[70] Third, reciprocally, was what could be termed 'the higher distrust', the need to avoid the ends of localism: uneven development, the disfavouring of less profitable industries, managerial bargaining over norms, and the manipulation of production and profits to local advantage. Fourth is the explicitly ideological attack upon the central role of profit, the motivating force of the capitalist system, and upon opponents of the State, which alone knows the profound interests of the workers and so must develop and guard social production, and of the plan, without which manpower surpluses and unemployment would be rife (as in the capitalist states) and discipline would slacken. Fifth is the self-defence of those in power at the centre of the system and their vested interests.[71]

All these factors defeated Liberman and are likely to defeat any proposals, however seemingly modest, that can be perceived as attacks upon the system itself. For what is at stake is the dominance of the centre, the political (control) system of the society and its accompanying ideology. Control of the system resides in the centre where it is exercised by the Party in the interests of the people; and so any proposal that could weaken that central control is a possible threat to the system as a whole and must be opposed.[72] Zaleski comments that the planning system was born in an authoritarian spirit of intolerance and is a by-product of excessive centralisation.[73] But it is not as though the planning system were the product of an isolated choice, that might have turned out differently if it had been undertaken in a different spirit. The economic system in the Soviet Union is the consequence of prior political determination — of who controls the system, in whose interests and how.

The 1965 Economic Reform

September 1965 saw not only the dissolution of Krushchev's economic structures but also new initiatives, launched by Kosygin, in procedural reform. Kosygin proposed that the problems of the production of low quality and unsold goods should be tackled by using volume of goods sold as a criterion of success and by making use of an index of profitability (the amount of profit per ruble of productive assets). Enterprises should retain profits in relation to their effective use of assets, the increase in the volume of goods sold, improvements in output quality and increased profitableness; and these profits should be used, through three new funds, to develop production, to improve techniques and to encourage workers, to improve working and living conditions. Further, enterprises should be rewarded more for the achievement of plans, involving new goods and better quality goods, than for overachievement.[74]

Following Kosygin's speech a series of major measures was introduced in October 1965, of which four were of special importance:

(1) The planning of all but eight of the 35–40 key indicators was devolved to enterprises. This was a substantial change despite the eight retained under ministry control being the most important of all: physical output of principal products; sales; profits and profitability; wages fund; payments into the state budget; capital investment from centralised funds; material supplies; and tasks for the introduction of new technology.

(2) Sales, profits and profitability were established as new success criteria and as new determinants of managerial bonuses[75] and of the new funds proposed by Kosygin.

(3) Payment from profits into the material incentive fund was made only for the actual fulfilment of the production growth plan.

(4) A charge was introduced for the use of invested capital.[76]

As is usual with Soviet reform measures, change was slow and it took until the end of 1967 for 7,000 enterprises (a mere 15 per cent of all industrial enterprises) to be brought under the new provisions, though they did represent 40 per cent of the value of total industrial output and 50 per cent of total profit.[77] However, as is also usual, beneficial effects were immediate: sales of these 7,000 enterprises increased by 11 per cent in 1966 and 12 per cent in 1967 and profits by 23.5 and 25 per cent respectively in the same years; malpractices disappeared; workers became cost-conscious; costs of materials were saved (that is, hidden reserves, legal and illegal, were uncovered); the turnover of working capital accelerated; and surplus equipment was sold or written off.[78]

But despite the introduction of new procedures, old rules were still retained, with contradictory and confusing results. For example, new profitability criteria led to a drive to economise on labour while the old rules did not allow the dismissal of labour without work to go to or without re-training. Similarly, the push to economise on capital led to a reduction in the investment fund which had been established as a percentage of capital employed.[79] Overall, the offering of greater local autonomy was contradicted by the retention under central control of output, consumption, investment and prices.[80] At the same time local uniformities were lost: some plants emerged as more profitable than others, and attracted workers; areas and industries lost uniformity in wages; bonuses became higher for light than for heavy industry and for white than for blue collar workers.[81]

Over time the number of plan indices crept up again, from eight to 15 and then to 20; and *glavki* and ministries, still with overall responsibilities for planning, continued to alter plans. Non-fulfilment of plans remained the bogey that it always had been so that the hoped-for more ambitious plans were not adopted.[82]

It seems clear from this brief comment on the reforms attempted in this period that in a system as complex as the Soviet economy, and in an incorrigibly *centralised* system, even piecemeal change is difficult.[83] According to Schroeder, the modest reforms of 1965 left untouched the real causes of inefficiency: taut planning; the planning and allocation of supply; irrational prices; lack of incentives for innovation; perverse success indicators; ministries in competition; bureaucracy.[84] According to Gregory and Stuart, while enterprise profits undoubtedly increased, profits remained a wholly secondary measure of economic success,[85] as indeed they must in a planned economy with changing priorities. Yet the change was visible. After the admittedly slow start in enterprises converting to the New Economic System in the first two years, conversion thereafter took off, to cover 54 per cent of enterprises in 1968, 72 per cent in 1969 and 83 per cent (41,000) in 1970. By 1970 92 per cent of total output was covered and 95 per cent of total profit.[86]

It is hard to escape the conclusion that there is a pattern of economic reform in the Soviet Union. First, a reform is launched with public acclaim but deliberate speed, for in so complex a system leaping impetuosity has been proved 'adventurist and hare-brained'.[87] Second, it achieves some visibility as spontaneous local initiatives are taken and as the central planners take stock of the real implications of the reform. Third, it honourably fades from sight as, in Schroeder's telling phrase, it is 'successfully assimilated and bureaucratized into impotence'.[88] In short, economic reform is a matter of procedures and modifications in procedures. It is not about systemic change.

Production Associations, 1973

Another reform that merits separate attention is the introduction in 1973 of economic or production associations (the *Ob'edinenie* reform). This is important in the context of the present discussion because it represents the Soviet move towards large economic units, comparable with the trend in the West toward mergers and the emergence of conglomerates. The associations are often large enough to cover several *raions*, while some cover *oblasts* and even republics.[89]

Previously, the enterprise was the lowest-level unit in the economic system and it was too small to evade what Smolinski has nicely called its 'traditional role of the toad beneath the harrow', with all legal and financial responsibilities but very few rights. In 1968 over 56 per cent of all industrial enterprises employed fewer than 200 employees each and accounted for only 11.6 per cent of aggregate gross output and 7.9 per cent of profits. They were too small to make any sense of schemes for decentralisation and too numerous for optimal central planning. Smolinski quotes a central planner's calculation that the reduction of the number of enterprises by a factor of eight (from 50,000 to 6,000) would reduce the complexities of planning by the cube of that factor, 512 times. To this simplifying end, mergers have been seen to be the means.[90]

Production associations, which are now the lowest-level administrative units in the economy, have been created from the combination of enterprises under one management directly by the economic ministries. The immediate object was to improve industrial performance, especially in quality, costs, labour productivity and the use of advanced technology, by the concentration and specialisation of production, by more subcontracting among enterprises, by the speedier introduction of technical improvements, by the simplification of administrative structures, and by the locating of research and development organisations within each association.[91] While overall planning, investment policy and technical progress remained the responsibility of the ministries, and R&D and new technology were to be financed by them, the association was to take note of consumer demand; redistribute profits, surplus working capital and material resources among its constituent enterprises;

receive and divide its plan; establish its own funds for R&D, the introduction of new technology, the development of export production and financial assistance to enterprises; and to operate on *khozraschet*.[92] By 1975, 2,314 associations controlled 25 per cent of industrial output; by 1977, 3,670 controlled 44 per cent.[93]

What is most noteworthy about the reform is the emphasis on specialisation and its benefits, a development that should have come easily in a stable economy but had been previously impeded by the structure of the industrial system. In the Soviet system the enterprise on its own could not specialise because of the inflexibility of its marketing arrangements and its lack of independence in planning. Thus specialisation has been dependent on at least mergers, and more rapidly advanced by the development of the far larger associations.[94] The larger formations have also allowed the transfer of knowledge and resources, the reduction of hoarding and pooling of reserves, and savings on management costs and administrative personnel.

The Development of Computerisation

Another reform dating from the period 1968–72 was the introduction of OGAS,[95] a four-level hierarchy of interacting automated systems of administration. Its sub-systems cover planning, statistics, material-technical supply, prices, and scientific and technological information. OGAS was believed to be the solution to all the economic, social and organisational problems of Soviet socio-economic development, a system that would encompass all planning and reporting at all levels of the management hierarchy and provide the technological basis for operational control of plan fulfilment. By 1978 half of the calculations for the national economic plan were aided by computers and in the second stage, 1978–85, the intention has been to make the planning system compatible with the systems for the collection of statistics and for material-technical supply. OGAS has in fact imposed great strain on the system's information-processing and co-ordination capacities,[96] and the flow of great masses of information through the complex and centralised hierarchical structure of the system has served to emphasise the extended lines of communication and the slow feedback that are its characteristics.[97]

Conyngham describes the difficulties that OGAS has encountered and comments on the need for the Soviet planners to build mathematical and organisational models (in preference to using computers principally for routine plan calculations), to harmonise conflicting interests, and to overcome social inertia and psychological resistance.[98] What he may not fully recognise is that the system of planning 'from the achieved level' is necessarily imperfect, that the conflicts of economic interest are inescapable, and that the new technology providing overwhelming amounts of 'better' information merely increases, and emphasises, the burden carried by the central planning authorites. Every 'technological fix', in Cocks's phrase, serves further to centralise the system.

Continuing Reforms

Reforms continued to be devised and promulgated all through the 1970s and into the 1980s. They are not easy to keep up with, partly because there is no equivalence between what is proposed and what actually occurs and partly because continual changes are made: new targets (including those of 'counterplanning'), new controls, new methods of planning and organisation, new incentives, new rules of procedure, new exhortations.[99] Schroeder refers to the 'treadmill of reforms', to the 'ceaseless search for panaceas', to constant changes in the 'rules of the game', and concludes that 'perennial administrative change is becoming part of the problem rather than contributing to its solution'. She even refers, Cassandra-like, to the Soviet economy's 'systemic arteriosclerosis',[100] but sees no plans for even minimal systemic change. Dyker, no more sanguine over the existing pattern of reform, simply looks for change to new political leadership.[101]

It is time then to look, in Chapter 6, at other groups and institutions with a very direct interest in the future of the economic system: at management, the trade unions and the role of the Party; and at how the system may be expected to respond to the continuing challenge of change.

Notes

1. The foregoing description is purposely based for simplicity's sake on one source only. See Lane (1976), Ch. 1; Lane & O'Dell (1978), Ch. 1.

2. See T.H. Rigby, 'Traditional, Market and Organisational Societies and the USSR', *World Politics*, vol. xvi, no. 4 (1964), pp. 539–57.

3. Lane (1976), Ch. 1.

4. Allen Kassof, 'The Administered Society: Totalitarianism without Terror'. *World Politics*, vol. xvi, no. 4 (1974), pp. 558–75. The quotation is from pp. 559–60. It is of no consequence in this context whether Kassof's title of 'administered society' is the most useful.

5. Gregory and Stuart (1981), Ch. 12.

6. Alexander Eckstein, 'The Background of Soviet Economic Performance' in Alex Inkeles and Kent Geiger (eds.), *Soviet Society: A Book of Readings* (Constable and Co. Ltd., London, 1961).

7. It covers an area of 8.6 million square miles. The next largest countries, Canada, China and the USA, cover areas of 3.8, 3.7 and 3.6 million square miles respectively. See *The Reader's Digest Great World Atlas* (The Reader's Digest Association Ltd., London, 1972).

8. Wilhelm (1979).

9. As Clarke has negatively put it, 'A regime which does not wish to command has no need of a command economy'. Roger Clarke, 'Dr. Abouchar and Levels of Inefficiency', *Soviet Studies*, vol. xxv, no. 1 (1973), pp. 77–87. The quotation is from p. 83.

10. Zaleski (1967), Ch. 1.

11. The terms directive or administrative planning are used interchangeably; the contrast is with indicative planning.

12. Nove (1977), Ch. 1.

13. Zaleski (1967), Ch. 1.

14. This section leans very heavily on Gregory and Stuart (1981), Ch. 5. This dependence is gratefully acknowledged.

15. Ibid., p. 123.

16. There are many other descriptions of the Soviet planning system but none superior, in the writer's view, to Gregory and Stuart's. Davies, in contrast, offer a 4-stage version — of directives, claims, plan compilation and disaggregation. See R.W. Davies, 'Economic Planning in the USSR' in Bornstein and Fusfeld (1970).

17. Commodities have a three-fold classification: funded commodities, planned commodities and decentrally planned commodities.

18. Hence the description of planning 'from the achieved level'. This policy is well evaluated in Birman (1978). See also Wilhelm (1979).

19. Gregory and Stuart (1981), p. 124.

20. Nove (1977), Ch. 4.

21. Wilhelm (1979).

22. Ibid.

23. Nove has commented that what Wilhelm takes to be limitations of the centralised planning model are in fact integral to it. See Alec Nove, 'Does the Soviet Union have a Planned Economy?' *Soviet Studies*, vol. xxxii, no. 1 (1980), pp. 135–7.

24. In this section also the clarity of Gregory and Stuart's account is acknowledged. The author has made good use of Gregory and Stuart (1981), Ch. 6.

25. See Chapter 6, pp. 148–50.

26. Zaleski (1967), Ch. 4.

27. Nove (1977), Ch. 2.

28. Levine does not claim to have proved his point, but others whose focus is the tautness of plans may be thought to have accepted it. Herbert S. Levine, 'Pressure and Planning in the Soviet Economy' in Bornstein and Fusfeld (1970).

29. Output has traditionally been targeted both as total gross value of output and as total value of marketed output; the plan also covers assortment or product mix.

30. The finance plan covers revenue, expenditure and profit.

31. The labour plan includes number of employees, average wage and total wages bill.

32. Nove (1977), Ch. 4.

33. Ibid.

34. Conyngham (1973), Ch. 10.

35. Zaleski (1967), Ch. 4.

36. Alan Abouchar, 'Inefficiency and Reform in the Soviet Economy', *Soviet*

Studies, vol. xxv, no. 1 (1973), pp. 66–76.

37. Nove (1977), Ch. 3.

38. Gregory and Stuart (1981), Ch. 5.

39. Nove (1977), Ch. 4.

40. Wilhelm (1979).

41. 'Storming' (*Shturmovshchina*) is the practice of greatly increasing production in a burst of effort towards the end of a plan period.

42. See Berliner (1957), Ch. 12; Wilhelm (1979).

43. See Birman (1978); Nove (1977), Ch. 4.

44. Berliner's managers found new products and processes were threats to the enterprise plan and, as a consequence, to premiums. Other kinds of innovation such as in workplace practices are possible and encouraged.

45. Zaleski (1967), Ch. 4.

46. Joyce's formulation in a sermon on St. Francis Xavier is, 'one thing alone is needful, the salvation of one's soul'. James Joyce, *Portrait of the Artist as a Young Man* (Jonathan Cape, London, 1916).

47. Michael Ellman, 'The Consistency of Soviet Plans' in Bornstein and Fusfeld (1970), p. 84.

48. Nove (1977), Ch. 4.

49. The post-Stalin period is chosen because the death and partial repudiation of Stalin is on all sides recognised as a watershed in Soviet history; and it is worth going back to the 1950s because the impetus to change then, after Stalin, was greater than at any time since.

50. Such a reader is referred to Nove (1972) and to Gregory and Stuart (1981).

51. Plan fulfilment could be simulated by substituting material inputs or by including unfinished, defective or inferior products in the enterprise plan. Conyngham (1973), Ch. 3.

52. Ibid.

53. Ibid., Ch. 5. By 1957 15,000 enterprises had been transferred to republic control.

54. *Gosplan* retained long-term planning but lost current planning to *Gosekonomkomissila*.

55. This number was reduced first to 103 and later, more severely, to 47, in 1963. Nove (1972), Ch. 12.

56. Plan periods were extended to seven and 15 years. See Michael Kaser, 'The Reorganisation of Soviet Industry and Its Efforts in Decision Making' in Gregory Grossman (ed.), *Value and Plan: Economic Calculation and Organisation in East Europe* (University of California Press, Berkeley, 1960).

57. Conyngham (1973), Ch. 5; Kaser, 'The Reorganisation of Soviet Industry'; Richman (1965), Ch. 2.

58. Kaser, 'The Reorganisation of Soviet Industry'.

59. Ibid.

60. The 'departmentalism' (*vedomstvenost'*) of the ministries, their tendency to maximise indicators of *their* plan performance at the expense of other levels of the system, was simply replaced by departmentalism at *sovnarkhoz* level. See Berliner (1983).

61. Nove (1977), Ch. 3.

62. Conyngham (1973), Ch. 5; Richman (1965), Ch. 2.

63. Conyngham (1973), Ch. 6.

64. Alec Nove, 'The Industrial Planning System: Reforms in Prospect', *Soviet Studies*, vol. xiv, no. 1 (1962), pp. 1–15.

65. Zaleski (1967), esp. p. 25.

66. Jerry F. Hough, 'Reforms in Government and Administration' in Alexander Dallin and Thomas B. Lawson (eds.), *Soviet Politics Since Khrushchev* (Prentice-

Hall, Englewood Cliffs, N.J., 1968).

67. Liberman's proposals first appeared in *Kommunist* in 1956; they next appeared in *Pravda* in 1962.

68. By which Liberman meant profits in relation to fixed and working capital.

69. See Yevsei Liberman, 'The Plan, Profits and Bonuses' in Bornstein and Fusfeld (1970). See also discussion in Zaleski (1967), Ch. 4.

70. See A. Zverev, 'Against Oversimplification in Solving Complex Problems' in Bornstein and Fusfeld (1970).

71. Zaleski (1967), Ch. 5 and Marshall I. Goldman, 'Economic Growth and Institutional Change in the Soviet Union' in Bornstein and Fusfeld (1970).

72. It must be noted that Liberman's proposals were debated and defeated precisely at the time that Krushchev was seeking greater Party control over the economy.

73. Zaleski (1967), Ch. 8.

74. Kosygin's speech entitled 'On Improving Management of Industry, Perfecting Planning, and Enhancing Incentives in Industrial Production', delivered to the Plenary Meeting of the Central Commitee of the CPSU on 27 September 1965, initiated and set the style of all subsequent economic reforms. See Bornstein and Fusfeld (1970). The three new funds were the Fund for Material Stimulation, the Fund for the Development of Production and the Fund for Social-Cultural Measures and Housing Construction.

75. This had been tried in 1962 but abandoned in 1964. Schroeder (1968).

76. Hitherto there had been no charge for the use of capital which, as a consequence, had been overapplied for—a practice which had long shocked Western economists.

77. Schroeder (1968).

78. Ibid.

79. Ibid.

80. *Gosplan* remained responsible for the consistency and optimality of the plan while others were responsible for its execution. Berliner (1983).

81. Schroeder (1968).

82. Liberman, 'The Economic Reform in the USSR' in Bornstein and Fusfeld (1974).

83. Berliner writes: 'genuine decentralisation of authority to enterprises is strictly limited by the directive nature of a detailed national economic plan'. Berliner (1983).

84. Schroeder (1968). The reader is referred to Schroeder (1972) for a discussion of attempted reforms to the supply system in 1965.

85. Gregory and Stuart (1981), Ch. 9.

86. Ibid., Table 26, p. 310.

87. The epithets attached to Krushchev's reform schemes, in retrospect.

88. Gertrude E. Schroeder, 'Recent Developments in Soviet Planning and Incentives' in Bornstein and Fusfeld (1974), p. 504.

89. Dunmore (1980). A *raion* is a small administrative territorial district, in a large city or an *oblast*; an *oblast* is the administrative designation of a province.

90. Leon Smolinski, 'Towards a Socialist Corporation: Soviet Industrial Reorganisation of 1973', *Survey*, vol. 20, no. 1 (1974), pp. 24–35.

91. Berliner has picked out as of special concern the slow rate of technological progress and the lack of enterprises' responsiveness to customers' requirements. Berliner (1983).

92. Dunmore (1980); Gorlin (1974).

93. Dunmore (1980). To operate on *khozraschet* is to operate on economic or commercial accounting principles.

94. The mergers that started to occur in the 1960s and the consequent formation of *firmy* are discussed in Gorlin (1974).

95. OGAS = the All-State System for the Collection and Processing of Information for Reporting, Planning and Management of the National Economy.

96. Conyngham reveals that in 1978 the circulation of written data was estimated at 120–170 billion bits per year, 90 per cent of them within enterprises. Conyngham (1980).

97. Conyngham (1980); Schroeder (1979).

98. Conyngham (1980).

99. See Schroeder (1979) and Gregory and Stuart (1981), Ch. 9. The most important reform was no doubt the Comprehensive Planning Decree of 1979. See Berliner (1983).

100. Schroeder (1979), esp. pp. 314 and 334.

101. David Dyker, 'Half-Hearted Reform: The New Planning Decree', *Soviet Analyst*, vol. 8, no. 20 (1979), pp. 5–8.

Select Bibliography

See end of Chapter 6, page 172.

6 INSTITUTIONAL INTERESTS AND THE CHALLENGE OF CHANGE

With the context of operations fully set out in the preceding chapter, we turn now to an examination of the principal powers affecting the system: management, the trade unions and the Party. Finally, we address questions raised by the challenge of change.

Soviet Management

In the early years of the Soviet Union there was a lack of professional management specialists sympathetic to the revolutionary regime. The hope of the Bolsheviks had been that the old entrepreneurs would simply be replaced by new management but it was quickly found that coercion and inducements were needed to obtain the services of these pre-revolutionary managers whom Azrael has called 'bourgeois specialists'. Lenin was clear that firm leadership was needed in industry and he enunciated the principle of one-man management (*edinonachalie*) that was brought in by legislation in 1920.[1] Any surviving ideas of collective workers' management were gradually suppressed.[2]

By 1925 these bourgeois specialists were paid ten times the wage of the lowest paid workers. At that time there were perhaps 20,000 industrial managers of whom as many as 25 per cent were what Azrael has typed as 'red directors', Old Bolsheviks whose advancement was a consequence of loyal service to the revolution and whose talents were turned after the civil war to the struggle for rapid industrial development.[3] For the Party was closely associated with industrial progress: by 1924 49 per cent of plant directors were Party members; by 1926 78 per cent; and by 1928 89 per cent, many of them in origin bourgeois specialists.[4] In 1929 according to Hardt and Frankel 95 per cent of directors were CP members.[5] In 1934–36 according to Granick the percentage reached 97 and most directors were civil war survivors, 'red directors',[6] at a time when the overall number had risen to 95,000.[7] If Party membership did not secure submission to the Soviet system, Stalin's purge in 1936–38 no doubt did.

Outside the Azrael typology, who were these men, in origin and education? In 1923, when the primacy of the Party in making economic policy and managerial appointments was asserted, Azrael shows that, of the red directors 9 per cent came from peasant background, 53 per cent from industrial worker (proletarian) background and 37 per cent from white collar (official or intelligentsia) background. Of this group 78 per cent had had only elementary education, 10 per cent had also had secondary education and 12 per cent had had higher education.[8] These men accepted Party discipline, contributed to Stalin's rise to power, and were then thinned out in purges after December 1934.[9]

By 1934–36, following Granick, the proportion of all executives who were sons of peasants varied from 23 to 29 per cent. Directors from proletarian backgrounds remained at approximately 50 per cent. The white collar contribution had evidently declined overall to 25 per cent, but sons of white collar personnel were now 50 per cent of chief engineers and more than 50 per cent of heads of *glavki*.[10] Two-thirds of directors had themselves started as industrial workers, while one-third of heads of *glavki* had done so and only 8 per cent of chief engineers. Of the directors in 1936, 40 per cent had had only elementary schooling.[11] In 1939 28 per cent had had higher education, and thus approximately 32 per cent must have had secondary education in this period. These figures for mid-1930s directors show them to be far more educated than mid-1920s directors but they remain less so than the contemporary heads of *glavki*, 60–65 per cent of whom had engineering degrees, or chief engineers, nearly 90 per cent of whom did so.[13]

Granick reveals one other significant fact about the mid-1930s executives. They were highly mobile. Only between 3 and 8 per cent had held their posts for longer than five years, and between 40 and 55 per cent had only held their posts for between one and three years.[14]

The last study available is Andrle's, of a sample of top directors. He found that 88 per cent of these were graduates, mostly of engineering;[15] only 27 per cent had started as industrial workers. As many as 65 per cent had held their posts at the time of the analysis for five or more years. Andrle corroborated his initial study with a newspaper survey that found no great turnover among directors, least of all among successful directors.[16]

This evidence about the changing Soviet director is slender but it is all consistent. At first the new regime had to make use of pre-revolutionary managers who were persuaded to lead the advance of industrialisation. These are Azrael's 'bourgeois specialists'. The Civil War threw up proletarian warriors of proven Party loyalty and a heroic record, and these were later found executive positions in industry; these were the new Soviet managers, the 'red directors'. The bourgeois specialists had played their part by the 1930s; the red directors were winnowed in the purge of 1936–38. By that time a new generation of Soviet-educated managers was available, more educated and predominantly engineers,[17] socialised under Stalin. By 1941 when, according to Hardt and Frankel, there were 153,000 professional engineers working in industrial establishments, this third group, named by Azrael the 'red specialists', was in the majority. By 1959 when the economy employed about 129,000 directors and 442,000 engineers and specialists their dominance was complete.[18]

In the early period when administrative ability and political skill were in short supply, mobility was inescapable in a centrally directed system. With the accumulation of experience and the spread of education this was greatly reduced.

Azrael's red specialists of the 1960s were educated,[19] idealist, authoritarian, loyal to Stalin, subservient to the system, accepting (perhaps through wartime experience) the need for sacrifice, and believing in a strong industrial State as the realisation of a classless society.[20] They were both proponents of scientific rationality[21] and strong-minded realists working in a framework of broad ideological orthodoxy. In the post-Stalin era, through the period of Krushchev's reform efforts, these men formed the conservative industrial establishment and enjoyed official prestige, economic preferment, social deference and privileges for their children.[22]

In the contemporary period we may suppose the majority of red specialists to have retired and the quality of redness to be less emphasised among the managerial specialists. According to Andrle the modern Soviet director is well educated, rational, an expert in management science in the service of peaceful socio-economic development, with a secure, orderly and even parochial career pattern. He is even cool, human-relations-oriented and socially responsible, and respected by the local specialist intelligentsia.[23] In this description he differs little from the manager in the West.

Managerial Motivation

He is, however, a State employee, paid a salary, whose motivation unlike his Western counterpart's is not the pursuit of profit. He is driven, explicitly and deliberately, by the tautness of enterprise plans. He does also, none the less, have a financial incentive, the increase of his premium: a bonus earned either for fulfilment or overfulfilment of the plan of his enterprise or for some particular, targetted successes (such as cost savings, economies in materials, improvements of product quality, innovations, etc.). Both his salary and the rate at which he is paid a premium are fixed by the ministry, but the actual amount received is dependent on known measures of success, affected by the manager's own decisions and efforts. Among the managers interviewed by Berliner maximisation of the premium was evidently a dominant goal.[24] Granick confirms this (as does Richman) but includes among managerial incentives promotion, the acquisition of fringe benefits (such as a car and housing) and social prestige.[25] Richman calculated that premium payments increased directors' salaries by 25–33 per cent.[26]

Management Powers

While Soviet industrial managers have been shown to work within the tight framework of the plan imposed from above, the manager does in reality have discretion in many areas, and he is reinforced in some sense of autonomy by the principle of *edinonachalie*. Above all, within the given annual plan, the director has authority over quarterly, monthly and other sub-divisions of the plan.[27] And prior to this management is centrally involved in providing to superiors the information from the enterprise upon which the plan is based. Management can also affect numerous operational decisions and details. Management can exert influence over quality standards; determine most labour utilisation norms and therefore influence manpower allocations and labour productivity targets; revise an assortment (product-mix) plan within a plan period; select suggestions for innovation;[28] revise utilisation norms for equipment in use and so influence capital allocations and production targets; and propose working capital norms and norms for material and technical supply. Naturally the extent of management influence varies, especially according to technology, production process and product: it is least in a mass-production plant.[29]

The Enterprise Plan

Much has been already been noted or implied about the Soviet industrial enterprise, yet it is important to consider further its predicament within the planned economy. The awesome effects of the planning system still need to be brought out more fully. The enterprise has no single plan, but many plans. In the short term alone it has an annual plan and quarterly and monthly plans. And within each planning period there are many sub-divisions of the enterprise plan. Inevitably there is a complex production plan which is likely to include gross output, marketable output, assortment targets, delivery schedules and quality control standards. In addition there will be plans for labour and wages; plant and equipment utilisation; finance — including details of working capital and profit and profitability targets; material and technical supply; and technical development.[30] The emphases and the priorities change but the range of information to be passed upwards and of actual plan implementation and decision-making varies little. Within the overall precept of enterprise autonomy within the framework of the plan much detailed work is left to the enterprise.

The enterprise prepares a preliminary draft plan and proceeds to negotiate with superior authority over the detailed targets for output, labour productivity, supply needs, etc. Finally the plan is settled and the enterprise must fulfil or overfulfil it although it may lack control over the element vital for fulfilment, supply of materials. Similarly plan changes may be incompatible with the supply possibilities (that is, the output plans of other enterprises). From this flow the undesirable practices already alluded to.

Informal Practices

There are three principal causes of informal practices in relation to the enterprise plan: the wish to manipulate the plan to local advantage, the effort to anticipate and avoid the supply difficulties that might otherwise lead to non-fulfilment of the plan, and the pressure to complete the plan. In practice they are hardly distinguishable.

The first kind of practice includes all forms of misinformation and misclaiming. The enterprise will overstate requirements for capital, manpower and supplies, and understate its likely output. It may also falsify its reporting, for example, recording goods still in process of manufacture as complete, thereby borrowing output from the next planning period.[31]

The main defence against anticipated difficulties of supply is to achieve a safety factor or slack (*strakhovka*), also by misreporting; stated potential should be less than true potential. More obviously the strategy is to hoard materials, usually by over-ordering (often as a result of having to order far in advance) or by taking advantage of excess or early deliveries or changes of plan, though also included is the false reporting of goods as spoiled, which can then be hoarded.

The final category of informal practice arises from pressure for plan completion: by last-minute 'storming', by the speeding up of repairs, by overproduction of items easy to produce, by deviation from the assortment plan or by reduction of quality, even if these practices result in substandard output, missed specifications, increased spoilage, or the disruption of delivery schedules, and therefore also cause problems for someone else's plan.[32]

What is significant is that all these practices are part of the system, necessary to make it work because of the paramountcy of meeting plan targets and also the constant undependability of supply. They are known to higher authorities who recognise this fact and therefore look the other way provided that the output plan is fulfilled and other plans are not substantially affected. There is a genuine joint interest in ignoring transgressions.[33] It is unfortunate that the practices lead also to inefficiency, waste, customer dissatisfaction and lack of innovation,[34] although it should not be forgotten that all economic systems produce these faults in some degree.

In the Soviet system the plan[35] has the force of law. Thus non-fulfilment is formally a violation of state discipline backed by the ultimate sanction of the criminal law. This is rarely invoked, however, since the enterprise is subject to the pressures of inspectors from the Ministry of Finance and the State Bank and, of greatest consequence, constant invigilation from the local Party. Dissatisfied workers may also call on the union in bringing criticism or resort to writing to the press. In any event it is more congenial to all concerned to deal with aberrant or unsuccessful directors by the simple devices of removal or transfer.[36] On his side the enterprise director may believe that he is the victim of interference or sluggishness from above or of unfavourable directives. He may take his complaints to his superiors or, if that is found wanting, to other higher administrative departments, to Party officials, to legal authority or to the press.[37]

Soviet Trade Unions

History

Before the First World War there was some syndicalism among

Russia's industrial workers — support for the running of factories by committees of workers.[38] In 1917 when the revolution came there were attempts to establish a collegial system of administration, but union leaders and the Bolshevik Party were hostile to this trend. The role of unions, fully recognised by the setting up of the CCTU in 1917 and the first All-Russian Congress of Trade Unions in 1918, thus became a subject of debate.[39] Should they be allowed to develop along the syndicalist road, or be subordinated to government and Party, or be given some independence within overall government and Party control? The issue was finally resolved with the adoption of the New Economic Policy in 1921:[40] unions were to be voluntary non-governmental organs, led and controlled by the Communist Party. In Lenin's own words unions were to be 'schools of administration, schools of management, schools of Communism'.[41]

Under the 1922 Labour Code union rights were established to bargain for improvements in working conditions. The right to strike was recognised in the private sector while unions were exhorted not to strike in the public sector; arbitration machinery was set up under the Ministry of Labour and joint management-union commissions in enterprises; outside enterprises, reference was to the Ministry of Labour or to the courts.[42]

The 1920s was a period of rapid expansion of the labour force which doubled between 1921 and 1929. The number of labour disputes and the number of workers involved increased despite a decline in the state sector; 70 per cent of the disputes were about the basic rate of pay. But at the same time the number of collective agreements increased, as did the number that were agreed after arbitration. In 1926 the government started wages planning. From 1924 to 1928 there was an increase in the number of disputes taken to the labour courts; from 1926 to 1928 there was also an increase in the number of cases taken for resolution to the Ministry of Labour.[43]

In the year 1928–9 there was a further rise in the number of disputes: the trend was toward more, small-scale disputes. But at the same time the attitude of government and of management shifted. The unions were urged to 'face toward production' and the Party began to toughen its control of the unions. In 1929 strikes were declared to be anti-proletarian and counter-productive; the management-union commissions began to agree to managements' proposals; the focus shifted to discipline[44] instead of wages bargaining and wage differentials came into favour. Finally the unions adopted training and the stimulation of productionism as their major role: socialist competition, shock workers and the Stakhanovite movement were all used as devices for increasing discipline and productivity.

The years 1930 to 1950 were a black period in Soviet trade union history. The unions were simply seen as the tools of management and of the Party. From 1932 to 1949 no Congress of Trade Unions was held. In 1933 large unions were split and regional inter-trade-union councils were abolished. In 1940 a law prohibited leaving a job without permission. In theory there were no disputes and actual disputes were blamed on ignorance, residues of capitalism or lack of clarity in legislation. Also in theory there was no unemployment and thus no provision for unemployment benefit. The unions were powerless to halt deterioration in working conditions and the increasing use of overtime. Discipline became increasingly ruthless.

However, in 1947 collective agreements were re-introduced — even if few were signed and those not always observed by 1956. In 1949 the 10th Congress of Trade Unions was held, and some self-criticism was admitted. In that year there were 28.4 million members, 87 per cent of all workers; of the delegates to the Congress 72 per cent were Party members. From that time onwards the responsibility of unions to the establishment was stabilised: for production, for safety and working conditions and for educational and cultural work.

Stalin's death allowed in the mid-1950s a renewed debate on union reorganisation. In 1955 the State Committee on Labour and Social Questions was set up which later became the State Committee on Labour and Wages. This Committee runs the Scientific-Research Institute of Labour. In 1954 membership stood at 40 million.[45]

By 1963 union membership had risen to 68 million, 94 per cent of wage and salary workers, including more than 10 million Party members.[46] In 1980 union membership had almost doubled to 128 million members in 31 industrial unions and including 700,000 factory groups and 500,000 shop committees.[47]

The Role of the Unions

Soviet trade unions, in the words of Emily Clark Brown, are 'mass public non-party organisations',[48] and their task is 'the mobilization of the masses for . . . creation of the material-technical base of communism, struggle for the further strengthening of the economic power and defensive right of the Soviet state, the steady growth of the material welfare and culture of the working people'.[49] This task is two-headed: to participate in economic construction — to serve the state; and to promote and defend the interests of the working people — to serve the workers. From the Stalinist era in which the interests of the state had primacy the unions have emerged with their more balanced responsibility in a system of democratic centralism, that is, under Party leadership.

The idea that unions have two roles is not that of a Western commentator who is incapable of seeing that the two roles are one. Unions expressly have the right to appear *representing* workers before government and other public organs and to *represent* workers on all questions of labour and life. It is stated in the 1963 union statute: 'trade unions defend the interests of workers and employees'.

At the top of the trade union structure is the CCTU which has a role in the drafting of labour legislation, shares in the issue of decrees, sets rules for safety inspections, works out the social insurance budget, controls six scientific institutions concerned with the protection of labour (for example, hygiene, and work clothing), and has general investigative, critical and supervisory powers. The CCTU and the *Sovprofs* (republic and regional trade union councils) have a role in the planning process. Union committees work with the State Committee on Labour and Wages, with the Institute of Labour and the Ministry of Health. The CCTU monitors the *Sovprofs* which themselves supervise the lower levels — regional committees of national industrial unions and plant unions — and provide an inspectorate for technical, legal and safety matters. Below the *Sovprofs* and the regional committees, every industrial union has its departments for labour, wages, safety and protection of labour, and international relations, under its central committee.

The modern period of Soviet trade union history began effectively in 1958 with a decree that established the rights of factory, plant and local committees of trade unions to broaden economic democracy, to check on management and to mobilise in defence of the workers. As a result unions represent workers and employees 'on all questions of labour, living conditions and culture'; participate in planning; take responsibility for production conferences and workers' meetings; offer opinions on managerial appointments; serve on joint commissions on labour disputes; criticise administrators; take joint responsibility for socialist competition; take part in the administration of the social insurance system; have the right to check on the observance of labour laws, the collective contract and the provision of services; and organise programmes and administer facilities (paid for by the enterprise) for cultural, educational, health-building and sporting activities.[50] It is the unions that oversee the clubs and houses of culture in industrial enterprises throughout the Soviet Union which provide the work-force with lectures, exhibitions, films; with performances by drama, dance and opera groups; with choruses, orchestras, and printing and sculpture classes. Over the period since 1958 unions have become more representative of the workers and less the servants of Party or government.[51]

At plant level the union elects a group organiser, an organiser of production-mass-work, an insurance delegate, a cultural organiser, a public inspector for the protection of labour, a physical culture organiser, and other officials. The group organiser is responsible overall for recruitment, collection of dues, production, protection of workers' rights, and educational and cultural activities. However, it is the union committee that has the principal powers. Its agreement is necessary in relation to such matters as overtime, discharge, transfer, vacation schedules, production standards and details of the wage system. Its contribution to joint decisions is required over the distribution of housing, socialist competition and expenditure from the enterprise fund. It must check on the observance of labour regulations, safety, and collective contracts. And it is the final authority for the settlement of individual labour disputes.

It is of course at plant level that the union is most active and its spread of interest widest. The mere list of factory commissions which involve union participation and of the range of matters that concerns factory union committees demonstrates this fact.

Exemplary of the concerns of factory commissions are the following: production, organisation, quality control, social insurance, pensions, education, labour protection, family and school, youth, housing, women and children, cultural matters, consumer services, and labour disputes. Such commissions are manned by volunteers, and their chairmen serve on the regional trade union committee.[52]

The factory union committee provides members of commissions. Outside the committee's formal duties in relation to improving the conditions of workers on the one hand and mobilising them to fulfil the economic plan on the other, it must popularise technical and scientific achievements; attend to recruitment; encourage rationalisers and inventors; raise productivity, lower costs and improve the quality of work; enlist workers in active criticism and self-criticism; and develop political consciousness and high moral values.[53]

It is at plant level also that union and Party are closely linked. In 1963 when one in nine of all workers was a member of the Party, 28 per cent of union committee members were also in the Party and 49 per cent of committee chairmen were so.[54] By 1977, 80 per cent of factory union chairmen were Party members.[55] Thus the Party has access to all union documents, and controls appointments to all positions of authority.[56] The Party has development plans relating to mechanisation, automation, labour conditions, production methods, social welfare, and workers' attitudes; all these mesh closely with the unions' interests and work.[57]

Workers' Rights

In 1970 the Fundamental Principles of Labour Legislation established workers' rights to appropriate employment, safe working conditions and adequate compensation, and recognised the role of the unions in protecting these rights.[58] In effect there are four workers' rights. First is the right to a labour contract, that is, a guaranteed job in accord with the worker's educational level, professional skills and other qualifications. Second is the right to a guaranteed and proper wage. This means that a base rate is guaranteed according to qualifications and type of employment to which may be added social wages, annual bonuses and premiums for socialist competition; union officials have a role in fixing the size of the pay-cheque. Third is the right to healthy and safe working conditions. All these rights are enshrined in annual collective agreements which have legal force when endorsed by a majority of the labour force and are reviewed quarterly.[59] Fourth is the right to trade union membership.[60] In addition workers are protected by a law which defines the permissible bases for discharge, by management's reluctance to dismiss a worker who has no job or training course to which to move, by the rights of unions to refuse consent to discharge and by the possibility of discharge being redressed outside legal process through protest to the press.[61]

Labour Disputes

Labour disputes inevitably arise concerning either collective or individual rights. Those which relate to application of the law or regulations or collective contracts are formally actionable, but most disputes arise in relation to the violation of individual rights, mostly those of production workers, such as abuses by management, breaches of discipline, or misunderstanding about obligations or rights, and can be resolved at the lowest level. If, however, this does not succeed, the matter is referred to a management-union commission (with equal representation from the two sides). The next level is the factory committee (*fabkom*) and finally, if local attempts at resolution fail, disputes may be referred to the People's Court.[62]

Collective disputes tend to be concerned with demands for improved working or living conditions and services; the establishment of rules and standards; violations of safety rules, labour laws and regulations; terms of collective contracts; and the rights of union committees.[63] Individual disputes occur in relation to wage calculations, vacation schedules, production standards, premiums, wage classification and cases of unfair discipline. Few disputes have to be referred to the *fabkom* and more than half of all claims are granted. Of those that went to court throughout the USSR in 1963, 70 per cent of wage claims and 73 per cent of all other claims were granted.[64]

Innovation

At shop floor level the encouragement to innovation is noteworthy. In 1970 the All-Union Society of Inventors and Rationalisers had a membership of 7.8 million and 15,000 schools for technical training provided for more than 400,000 workers. In 1965 more than 28 million proposals for inventions or rationalisation were submitted by the work force, and of these 18.5 million were accepted.[65]

In this process management has stated responsibilities. By law it must provide an adequate technical and organisational environment for inventors' suggestions; respond to any suggestions within two weeks; pay according to the value of the proposals; allow appeals against decisions not to act upon suggestions; and give workers access to relevant documents. The policy of so much involving the labour force in promoting innovation harnesses the workers in two different ways. On the one hand it draws upon the creativity of workers to compensate and correct for poor design and to induce a receptive environment for the introduction of new technology. On the other hand it is a surrogate for workers' greater control of their work lives by closing somewhat the gap between manual and mental work. The workers' energies are thus mobilised in support of production and the goals of the planning system.[66]

Conclusion

This quite full account of the role of trade unions shows them in all respects to be a firm pillar of the industrial system, and in no way a source of challenge to it. The energies of workers to innovate are harnessed to the promotion of minor types of change. Workers have become, in Lane and O'Dell's phrase, 'incorporated' into the system, with stable employment, a rising standard of living, a sense of solidarity with the factory and its administration, and a sense of participation in promoting the national interest. Workers and their unions are thus a support to the stability and continuance of the system.[67] In Durkheim's terms Soviet workers have bases for association and for solidarity provided both by enterprises and by unions. They have a third basis offered by the local Party organisation.

The Role of the Party

While the role of the Communist Party in the industrial system has been alluded to at various points, in this section it will be more fully explored. The Party is the controlling power in the Soviet state and although there are governmental, administrative and industrial structures in the Soviet Union just as in any other state, there is a parallel Party structure behind them which watches over them and ultimately controls them — for the Party is understood to embody the will, vision and energies of the people as a whole.[68]

This arrangement immediately raises two problems. First, how in practice do the parallel structures, not infrequently competing and occasionally conflicting, resolve their differences? Second, how is the Party structure itself managed, how are the sub-units and local officials of the Party supervised from the centre? The answers to these questions will emerge in what follows.

According to Hough, at all levels of Soviet society — republic, *oblast* (region), city and *raion* (district) — the local Party organs are the prefects of the system.[69] In relation to the enterprise the local Party has three broad areas of responsibility: for performance, for people and for political stability. The Party has to check on performance, on fulfilment of the plan. Ordinarily it oversees rather lightly and formalistically,[70] but it can correct or guide local enterprises and their management, and if necessary it can formally investigate them, often with a commission that includes outside members. The threat of investigation lies behind the normal exercise of Party influence.

But naturally, since it is a power structure with which industrial management works closely, the Party can assist as well as quiz local management; indeed it is charged with aiding and strengthening management.[71] The Party can help in obtaining supplies or it can influence investment decisions in favour of one plant rather than another. It can also help to mobilise the workers to fulfil the plan.

The Party's second interest is in personnel. It is involved in all decisions of personnel selection and replacement, formally approving senior appointments and those on the *nomenklatura*. It can force the dismissal of administrative officials. It has responsibilities for the development of human potential: for the raising of educational, technical and moral standards; for the struggle against parasites, loafers and drunkards; in general, for looking after the work-force and for humanising the processes of government.

Finally, the Party is responsible for mobilising mass support for the Soviet regime and for the building of socialism. Within the industrial plant it praises the value of socialist competition which it stimulates both through individuals and by regular meetings of workers. Thus the Party runs political schools, circles and Universities of Marxist-Leninism; recruits lecturers and propagandists; organises training sessions on selected themes — all in the pursuit of adult political education.

The Party should not bypass the organs of the administration and thus at plant level, while the Party organisation as a whole formally has the power to enforce its will over management, the local officials are expected to work closely with and through the plant director. In this manner information should be shared and maximum participation harnessed at all levels. The exact relationship between directors and Party officials is in general unclear since the formally greater power of the Party is balanced by the greater technical and management expertise of the director and the greater time that he has to devote to enterprise problems. This sounds uneasy, but significantly, it means that the actual nature of relations is decided informally, in a personal, face-to-face manner in a situation in which the greatest interest of all is shared — plan fulfilment — and in which Party secretaries are expected to work harmoniously with the director since they also are rewarded with premiums for the enterprise's success.[72] As Andrle points out, directors and Party secretaries are members of a local political elite; directors can normally achieve security by informal bargain.[73] Local Party organs (not plant cadres) exercise their greatest influence outside the enterprise, resolving area and inter-area problems and disputes, balancing the plan fulfilments of local enterprises[74] and acting as an advocate for their localities at higher levels of the system.

Krushchev's Reform

Apart from the introduction of the *sovnarkhozy*, Krushchev also initiated reform of the Party. In 1962 he split the local Party organisation into two functional specialisms, one to deal with industry and the other with agriculture, thus ending the principle of territorial (local) integrity.

Krushchev's objective was to achieve increases in industrial and agricultural production. He hoped that the local Party organs, once they became more specialised and knowledgeable, would be more effective in increasing the efficiency and responsiveness of industrial managers, in countering localist tendencies, in solving more of the problems of material-technical supply and in generally exploiting local economic potential. He also believed that local Party officials would achieve greater influence in economic and technical decision-making that would balance more satisfactorily the power of the centre and revitalise and mobilise the workers. The *sovnarkhoz* innovation had given the Party greater access to information and decision-making at that regional level; *obkom* officials had gained more influence over intermediate level management. The Party reform was to carry this change down to the local level, achieving greater integration and dynamism throughout the system.[75]

It did not work. The local Party organs lacked the capacity to play a greater role in the economic and technical sphere, yet the reorganisation violated the principle of one-man management. Thus on the one hand production discipline and the authority of management were weakened and the issue of accountability was unfruitfully complicated, while on the other the Party's capacities were fragmented and its efficiency reduced. Hence Party officials, who were not slow to recognise the anti-*apparat* overtones of the proposals,[76] were themselves opposed to Krushchev's initiative, which in due course was reversed. Thus although the powers of the Party were enlarged, it remained the monocratic, hierarchical and centralised structure that it had always been. The reform merely introduced a new source of imbalance into the command economy and, as a consequence, more intervention, more disorganisation and less efficiency.[77]

Quite possibly part of the cause of Kruschchev's failure and dismissal lay in his personality and his mode of operation — impulsive, over-confident and populist. But regardless of this his reforms inevitably encountered opposition as a result of the structure of the Party, its habitual practices and the vested interests of Party officials. Opposition to 'economics over politics' was natural to officials in an organisation that embodies the principle of politics over all; the role of technocrat was alien to, and at variance with, the customary roles of a political elite: human relations facilitation, political mobilisation and the guarantee of ideological purity. Involvement of the Party in the administrative process was contrary to the tradition of Party separateness and independence from government and industrial bureaucracies.[78]

There are, in fact, a number of dilemmas and contradictions at the heart of Soviet Party orthodoxy. The first arises from the dual role of the Party as the source of central direction and the channel for the release and emergence of the energy of the masses. On the one hand the Party should act as a general staff, giving instructions from the centre on every political and organisational question. It should therefore be demanding. On the other hand the Party should be constantly tapping local initiative and energy. It should be trusting. The second dilemma for the Party is the clash between the principles of *rukovodstvo* and *kontrolirovat* and that of *edinonachalie*: between the Party being empowered to participate in decision-making, to control policy issues, to intervene and to check, and the principle that modern industrial management should be subordinate to a single will — that of the director. This tension is further confused by the local Party's dual responsibility, within its jurisdiction, to monitor management and to ensure fulfilment of enterprise plans by which the leadership is principally judged.[79]

It is evident that what have been called dilemmas need not be disabling, provided that the Party is operating on a small scale. But once the Party is working on the scale required by the Soviet Union its own structure becomes so complex that a loss of essential flexibility becomes inevitable. A mode of governance that depends upon the release of spontaneous initiative at local level cannot be satisfactorily administered by a giant bureaucracy. Hence the system must alternate between longer periods of routine and stable administration and short episodes of extra-bureaucratic shake-up that lead to the renewal of flexibility and creativity.

The Challenge of Modernisation

There is much speculation about what will be the effects upon the Soviet economic and political system of the continuing process of modernisation. Various meanings are attached to the notion of modernisation but it will be taken here to mean the application of the fruits of the scientific and technological revolution (STR), a shorthand for such developments as the introduction of modern management techniques, mathematical modes of analysis, the systems approach and computerisation. Given that the Soviet Union cannot eschew these products of the STR, since if it did so its economy in general and its defence industry in particular would be immediately handicapped, will their use affect the way in which the Soviet leaders think about their society, will it push aside the traditional ideological approach to decision-making, will it limit the role of the Party, will the new New Class of managerial technocrats usurp the power of the politicians? These are some of the questions raised in this context, often by those who are searching for 'cracks in the system' and signs of its impending disintegration. Some observers tend to conclude either that the changes that are visible are in process of altering the fundamental lineaments of the system or that the system is so rigid and inflexible ('bureaucratic') that it cannot adapt and so will at some future point inevitably suffer radical transformation.

A realistic view is both more humdrum and less grudging. On the one hand all contemporary advanced societies are alike in finding the process of adapting to the scientific and technological revolution continuingly challenging and strenuous and at times threatening to the very fabric and the no longer consensual value systems of society. On the other hand the Soviet system has already proved itself capable of, by any standards, massive adaptation. It possesses in the Party an instrument of change that has not so far been found wanting and in which its leaders place greater faith than in the inexorable forces of history. It is well to remember Stalin's own words: 'Victory never comes by itself. It has to be dragged by the hand'.[80] The Soviet Union has in the Communist Party a structured and elaborated institution designed to grip the society in one hand and reach out to victory over the challenge of modernisation with the other. It has in its governmental administration and the Party a system of dual authority that, it is not unreasonable to believe, could give it some advantage over other societies in adapting to the future.

Thus we have turned the issue on its head to consider, not the question 'will the Soviet system be able to cope with modernisation' but rather, 'in coping with it will the system be substantially affected?' The answer seems to be that there is no evidence that it will be affected — unless it is strengthened.

The major post-war social adaptation faced by the Soviet Union has been the adjustment to the end of Stalin's reign of terror. Manifestly this had many reverberations. Krushchev experimented with a decentralisation of the economic management system; he also developed the Party more widely than before in the economic sphere and involved Party rank-and-file and even non-Party members in Party affairs. Groups and specialists whose previous overriding concerns had been to keep a low profile began to take pride in their expertise and freely offer their professional advice; political, social and cultural issues were widely and fervently debated. The society breathed more freely and a period of flexibility, even of innovation and experimentation, resulted. The economic reforms of 1957 and the debate about the management of the economy led Western commentators to declare that the directed society based on coercion and terror was a thing of the past and to apply interest group analysis to the Soviet system very like that appropriate to analysis of the US society and polity.[81]

But reaction followed, and from 1970 the trend has been to reassert control from the centre and to use every available modern method to do so.

The Politics of Administration

There is a tradition of considering governmental administration — a civil service — to be a politically neutral machine whose organisation is a matter of non-political efficiency, but Michael Reagan has pointed out that 'a choice of organisation structure is a choice of which interest or which value will have preferred access or greater emphasis'.[82] The framework within which managerial technocrats work and the attention paid to managerial attitudes, organisational structures and administrative techniques are thus of crucial political importance. Brezhnev himself bore witness to this in his much-quoted statement, 'the science of victory in building Communism is in essence the science of management'.[83]

The Soviet leadership has increasingly used management techniques[84] to reassert its authority over a bureaucratic establishment that was fragmented, inefficient and insufficiently responsive to guidance, and to escape from bureaucratic politics, bargaining and 'muddling through'. Hence arose its interest in systems analysis and in PPBS (Planning-Programming-Budgeting System) with which it aimed, in Cocks's words, 'to transcend and circumvent group politics, to reform and broaden managerial perspectives, to reassert the primacy of general interests, values, and needs of the "system" as a whole over the special and limited interests of bureaux, organisations and regions'.[85]

This aim itself arose from twin motives: to overcome the Soviet Union's technological and organisational backwardness and to reassert strong executive leadership, the second being a prerequisite of the first but also a goal in itself. The outcome has been a steady growth of administrative and management science, at the behest of the Party and under Party control.

The Dual Authority System

The problems with any settled administration are the inevitable development of routine, inertia and vested interests and, as a consequence, a resistance to innovation, and the problems are magnified in a turbulent environment where the need for flexibility is all the greater. This complex of difficulty was not perceived by the early Western theorists of administration and bureaucracy in this century[86] whose aim was to exclude uncertainty from administrative functioning through what Cocks has nicely called 'conceptual closure of organisation'.[87] It was, however, recognised, no doubt instinctively, by Stalin, who with the slogan 'Cadres Decide All' used the Party to enforce total control of Soviet society in an international context of continuing constraint and antagonism, and thereby institutionalised the Party as the watchdog and goad of the administrative bureaucracy.

The state administration in the Soviet Union is thus responsible for administrative and technical tasks. The Party is responsible for organisational and political tasks, for eradicating the dysfunctions of 'rational' bureaucracy'[88] and for the maintenance of the primacy of politics over administrative efficiency, for 'only the Party is capable of determining how power should be used'.[89] The two elites thus complement each other, working in tandem, to form a joint establishment; their relationship is further smoothed by their memberships being composed of the same people, well educated and of proven ability.[90]

The Uses of Computers

The Soviet leadership was slow to recognise the possibilities of computers and as a result the Soviet computer industry for long remained fragmented and uncoordinated. There were no incentives for hardware improvement, for software development or for the replacement of labour by computers. No enterprise welcomed the risks of the unknown technology and the uncertain response of the bureaucracy.[91] There was also much resistance to the introduction of computers, especially on the part of older officials and generalists, which was further exaggerated in the Party bureaucracy itself.

Nevertheless, the overwhelming potentialities of the computer for information storage, retrieval and analysis were duly recognised and corresponding efforts, albeit piecemeal, haphazard and cautious, were made to introduce computer use at all appropriate levels of the planning process and of government administration.[92]

But there is no evidence either of a pressure group of computer specialists (or indeed that such specialists form a group in any meaningful sense) or of a loss of control by the Party orthodoxy to this new profession. On the contrary, the introduction of computers has further concentrated power at the centre of the system where top officials and politicians make decisions on the basis of more information than ever before. Technology does not change a political system if it is available to those who have power in the system. It merely reinforces the existing distribution of power.[93] So, in the Soviet Union computers are yet another aid to the leadership in promoting its objective 'to combine organically the achievements of the scientific and technological revolution with the advantages of the socialist economic system'.[94]

The Stability of the System

The reader will have noted the constant assertion that the Soviet system has stability. It has endured and it has changed. Kassof wrote in 1968 that the Soviet Union has emerged as 'a more or less benevolent authoritarianism of great vitality and long-range durability',[95] and there is little reason to revise that verdict. Reforms, changes, advances take place within the system.

The management group or stratum has, as already noted, changed over the years but it has shown no disposition to change the economic and social system itself. The managers' view of the good society has not changed significantly since Azrael wrote:

their composite image of the good society is and is likely to remain one in which such cardinal attributes of the system as the dictatorship of the party, the primacy of the party apparat, the canonisation of Marxist-Leninist ideology, the comprehensive institutionalisation of collectivist forms of social and economic organisation, and extensive central planning are combined with such 'new' attributes as stabilised policy-making procedures, a substantial devolution of authority to specialised functionaries of proven political reliability, and reliance on material and honorific incentives as the principal means of social and economic mobilisation.[96]

The 'gravediggers of Communism' thought likely by hostile Western observers to arise from professional management ranks seem no more in evidence today than they were in 1966.

What is noteworthy about these observations by Kassof and Azrael is that they were made in the 1960s when the post-Krushchev inheritance was by no means clear, and well before Brezhnev had consolidated his leadership. Since that time the leadership and the Party have regained, in Cocks's words, 'the momentum and march of an administered state' and the longstanding primacy of politics is yet more firmly assured.[97]

The focus of this study is too narrow to encompass an analysis of the inequalities of Soviet society or a scrutiny of its system of stratification. Yet it seems clear that these pose no threat to the stability of the system. The Soviet people as a whole feared Stalin's reign of terror and its arbitrary character; they have not, historically, dreaded stern control as such. They are not normally politically active; they accept leadership and expect their leaders to get on with the job of ruling the country. They are patriotic. They have benefited from a rising standard of living, despite the system's casualness about consumers' interests, but the level of their material expectations is not high by Western standards. Thus the Soviet government's task is one of the satisfactory management of expectations and that is another task at which the Party has proved itself effective. There is no class struggle, merely non-antagonistic contradictions which Griffiths has identified with a conflict of tendencies within a system-dominated society.[98] Dissenters there are, among the intelligentsia, but they are few; their dissent is, for most, over a narrow range of issues.[99] Most of those who wish for change are inside, and work for change within, the official institutional framework; in Hough's view, institutional forces are responsive to broader societal forces, including the interests of clients and subordinates.[100] Citizens at large make use of the press to express complaints and criticisms of at least some aspects of the system and of officials in authority within it.[101] It is not easy to believe that any stifling of opposition could seriously threaten to undermine the system from within.

The Threat of Conservatism

Indeed the largest threat may still be the system itself, with its belief in what Gregory and Stuart call 'organisational shuffling', Cocks's 'reorganisation as an all-purpose cure'.[102] In Cohen's view Stalin's death unleashed a decade of reformism that was utterly disproportionate to its real strength with the result that, when it was spent, a profound underlying conservatism reasserted itself, dedicated to stability, security and predictability.[103] According to this view economic reform remains *an official idea*[104] but the reform itself is conservative, retaining the very centralisation of the planning of inputs and outputs, of the administration of prices and of the allocation of investment that is perceived as the obstacle to real economic change.[105]

Certainly other economists foresee scenarios of catastrophe. Hunter admittedly offers three alternative scenarios for Soviet economic policies: a 'muddling through scenario', a 'liberal scenario' and a 'conservative scenario'. But only the 'liberal scenario' offers any hope, with its vision of new initiatives, products and processes; market forces; revised incentives and disincentives, labour and investment policies; higher productivity; greater growth of GNP; concern for consumers; and higher morale in general.[106] This is a wholly fanciful scenario as, more knowingly, is Nove's expression of a fictional Soviet committee's views that

> The errors and distortions of centralized planning arise essentially not from human stupidity or organisational inadequacies, but because microeconomic control from the centre *cannot* of its nature be efficiently carried out, despite computerization. Bureaucratic fragmentation, conflicts, inconsistencies, waste are inescapable, *unless* the path of radical reform is chosen

and by 'radical reform' is meant changing the whole system in fundamental ways.[107] Both economists foresee doom for the Soviet system without 'radical reforms'.

Cocks would seem to endorse these unfavourable views of the present Soviet system's adaptability when he comments that the complexity of the society has defeated attempts at radical systems engineering; that the system itself is neither integrated nor coherent; that the vaunted systems approach is merely a rhetorical device; and that the scale of priority problems exceeds the competence of any agency to deal with them. He concludes:

Technique has become a fetish and exaggerated expectations are the result. In the course of practical application, initial hopes invariably give way to disappointment, to a sobering of estimates, and ultimately to a new line of organisational panaceas and technological fixes upon which everything is supposed to depend. That is the perennial story of all Soviet reforms.[108]

Most recently, and more judiciously, Berliner has suggested four alternative models of development for the Soviet industrial system: conservative, reactionary, radical and liberal. With the conservative model the commitment to central planning remains and attempts are made to improve the quality of production or to promote technological progress through 'administrative measures' (such as changing structures of authority and clearly assigning responsibilities). With the reactionary model the emphasis is on greater order and discipline; there would be more centralisation and tighter labour discipline. With the radical model both planning and management would be decentralised; in the Hungarian style, there would be central planning but without directive targets for enterprises. With the liberal model traditional central planning would be combined with fewer restrictions on *private* initiative (somewhat on NEP lines).

Berliner prefers the liberal model because he believes that some private enterprise would release untapped sources of initiative that are now needed to promote technological innovation in the matrix of a centrally planned economy, now that the borrowing and application of the results of others' research can no longer suffice. But if he discounts the radical model because the reintroduction of profit criteria would be contrary to 40 years of Soviet practice, it is hard to give the liberal model any greater credibility. While Berliner believes the reactionary model would attract the most political support, he settles for the conservative model (that of the status quo) as the most probable for the future of the system.[109]

The Prospect of Incremental Change

Surely at this point, and in an unfamiliar context, we have strayed into the world of Popper's 'piecemeal social engineering'? Popper offered his path of realism toward the future directly counter to the nostrums and panaceas of Marxist-Leninist theory.[110] But if the wise way into the future is step by experimental step rather than by gambling recklessly upon a prophetic leap, then the wisdom, *pace* Hunter and Nove, is fit for the Soviet Union too.

Nor are Hunter's 'muddling through' scenario and Berliner's conservative model necessarily as disappointing or limited as the authors seem to suppose.[111] They promise continued centralised bureaucratic management of the economy; politically determined resource allocation through the medium of administrative procedures, open only to routine reform; slow technological progress; tendencies to overstaffing, low productivity and lopsided investment in enterprises; slow growth of GNP. In other words in a 'muddling through' scenario the centralised political control of the economy will continue, which is certain; and the associated difficulties will be little different from those experienced by many contemporary capitalist economies. There is assuredly no room for complacency here but also no prospect of systemic convulsion or transformation.

Conclusion

We have noted already in this chapter how the Soviet system provides for industrial workers a variety of forms of association that can offer bases for solidarity. Durkheim would surely have recognised an advanced form of 'organic solidarity' underpinned by the State,[112] even if he regretted the diminution of individualism allowed by the prevailing ideology. To Weber the Soviet Union would have provided an example of a nation-wide bureaucratic system that fulfils his worse forebodings of 'a house of bondage' in which democratic and bureaucratic principles are in conflict and incompatible. Yet he would have understood the inevitability of the extension of the bureaucratic system in the attempt to bring this vast and complex society under rational administration.

Throughout our discussion of the Soviet Union I have emphasised the fact that it is a social system in which politics are in command. Thus any knowledge elite, the product of the advance of science, scientific research and education (such as Bell might recognise), or any equivalent of Galbraith's technostructure will be firmly subordinated to political, that is Party, control. Likewise, an ideology of technological rationality, which Habermas, Mandel and Marcuse all find to be rampant in the systems of Western capitalism, would in the Soviet system be subordinated to the ideology of Marxism-Leninism. Yet we may surmise, notwithstanding the evident stability of the system upon which we have commented, that tensions leading toward change will in the future be felt precisely at these pressure points: where the knowledge elite challenges the political leadership and where the ideology of technological rationality suggests revision of the ideology of Marxism-Leninism. No doubt the system will be able to respond to these pressures but no doubt also evolutionary changes in the system will occur.

Notes

1. Lenin advocated 'a single will linking the entire working personnel into an economic organ operating with the precision of clockwork'. Quoted in Nove (1972), p. 57.
2. Azrael (1966), Ch. 3.
3. Hardt and Frankel (1971).
4. Many disappearing in the purge of technical intelligentsia, 1928–32. Azrael (1966), Ch. 3.
5. Hardt and Frankel (1971).
6. Granick (1954), Ch. 3.
7. Hardt and Frankel (1971).
8. Conyngham refers to a 1928 sample of plant directors among whom 58 per cent of non-Party members had higher education but only 2.8 per cent of Party members. Conyngham (1973), Ch. 1.
9. Azrael (1966), Ch. 4.
10. Granick (1954), Ch. 3.
11. Ibid.
12. Hardt and Frankel (1971).
13. Ibid.
14. Granick (1954), Ch. 3. This mobility is confirmed by Berliner's study of managers from the 1938–42 period: the average term of the 41 managers he interviewed had been two years. Berliner (1957), Ch. 4.
15. Conyngham states that by about 1948 77 per cent of plant directors had higher education. Conyngham (1973), Ch. 3.
16. Andrle (1976), Ch. 6.
17. This was entirely suitable to a group working predominantly in heavy industry. Engineering may also be thought of as politically safe.
18. Hardt and Frankel (1971).
19. In 1967, 68 per cent of directors had had higher education, more than double the proportion in 1939. Ibid.

20. Andrle (1976), Ch. 1; Azrael (1966), Ch. 6.
21. As was Lenin, a disciple of aspects of F.W. Taylor's scientific management.
22. Azrael (1966), Ch. 5.
23. Andrle (1976), Ch. 7.
24. Berliner (1957), Ch. 3.
25. Granick (1954), Ch. 11; Richman (1965), Ch. 7.
26. Richman (1965), Ch. 7. He estimated that potentially this increment was 40–60 per cent.
27. Andrle (1976), Ch. 2.
28. Made by 'rationalisers and inventors'.
29. Richman (1965), Ch. 4.
30. Ibid., Ch. 3.
31. Berliner (1957), Ch. 10.
32. Berliner (1957), Chs. 8–10; Richman (1965), Ch. 8.
33. Berliner (1957), Ch. 14.
34. Richman (1965), Ch. 8.
35. This refers only to current, short-term plans.
36. Granick (1954), Ch. 11.
37. Andrle (1976), Ch. 2.
38. McAuley (1969), Ch. II.
39. Brown (1966), Ch. III.
40. McAuley (1969), Ch. II; Ruble (1981), Ch. 1.
41. Brown (1966), Ch. III.
42. McAuley (1969), Ch. II.
43. Ibid.
44. Severe limits were imposed on labour mobility.
45. Brown (1966), Ch. X; McAuley (1969), Ch. II; Ruble (1981), Chs. 1–2.
46. Brown (1966), Ch. I.
47. Ruble (1981), Introduction.
48. Brown (1966), Ch. III.
49. Ibid., p. 48.
50. Lane and O'Dell (1978), Ch. 2, record there being 200,000 union-run sports stadiums.
51. Brown (1966), Ch. V.
52. Ruble (1981), Ch. 3.
53. Lane (1970).
54. Brown (1966), Ch. VI. Lane and O'Dell (1978), Ch. 2, note 54 per cent of factory managers as Party members.
55. Ruble (1981), Ch. 3.
56. On the *nomenklatura* system officials selected by the union's central committee are endorsed by the Party before election. See Blair A. Ruble. 'Factory Unions and Workers' Rights' in Kahan and Ruble (1979). The *nomenklatura* is the list of offices requiring Party approval or designation. For discussion of the workings of the *nomenklatura* system see Bohdan Harasymiw, 'Nomenklatura: The Soviet Communist Party's Leadership Recruitment System', *Canadian Journal of Political Science*. vol. ii, no. 4 (1969), pp. 493–512.
57. Lane and O'Dell (1978), Ch. 2.
58. Ruble (1981), Ch. 4.
59. These collective contracts also commit workers to production and productivity targets and state the responsibilities of all parties. Brown (1966), Ch. VII.
60. Ruble in Kahan and Ruble (1979).
61. Brown (1966), Chs. VIII and XI.
62. Brown (1966), Ch. VIII; McAuley (1969), Chs. VI–VII.
63. Brown (1966), Ch. VIII.

64. McAuley (1969), Ch. VII.

65. Lane and O'Dell (1978), Ch. 2.

66. Rensselaer W. Lee, III, 'The Factory Trade Union Committee and Technological Innovation', in Blair and Ruble (1979).

67. Lane and O'Dell (1978), Ch. 8.

68. The primacy of the Party's leadership role is known as *rukovodstvo*; in every sphere the Party has the power to invigilate (*kontrolirovat*).

69. Hough (1969), Chs. I–II.

70. Andrle (1976), Ch. 3.

71. Hough (1969), Ch. III, found local party officials to be similar in background and career experience to enterprise directors.

72. Richman (1965), Ch. 11.

73. Andrle (1976), Ch. 3.

74. By exercising what Hough terms 'brotherly patronage'. Hough (1969), Ch. XI.

75. Conyngham, (1973) Ch. 9; Hough (1969), Ch. X. An *obkom* is a provincial Party committee.

76. Elements of the programme relied upon the use of volunteers and were clearly anti-bureaucratic. Conyngham (1973), Ch. 7.

77. Ibid., Ch. 9.

78. Ibid., Chs. 8–10.

79. Ibid., Chs. 8 and 10.

80. Quoted in Cocks (1978), p. 52.

81. This movement is well exemplified in the work of Hough and fully (and critically) discussed by Griffiths. See Hough (1969 and 1977) and Franklyn Griffiths, 'A Tendency Analysis of Soviet Policy Making', in H. Gordon Skilling and Griffiths (eds.), *Interest Groups in Soviet Politics* (Princeton University Press, Princeton, N.J., 1971).

82. Quoted in Cocks (1976), p. 162.

83. Quoted in *Pravda*, 13 June 1970. See Cocks (1976).

84. Cocks has pointed out that administrative science disappeared in the Soviet Union during Stalin's regime. The post-Stalin period required some years before the process of borrowing ideas from capitalist management (approved by Lenin) could recommence. Cocks (1977).

85. Cocks (1976), p. 165.

86. Many examples could be given. The classic characterisation of an ideal-typical bureaucracy (functioning in a stable environment) is that of Weber. See Weber (1947) and Chapter 2, pp. 9–10.

87. A further article by Cocks has been freely drawn upon in this section and is respectfully acknowledged. See Cocks (1978).

88. Hough (1969), Ch. XIV, has noted that classical bureaucracy has been virtually unknown in the Soviet Union where tenure has often been conditional and ideological loyalty prized above detached neutrality.

89. Cocks (1978), p. 51.

90. Hough (1977), Introduction.

91. Richard W. Judy, 'The Case of Computer Technology' in Bornstein and Fusfeld (1974). In fairness, Hoffman points out that computers were introduced slowly enough in the USA. See Erik P. Hoffman, 'Technology, Values and Political Power in the Soviet Union: Do Computers Matter?' in Frederic J. Fleron, Jr. (ed.), *Technology and Communist Culture: The Socio-Cultural Impact of Technology under Socialism* (Praeger Publishers, N.Y., 1977).

92. Hoffman, 'Technology, Values and Political Power in the Soviet Union'.

93. Ibid. The notion that knowledge is power is widely misunderstood. It is not that knowledge specialists gain political power but political leaders served by the specialists enhance theirs.

94. The words are Brezhnev's, quoted in ibid., p. 423.
95. Allen Kassof, 'The Future of Soviet Society' in Kassof (ed.), *Prospects for Soviet Society* (Pall Mall Press, London, 1968), p. 506.
96. Azrael (1966), pp. 170–171.
97. Cocks (1976), p. 176.
98. Griffiths in Skilling and Griffiths (eds.), *Interest Groups in Soviet Politics*. By system-dominance Griffiths refers to a situation in which all actors' activities, despite appearances of autonomy, are subordinated to the whole.
99. There are many sources on Soviet society as a whole. Two used here are Lane (1976) and Walter D. Connor, 'Workers, Politics and Class Consciousness' in Kahan and Ruble (1979).
100. Hough in 'The Soviet System: Petrification or Pluralism?' *Problems of Communism* (March-April 1972); also in Hough (1977).
101. This is amply witnessed in many sources. See, for example, Brown (1966), Ch. VIII.
102. Cocks (1980), p. 231; Gregory and Stuart (1981), Ch. 9.
103. Stephen F. Cohen, 'The Friends and Foes of Change: Reformism and Conservatism in the Soviet Union', *Slavic Review*, vol. 38, no. 2 (1979), pp. 187–202.
104. Ibid.
105. Gregory and Stuart (1981), Ch. 9.
106. Holland Hunter, 'Soviet Economic Problems and Alternative Policy Responses', in *Soviet Economy in a Time of Change* (Joint Economic Committee, Congress of the United States: U.S. Government Printing Office, Washington, D.C., 1979), vol. 1, pp. 23–37.
107. Alec Nove, 'The Economic Problems of Brezhnev's Successors', *The Washington Papers*, vol. VI, no. 59: *Soviet Succession: Leadership in Transition* (Sage Publications, London, 1978), pp. 59–72.
108. Cocks (1980). The quotation is from p. 253.
109. Berliner (1983).
110. Karl Popper, *The Open Society and Its Enemies*, vol. II (Routledge, London, 1966). Cocks recognises this when he writes, 'Change is not a single action. A situation cannot be radically altered by political fiat or by one structural blow of the organizational cudgel'. Cocks (1980), p. 249. Vidmer also echoes Cocks in the statement: 'specialists and their political patrons have come to recognise that total solutions simply do not exist'. Richard F. Vidmer, 'Soviet Studies of Organization and Management: A "Jungle" of Competing Views', *Slavic Review*, vol. 40, no. 3 (1981), pp. 404–22.
111. 'Muddling through', we may note, is what the practical, utilitarian, and firmly non-ideological British have always *prided* themselves on doing.
112. See Chapter 2, pp. 11–13.

Select Bibliography

Andrle, Vladimir (1976) *Managerial Power in the Soviet Union* (Saxon House, Farnborough).
Azrael, Jeremy R. (1966) *Managerial Power and Soviet Politics* (Harvard University Press, Boston, Mass.)
Berliner, Joseph S. (1957) *Factory and Manager in the USSR* (Harvard University Press, Boston, Mass.)
———— (1983) 'Planning and Management' in Bergson, Abram and Levine, Herbert S. (eds.) *The Soviet Economy: Toward the Year 2000* (George Allen and Unwin, London)

Birman, Igor (1978) 'From the Achieved Level', *Soviet Studies*, vol. xxx, no. 2, pp. 153–72.

Bornstein, Morris and Fusfeld, Daniel R. (eds.) (1970) *The Soviet Economy: A Book of Readings* (Richard D. Irwin Inc., Homewood, Illinois, 3rd edition)
_____ (1974) Ibid., 4th edition

Brown, Emily Clark (1966) *Soviet Trade Unions and Labor Relations* (Harvard University Press, Boston, Mass.)

Cocks, Paul (1976) 'The Policy Process and Bureaucratic Politics' in Cocks, Paul, Daniels, Robert V., and Heer, Nancy Whittier (eds.) *The Dynamics of Soviet Politics* (Harvard University Press, Boston, Mass.)
_____ (1977) 'Retooling the Directed Society: Administrative Modernization and Developed Socialism' in Triska, Jan F. and Cocks, Paul (eds.) *Political Development in Eastern Europe* (Praeger Publishers, New York)
_____ (1978) 'Administrative Rationality, Political Change and the Role of the Party' in Ryavec, Karl W. (ed.) *Soviet Society and the Communist Party* (University of Massachusetts Press, Amherst)
_____ (1980) 'Rethinking the Organizational Weapon: The Soviet System in a Systems Age', *World Politics*, vol. xxxii, no. 2, pp. 228–57.

Conyngham, William J. (1973) *Industrial Management in the Soviet Union: The Role of the CPSU in Industrial Decision-Making, 1917–1970* (Hoover Institution Press, Stanford University, Stanford, Calif.)
_____ (1980) 'Technology and Decision Making: Some Aspects of the Development of OGAS', *Slavic Review*, vol. 39, no. 3, pp. 426–45.

Dunmore, Timothy (1980) 'Local Party Organs in Industrial Administration: The Case of the *Ob Edinenie* Reform', *Soviet Studies*, vol. xxxii, no. 2, pp. 195–217.

Gorlin, Alice C. (1974) 'The Soviet Economic Associations', *Soviet Studies*, vol. xxvi, no. 1, pp. 3–27.

Granick, David (1954) *Management of the Industrial Firm in the USSR* (Columbia University Press, New York)

Gregory, Paul R. and Stuart, Robert C. (1981) *Soviet Economic Structure and Performance* (Harper and Row, New York)

Hardt, John P. and Frankel, Theodore (1971) 'The Industrial Managers' in Skilling, H. Gordon and Griffiths, Franklyn (eds.) *Interest Groups in Soviet Politics* (Princeton University Press, Princeton, N.J. 1971)

Hough, Jerry F. (1969) *The Soviet Prefects: The Local Party Organs in Industrial Decision-Making* (Harvard University Press, Boston, Mass.)
_____ (1977) *The Soviet Union and Social Science Theory* (Harvard University Press, Boston, Mass.)

Kahan, Arcadius and Ruble, Blair A. (eds.) (1979) *Industrial Labor in the USSR* (Pergamon Press, Oxford)

Lane, David (1970) 'Management, Trade Unions and the Party in Industry' in *Politcs and Society in the USSR* (Weidenfeld and Nicolson, London)
_____ (1976) *The Socialist Industrial State* (George Allen and Unwin, London)
_____ and O'Dell, Felicity (1978) *The Soviet Industrial Worker: Social Class, Education and Control* (Martin Robertson, Oxford)

McAuley, Mary (1969) *Labour Disputes in Soviet Russia 1957–1965* (Oxford University Press)

Nove, Alec (1972) *An Economic History of the USSR* (Penguin Books, Harmondsworth and London)
_____ (1977) *The Soviet Economic System* (George Allen and Unwin, London)

Richman, Barry M. (1965) *Soviet Management* (Prentice-Hall, Englewood Cliffs, New Jersey)

Ruble, Blair A. (1981) *Soviet Trade Unions: Their Development in the 1970s* (Cambridge University Press)

Schroeder, Gertrude E. (1968) 'Soviet Economic "Reforms": A Study in Contradictions', *Soviet Studies*, vol. xx, no. 1, pp. 1–21.

_____ (1972) 'The "Reform" of the Supply System in Soviet Industry', *Soviet Studies*, vol. xxiv, no. 1, pp. 97–119.

_____ (1979) 'The Soviet Economy on a Treadmill of "Reforms"', *Soviet Economy in a Time of Change* (Joint Economic Committee, Congress of the United States: US Government Printing Office, Washington, D.C.) vol. 1, pp. 312–40.

Wilhelm, J. (1979) 'Does the Soviet Union Have a Planned Economy?', *Soviet Studies*, vol. xxxi, no. 2, pp. 268–74.

Zaleski, Eugene (1967) *Planning Reforms in the Soviet Union 1962–1966* (University of North Carolina Press, Chapel Hill)

PART FOUR

THE JAPANESE INDUSTRIAL SYSTEM

7 THE PROCESS OF DEVELOPMENT UP TO WORLD WAR II

The Pre-Tokugawa Period

Years before the advent of the Tokugawa period the stability and continuity of the Japanese nation and its values were already established. The statesman Shotoku Taishi introduced the idea of the Emperor's heavenly descent, thus placing the position of the supreme ruler outside factional rivalries, as early as the 7th century, and the idea was not disputed. From 1182 a system of dual administration was set up whereby the Emperor's civilian government was separated from the military administration of the *Shogun*. *Shoguns* might change but the continuity of the Emperor's government was not at risk. It seems likely that this system gave rise to a sense of continuity of history and traditions among the Japanese people that is without parallel. The ruling family in Japan has been without rivals for more than a thousand years; there has been but one imperial dynasty.

During the period 1467–1567 Japan was racked by constant civil war, which had the effects of creating a specialised warrior class, the *samurai*, and of separating the *samurai* from other groups in the population. Also in the 16th century it became customary for lords and *samurai* to move from fief to fief according to the Emperor's orders. Whether by imperial design or not, the consequence was that the *samurai*, while clearly part of the ruling class, were quite detached from the land and from any productive economic role. The creation of this elite social group was to have significant long-term consequences.[1]

Tokugawa Japan (1615–1868)

The Tokugawa period was a period of exceptional stability. It is well-known that Japan kept itself in large degree protected from foreign influences. It is equally important to recognise that the society developed, at least sufficiently, we may say in retrospect, to provide a basis for a later phase of modernisation and partial Westernisation.

Had the society remained truly static from the seventeenth century onward it could not have sustained its traditional continuities at the same time as it adopted and adapted outside institutions and values.

In brief, during the Tokugawa period the Japanese people became a nation and developed the economic sub-structure of their society at an unforced pace. Japan was free of wars and of tyrants and by policy kept external influence carefully filtered. Social change thus occurred slowly and incrementally.

The monarchy was 'above the clouds' and unchallenged. The government of the *Shogun* was weak in relation to the nearly 300 semi-independent provincial magnates (*daimyo*) and dependent on its high officials, but its very weakness preserved it from being fought over, and it was sustained by the emperor's presence. But the magnates were themselves reined in (from 1635) by the system of alternate residence whereby for part of the year they were obliged to sojourn at the Emperor's court.[2] Thus they were at times hostages to the imperial pleasure and at the same time burdened by the expenses of two residences. And there was no escape in foreign adventure since in 1637 the death penalty was introduced for any who attempted to leave the country or to return to it having once gone abroad.[3]

The alternative residence system had other effects. It led to the development of good communications, especially to an effective network of roads that was invaluable in permitting the growth of internal trade. It spread knowledge and understanding of customs and norms, and helped in the standardisation of the Japanese language.[4] The regular movement of nobles, *samurai* and traders effortlessly united the nation.

The economy did not stagnate. The policy of alien exclusion was one of protectionism that benefited the traditional crafts. Skills were maintained, workshops were developed.[5] Small amounts of capital and small advances in technical method led to substantial advances in the older industries. Local production of everyday articles — of food, of clothing, for the household — articles that into the twentieth century have remained peculiar to Japan, flourished in the Tokugawa period. Small producers made a good living in the textile trades, in *sake*-brewing, and in wax manufacture. Modest entrepreneurs developed the country's resources in gold, silver, copper, iron ore and coal. Housebuilding was naturally in the hands of local, labour-intensive builders. A start was made in the development of manufacturing: in rural areas using part-time and casual employees. But the pursuit of profits was not a selfish imperative; it was a public duty.[6]

The management of the economy was capricious. The *samurai*, unemployed in peaceful times, became an intelligentsia supported by stipends according to rank. The *daimyo*, their feudal lords, but administrators rather than owners of land and still, as in earlier times, liable to movement round the country, lived by printing their own money, by forced loans from merchants, and by securing monopolies from the same merchants.[7] The merchants themselves were heterogeneous, ranging from city traders and those who developed the early banks and financial institutions to the small entrepreneurs in the rural areas. Below them, honoured above merchants but exploited by all, were the farmers, heavily and consistently taxed to sustain the administrative institutions and the leisured elite above.[8]

The system developed haphazardly but it had stability. It was held together by a structure rather than by leadership, essentially by disciplined bureaucracy at all levels of administration. And it was economically sustained by a dependable agricultural surplus.[9] During the Tokugawa period there was peace; there were no political or constitutional disputes; and there was no accumulation of vast wealth based on land or trade or industry. Uniquely, there was a military elite which faced no military challenges, and accordingly became a leisured class without clear economic function but with the abilities to develop an effective bureaucracy.

The innovative institution in this period was the merchant house. The house was based not on a blood group but a name group. Thus non-related individuals could become adopted into what may have started as a family enterprise, and the organisation was then run as an artificial kinship group.[10] A boy might become apprenticed to a merchant at the age of 10, be a regular employee at 18 and a manager about 20 years later. At that point he might well set up his own business as an off-shoot of his master's house.[11] There is no direct development from these houses to the full-fledged lifetime employment system of the modern period. Equally it is clear that the merchant house does exemplify crucial features of Japanese business practice: the kinship model, sustained employment from the first job onward, the focus on the importance of correct recruitment, certain advancement for good service. Nor was the house a haphazard growth. The family was expressly subordinated to the House; the heir to the business was frequently adopted from outside; written contracts of employment were drawn up to cover as much as 10 years of service and monitored by guilds; above all the House was earnestly exhorted and minutely supervised by its House Rules.[12]

There were five classes of labour during the period: the *samurai*-bureaucrats and the merchant house employees already noted; craftsmen, with their apprentices and journeymen; urban labour bosses with their gangs of unskilled workers; and the casual workers of the rural labour market.[13]

Traditional Values

Japanese society draws on three major religions and ethical traditions: the Confucian, the Shintoist and the Buddhist.[14] While the Shintoist is native to Japan, the other traditions reached Japan from overseas and have become adapted to Japanese culture over time.

The prime values of Confucianism are benevolence — that affection that is natural between relatives in a family extended to all others — and filial piety — a dutiful obedience to one's seniors and to the older generation. Society should be well-ordered, service is highly valued, the individual is governed by conscience to act in accord with prevailing norms, the ruling group is justified. Learning and devotion to learning are accorded the highest respect.

Confucianism has long been valued in Japan[15] but two influences have modified it. First, it comes from China with an acceptance of 'China as the centre of the world'. With some sense of inferiority toward China the Japanese could not accept Confucianism wholly unamended. Second, the military tradition established in the Japanese civil war had to be accommodated. The outcome, argues Morishima, is a Japanese Confucianism in which loyalty is emphasised rather than benevolence and devotion to a lord more than truth to one's conscience.[16] This military version of Confucianism has been defensively nationalistic, and at times has expected unflinching loyalty to those in authority.

In place of the reverence for China as the world's centre Japanese Confucians borrow the Shintoist idea of Japan as the 'land of gods', with its divine ruler — a conception later exploited in the cause of nationalism.[17]

Yet Confucianism was the latest of the three systematic sources of values and in origin its appeal was to the ruling elite. The earliest underpinnings of traditional values are the Shinto myths, finally written down and codified on the orders of the Emperor Temmu, in 712. This codification, in the *Kojiki*, was ordered not only to place the myths and legends beyond controversy but also to settle definitively the Imperial genealogy. Thus it was Shintoism that established the orthodoxy of the developing society.

Buddhism, the third system of belief, was in fact established first; introduced in 522, it became the religion of the state and of the aristocracy in 592.[18] However, its concerns are primarily with the transcendental so that it has traditionally remained aloof from the commercial sphere and has little influenced its development. In Norbeck's words, 'the relationship between Buddhism and practical, worldly morality is remote'.[19]

In conformity with Confucian tenets, the guiding principle of conduct was conformity to family expectations; filial piety was the axis of family morality. The household (*ie*) existed through time, uniting living members with ancestors, and the custom of primogeniture ensured its preservation. Each individual had a clear status within the family and each family a clear status within the locality. Hence by tradition the individual was subordinate to the group and hence conduct was governed, as Fukutake points out, by 'supremacy of custom' and by 'submission to authority'. Thus the thrust into modernity when it came was in no way associated with self-conscious individualism, as in all Western societies, but with the enduring salience of the group.[20]

The Meiji Restoration

The early industrialisation that took place in Japan during the Meiji period is remarkable in two respects: the programme of modernisation was government-led, and there was no bourgeois class already at hand to implement the programme. We may note in passing that the industrial development of Russia in 1917 was clearly in advance of that of Japan in 1867.

The driving force for modernisation was the intelligentsia drawn from the nobility and from the *samurai* class. The actual power of government lay in the executive, the Council of State, composed of nobles and reformers. Those who implemented the reform programme and especially the industrial development were the lower-ranking *samurai*.[21]

The aim of the reformers was modernisation in the material and physical domain, explicitly recognising and following the example of the Western industrial nations. Hence the copying of Western models was the only rational course, and delegations were despatched to Europe to review the industrial, scientific, educational, economic and political practices of the industrial nations, in order to assess which practices and policies to adopt. In the Emperor's Charter Oath of 1868 was the affirmation: 'knowledge shall be sought for all over the world and thus shall be strengthened the foundation of the imperial polity'.[22] Thus foreign developments were scrutinised with a view to securing the *foundations* of the polity, but there was no wholesale abandonment of tradition. In Hirschmeier and Yui's formulation, modernisation was undertaken for the sake of tradition: the ancestors retained authority, the vertical order was maintained, learning and public service remained the proper sources of social esteem.[23]

Reforms were pragmatic, not patterned after an ideology. Given the long period of virtual exclusion of Western influence, and the reformers' recognition that Japan's internal weaknesses and in certain spheres 'backwardness' precluded the continuation of this policy, then the obvious course was to end it and instead to control rather than exclude the insistent threats, military and commercial, of foreign science and technology.

The pride of the nation was not to be diminished. The reforms were nationalistic.[24] The winning argument over 'exclude the barbarians', now exhausted, was 'admit them, temporarily, in order to overcome them'. Thus there had to be some cost, for to plan to catch up and to overcome implied a present inferiority; and this psychological admission necessarily carried a resentment which was inevitably nursed by the group most put out of face by the reforms, the military.

The feudal system and its privileges were abolished. But this was 'restoration' rather than revolution, for the surrender of fiefs to the Emperor restored to the Emperor his legitimate rights.[25] In 1869 the social classes were declared equal.[26] New freedoms were established: to buy and sell land, to travel and reside according to choice, to choose an occupation. Education was massively developed. In 1870 university education was introduced. In 1872 general education for all children aged 6 to 13 was established by decree (and by 1896 96 per cent of eligible children were enrolled). In 1877 the University of Tokyo was founded.

In 1873 a number of major reforms were carried out. The land tax was reformed, placing the tax upon owners rather than cultivators, which then provided the bulk of fiscal revenue. The traditional military privileges were set aside and a conscript army introduced. Between 1873 and 1876 the stipends paid to *samurai* were phased out and replaced by bond issues.[27] The government had been supporting 400,000 households of former *samurai* which was absorbing 40 per cent of its budget at this time.[28]

These changes were bitterly opposed and opposition reached its climax in the Satsuma Rebellion in 1877. Just as the Meiji regime considered that it was a restoration, so the rebels led by Saigo considered that they were supporting the Emperor, fighting for him to restore traditional practices from which his new advisers had so evilly led him. The defeat of the rebels was of peculiar bitterness, for the endeavour to restore the military caste to its traditional place was defeated by an army of conscripts.

Unfortunately, the defeat of the rebellion did not settle what was a proper role for the military in the modernising state. It may also be thought unfortunate that the constitutional model adopted from Europe should have been that least sympathetic to democratic control, namely that of Bismarck's Germany.[29] The elected assembly which was introduced was controlled by the executive which was responsible to the Emperor; the House of Peers was equal to the House of Representatives but with a power of veto; the suffrage was given to 1 per cent of the population. Under the 1889 Constitution, the Emperor himself exercised legislative power, with the Diet's (the two Houses') consent.[30]

In this way was a compromise reached with the Western forces of modernisation. The political system, unleashing as it did the pressures for change, remained the guardian of centralised power and of the people's values. The 1890 Rescript on Education required of all students the duties of filial piety, obedience, benevolence and service to the State;[31] a form of Confucianism with a stern political overtone was thus spread to the entire nation.

In the field of industry there was an additional reason for the government's leadership beyond the desire to lead and to prime industry, at least temporarily, at a period of crisis.[32] The government already (in the 1860s and early 1870s) ran its own mines; in gold, silver, copper, coal and iron ore it owned and worked 9 mines. The government now acted as entrepreneur. It imported Western machinery and foreign technicians. It invested capital raised from land taxes in manufacturing establishments. It built and operated cotton-spinning mills, silk factories, and tile, cement and bleaching works. It re-equipped shipyards and munitions factories. It took over more mineral properties.[33] And above all it employed the *samurai* with no economic role and declining income as its managers.[34] Thus with extraordinary rapidity a managerial class was created that was beholden to government and came out of a long tradition of public service. Other *samurai* not directly employed by government were helped into business or agriculture with loans for joint-stock enterprises.[35]

A second stage followed. The government and its managers were industrially inexperienced, thus too high wages were paid and firms accumulated heavy losses. Faced with high inflation, the government sold off its factories at advantageous prices to its own protegés (*seisho*). Again with great rapidity, from the managers a class of large capitalists was created, favoured by government, accepted by all, loyal to the nation.[36] The large firms that resulted gave further opportunities for *samurai* as they were turned into profitable enterprises, and gave employment as operatives to their daughters.[37] They also gave rise to a new form of enterprise, the subcontractor to the large manufacturer, independent but under guidance.

The developments were focused on heavy industry: mining, shipbuilding, armaments, machinery and railways. Interdependently arose a modern banking system of joint-stock banks, modern communications and transport, and an education system, founded on the pre-existing Tokugawa structure,[38] to serve the industrial system. The sole manufacturing industry in private hands during the period 1868–1890 was the textile industry. This was organised very simply, on a family workship basis.[39]

Characteristic features of the Japanese industrial system appeared in this period. On the one hand very large firms emerged, the *zaibatsu*, and the dual structure of the large firms and their small subcontracting subordinate firms. On the other hand, *among white-collar workers*, a form of employment appeared that would subsequently, in large firms, spread to all categories of employee.

The growth of *zaibatsu* may be exemplified by the two most notable instances. Mitsui (its original house having been founded in 1672) by the mid-1880's had expanded well outside the original drapery business. It was in mining and it had established its own bank and trading company (Bussan). Mitsubishi (founded in 1873 by Iwasaki) extended its interests rapidly from shipping into shipbuilding, banking, insurance and trading.[40]

White-collar workers were recruited to the new firms by recommendation. Promotion and pay were according to length of service, and workers were expected to stay with their employer until retirement. Loyalty was seen as a more important source of motivation than money.

At this time blue-collar workers were not so privileged. Labourers were of three kinds: they were craftsmen, re-trained as skilled factory workers; day labourers, mostly women, recruited as apprentices from the children of *samurai* and craftsmen, the peasantry or the destitute; or unskilled workers provided through the traditional boss-labour system.[41] They certainly had little job security at this time and there was much labour mobility.[42] To keep recruitment costs (that is, fees paid to recruiters) low, manufacturers cut all non-wage expenses. Absenteeism, desertions, strikes and sabotage followed, and as a result of the high turnover employers resorted to poaching labour from their competitors.[43]

In the period from 1880 up to the beginning of World War I a new approach to employment practice emerged among the employers. Their first attempt to stabilise the labour market was through joint action. Employers developed controls to prevent poaching and agreed to restrict the workers' choice of employer and to force them to re-contract with employers whom they had sought to leave. This harsh approach was subsequently softened by government through prohibition in the Civil Code of employment contracts for more than 5 years[44] and by employers through offers of various benefits, security and humane treatment. But this was hardly benevolence, for the situation was one of labour shortage, and especially of skilled labour;[45] joint arrangements could not work satisfactorily in a time of competition among employers. Thus a form of paternalism emerged, not out of high principle but from economic rationality. In such a context the two approaches are, as Taira has remarked, indistinguishable.[46]

Employers competed in the benefits they offered. These included the payment of bonuses for regular attendance; profit sharing schemes; recreation facilities; increments related to length of service; and the provision of dormitories and other welfare facilities. The aim was to secure a stable labour force by making factory work more attractive than rural family life, and in the individual firm's case, more attractive than work for a rural enterprise. The fact that employers would also hire a second set of temporary workers to cover absentees perhaps indicates that a stable labour force was their primary consideration. None the less, even if the principal motivation was to control the labour market, the new practices found their framework in traditional values. On the one hand the merchant house provided a model for a system of apprenticeship (and was anyhow carried into the industrial age in the treatment of white-collar workers), and on the other hand the family itself provided a pattern for various industrial practices.[47] The *oyabun-koyabun* system was expressly modelled on the family, whereby, away from kin, younger men became symbolic children of an older man who was their ritual parent. Such a group was bound together by ties and expectations of equal force to those in a real kinship group. This system became a framework for work apprenticeship, it facilitated both geographical and social mobility, and it provided social security. Before the modern industrial system was fully formed it was an invaluable transitional institution, reaching its peak around 1900, functioning equally effectively in peasant recruitment, work crews, labour organisations and business associations.[48]

The employers came to have links with particular rural localities indirectly, the recruiters directly. So 'connections' developed, and so personal recommendations became all-important in recruitment. When no relevant experience or training could be offered, a personal assessment of background and of moral qualities was the only stable information. This process had the additional and cumulative effect of gradually drawing into the modern economy even the most economically backward areas of the country, sources of the cheapest labour. In Taira's view it was the poor who built modern Japan.[49]

The employers did not live in a vacuum where only their competitors brought social pressures to bear. Reformers were appalled by the conditions of work and called for improvements, and above all the workers themselves attempted to mobilise in self-defence. As in the Western industrialising nations the first unionist ventures were for mutual benefit and self-help, to upgrade the social position of workers. Again, as in the West, they suffered oppression from both employers and police. In 1897 the Society for the Promotion of Trade Unions was formed. In 1900 the Public Peace Preservation Act was passed to control public demonstrations of discontent, which became infrequent, and to outlaw the use of organised power for 'instigation', 'temptation' and 'violence'.[50] Years of fitful organisation and repression led in some areas to an accumulation of resentment. Between 1903 and 1907 107 strikes occurred, involving 20,789 workers.[51] In 1907 labour riots erupted in the Ashio and Besshi copper mines. Thus employers were under constant pressure to improve their employment practices. While in 1912 only 49 labour disputes were recorded, by 1919 the number had multiplied tenfold, to 497, involving 63,000 workers.[52]

So during the period from 1890 to 1920 a new employment situation emerged. The pressures for it came from many sources: high labour turnover,[53] lack of skilled labour, the need for labour discipline and for better human relations, the revelation of unacceptable working conditions, the lack of direct management (because of the prevalence of sub-contracting systems, of *oyabun-koyabun* groups).[54]

Management in the large modern enterprises reacted, rationally, by gradually elaborating a more employee-oriented and attractive system and by developing an ideology that underscored the continuity of new practice with older merchant-house forms of organisation and that revitalised an older value pattern.[55] The smaller firms lacked the resources to follow the example of the larger firms but also, by definition, with small work forces, they lacked the incentive; they took up a client status in relation to the large firms. Thus the large and small firms drew apart in their mode of employment and a dual system arose. In the larger firms management became less arbitrary; more graduates were recruited into management; employment assumed a commitment to the firm and tended to become permanent; training programmes were introduced; a hierarchy of graded ranks appeared based largely upon seniority; and welfare programmes met family needs and induced a communal, even familial, spirit. In contrast, in the small firms in traditional industries, no such elaboration took place; management remained more arbitrary and employment remained casual, temporary and harsh. Pay was also less in small firms, which lacked the resources to elaborate a pay structure with incentive payments, allowances and bonuses such as the large firms introduced. From this period onward the differentials between small and large firms became evident and widened.[56] It was in both spheres a matter of management choice. Management were firmly in control of the labour market. Unions were slow to develop as a permanent industrial working class only fitfully formed,[57] and the work force acquiesced to the emergent employment policy. In this manner a new employment system was fashioned to overcome the difficulties employers had suffered from a mobile and unstable work force, but a new system sustained by honourable traditional values.

The contrast in both practice and ideology was conspicuous in certain sectors where large and small firms co-existed. This was especially so in heavy industry and also in textiles, paper-making, glass and cement manufacture — in short, in modern or modernising (mechanising) sectors. In traditional industries, such as food and drink manufacture, construction, furniture-making and so forth, small firms predominated and traditional practices were not threatened. In either circumstance it was management that decided upon the most advantageous practice and labour that acquiesced.

The Role of Government

Government had largely stepped out of direct industrial entrepreneurship by 1900, but its closeness to industrial development remained. In 1896 and 1899 it had subsidised the ship-building industry. In 1901 it founded the Yawata Iron Works. In 1906 it nationalised the railways. The state intervened for a variety of reasons. It sustained those sectors, such as shipbuilding and railways, that were important for national defence. It kept an oversight over the continuing modernisation and development of the economy. It underwrote the banking system in the absence of a suitably large group of private investors. By developing its own enterprises it provided a model of management for private capitalists. By selling off its own enterprises for profit, the government effectively sponsored the concentration of holdings in the more modern sectors, and it continued to influence development through close contact with large firms. It was in no way trammelled with an ideology of *laissez faire* which inhibited government involvement in industry.[58]

The Banking System

Like industry, banking developed a dual structure. Traditional enterprise was adequately served by a network of small, local banks. This system sufficed for individuals' savings, for commerce and for traditional sectors such as silk manufacture, weaving and food processing. A new system, however, had to evolve to meet the needs of the capital-intensive modern sectors: mining, metals, shipping, railways, electricity. In 1900 the Industrial Bank of Japan was founded, expressly to provide loans to firms in large-scale industry and to public utilities. Around it arose large investment banks, closely allied to government and sited in large cities. This sector was highly concentrated, effectively dominated by just five city banks.[59]

The core of the modern economy was thus established: large firms supported by a few large banks, all working in close association with government.

Between the Wars

The inter-war period saw Japanese industry working within an increasingly restrictive and ultimately oppressive political framework. None the less it was essentially a period of consolidation of trends set in motion in an earlier period. The employment system continued to develop as the labour force responded to modernisation. The *zaibatsu* became yet more dominant and powerful.

The *zaibatsu* developed massively. They were larger than other firms, more modern — because ahead in the applications of technology and the recruitment of educated manpower — more influential, more wealthy. In 1916 the Industrial Club was formed among the larger firms to act as a political lobby. In 1922 came the Japanese Economic Association, the lobby of finance capital. In 1925 the Law on the Organisation of Important Industries promoted cartels and by 1932 all major industrial sectors were cartelised: there were 33 cartels in heavy industry, 31 in chemicals, 11 in textiles, 8 in food processing, 18 in the financial sphere, and 7 others — 108 in all.[60] During this period the commercial bank, designed to meet the needs of industry, was not permitted long-term lending. Hence the *zaibatsu* extended their own banking activities. They also formed holding companies to control a network of joint stock companies. Non-executive directors were appointed to these companies but they were company employees who did not dilute the concentration of power in the centre.

Beyond the large firms were numerous medium-sized and small enterprises, of three kinds. In small towns and villages traditional enterprise continued in housing, food and clothing. In large towns and cities there were numerous small producers of modern foods, most of them employing imported modern technology. Alongside these were the subcontractors of the large firms. These various firms employed the greater part of the labour force; in 1930 firms with less than 100 employees accounted for 79 per cent of the industrial labour force. But their influence, economically or politically, was negligible when compared with the giant firms.[61]

The large firms now began to offer lifetime employment to their blue-collar workers as well as their white. Their wealth allowed them to afford the new technology which promoted higher productivity which in turn allowed higher wages. (By 1932 the wages of the smallest firms were no more than 26 per cent of those paid in the largest.) Their workers were becoming male-dominated with the growth of modern industry: heavy industry and the chemical industry predominantly recruited men and by 1942 88 per cent of the employees of large firms were working in these sectors. Thus the proportion of women in the labour force in manufacturing industry declined from 60 per cent in 1914 to 48 per cent in 1919 and to 31 per cent in 1942.[62] The large firms' workers were becoming unionised. Their managers were becoming better educated.[63]

Outside the large firms the labour force was relatively unskilled and drifting, often only employed part-time or seasonally. In the pre-industrial outlook that still prevailed the antipathy to paid employment as a way of living, and to sustained rather than casual, remained deep, only overcome by payment of a premium that only large firms could afford. Firms that could not, made do with the least skilled, least educated and least desirable of a still largely migrant labour-force supplied by 'labour-supply agents'.[64]

The prevailing culture was not hospitable to trade unions, which were thought to undermine the loyalty of the workers. In 1925 a Conciliation Society was formed expressly to diffuse the ideology of management familism and the new provision of welfare benefits and workers' councils.[65] But two types were emerging. In the 1920s in the large firms the first enterprise unions appeared. In these at least loyalty to the union did not wholly conflict with loyalty to the firm. In the local labour market craft or industrial unions developed, often very radical and sharply opposed by government.[66] All the unions were modest in both growth and achievement, struggling against political opposition, employers' mistrust and the traditional values of loyalty and familism.

Notes

1. Morishima (1982), Ch. 1.
2. Hirschmeier and Yui (1975), Ch. 1; Morishima (1982), Ch. 1.
3. Storry (1960), Ch. 2.
4. Morishima (1982), Ch. 2.
5. Ibid.
6. Allen (1972), Introduction and Ch. I; Hirshmeier and Yui (1975), Ch. 1. This

attitude to the pursuit of profits is still exemplified today by the leading entrepreneur, Matshushita, who has said, 'Profits should not be a reflection of corporate greed but a vote of confidence from society that what is offered by the firm is validated'. Quoted in Pascale and Athos (1982), p. 49.

7. Allen (1972), Ch. 1.
8. Morishima (1982), Ch. 1.
9. Hirschmeier and Yui (1975), Ch. 1.
10. Yoshino (1968), Ch. 1.
11. Taira (1970), Ch. 5.
12. Hirschmeier and Yui (1975), Ch. 1.
13. Taira (1970), Ch. 5.
14. There is also a Christian tradition in Japan but it is of much lesser importance. Between 1640, when all foreign missionaries were killed or expelled from Japan, and 1873 Christianity was a banned religion.
15. It spread through Japan between the third and the sixth centuries.
16. Norbeck confirms Morishima's view: 'filial piety and loyalty were stressed, and loyalty was raised to pre-eminence'. Edward Norbeck, *Religion and Society in Modern Japan: Continuity and Change*, Rice University Studies, vol. 56, no. 1 (1970), p. 142.
17. Morishima (1982), Introduction.
18. Dates are taken from Odette Bruhl, 'Japanese Mythology' in *Larousse Encyclopedia of Mythology* (Batchworth Press, London, 1959), p. 414.
19. Norbeck, *Religion and Society in Modern Japan*.
20. Fukutake (1982), Chs. 3 and 5. See below for a discussion of societal characteristics today.
21. Hirschmeier and Yui (1975), Ch. 2.
22. Storry (1960), p. 103.
23. Hirschmeier and Yui (1975), Ch. 2.
24. Byron K. Marshall, *Capitalism and Nationalism in Prewar Japan: The Ideology of the Business Elite, 1868–1941* (Stanford University Press, Stanford, Calif., 1967), Chs. 2–3.
25. Storry (1960), Ch. 4.
26. Allen (1972), Ch. II.
27. Morishima (1982), Ch. 2.
28. Mikio Sumiya, 'The Emergence of Modern Japan', Ch. 2. of Okochi *et al.* (1974).
29. At the same time it was perhaps inevitable. Germany above all Western nations which were industrially advanced retained a sovereign whose remaining powers could be seen to be closest to what continuity in the Japanese constitutional system required.
30. Storry (1960), Ch. 4.
31. Ibid.
32. Marshall, *Capitalism and Nationalism in Prewar Japan*, Ch. 2.
33. Allen (1972), Ch. II.
34. New technology brought a need for new knowledge and the ability to grasp it. This gave the advantage to the educated, the *samurai*. Yoshino (1968), Ch. 3. The *samurai*'s government bonds attracted only 7 per cent interest which was soon eroded by inflation. Sumiya in Okochi *et al.* (1974), Ch. 2.
35. Hirschmeier and Yui (1975), Ch. 2.
36. Morishima (1982), Ch. 2.
37. The preponderance of women in the manual worker labour force is discussed below.
38. See Ronald Dore, *Education in Tokugawa Japan* (Routledge and Kegan Paul, London, 1965).
39. Clark (1979), Ch. 11.

40. Hirschmeier and Yui (1975), Ch. 2.
41. Hirschmeier and Yui (1975), Ch. 2; Sumiya in Okochi *et al*. (1974), Ch. 2; Taira (1970), Ch. 5.
42. Yoshino (1968), Ch. 3.
43. Taira (1970), Ch. 5.
44. Ibid., Ch. 6.
45. Clark (1979), Ch. II.
46. Taira (1970), Ch. 5.
47. Abegglen (1958) has argued that factory organisation is a logical development from pre-industrial family structure: the company was merely an extended family, complete with hierarchy.
48. See Iwao Ishino, 'The *oyabun-koyabun:* a Japanese ritual kinship institution', *American Anthropologist*, vol. 55, no. 5, Pt. 1 (1953), pp. 695–707. The *oyabun-koyabun* system was equally prevalent in politics and in racketeering, other growth areas in modernising Japan.
49. Taira (1970), Ch. 5.
50. Ibid., Ch. 6.
51. Cole (1979), Ch. 1.
52. Hirschmeier and Yui (1975), Ch. 3.
53. Dore notes turnover rates for labour of 50–100 per cent in 1900. Dore (1973), Ch. 14.
54. Hirschmeier and Yui (1975), Ch. 3.
55. The 19th century household (*ie*) system and the kin-linked household confederation (*dōzoku*) system had offered permanent employment to male workers (see pp. 179–180).
56. Dore (1973), Ch. 14; Hirschmeier and Yui (1975), Ch. 3.
57. This is a point interestingly examined by Cole and Tominaga. See Robert E. Cole and Ken'ichi Tominaga, 'Japan's Changing Occupational Structure and its Significance' in Patrick (1976).
58. Allen (1972), Chs. II–III. Indeed according to tradition, the Japanese state is very properly concerned with every aspect of society. See Robert A. Scalapino, 'Ideology and Modernization — The Japanese Case' in David E. Apter (ed.) *Ideology and Discontent* (Free Press, Glencoe, 1964).
59. Allen (1972), Ch. III. See also Juro Teranishi, 'Availability of Safe Assets and the Process of Bank Concentration in Japan', *Economic Development and Cultural Change*, vol. 25, no. 3 (1977), pp. 447–70.
60. Hirschmeier and Yui (1975), Ch. 3.
61. In 1930 among representatives in both Houses of Parliament one-third were businessmen from large firms. Hirschmeier and Yui (1975), Ch. 3.
62. Morishima (1982), Ch. 4.
63. Sumiya in Okochi *et al*. (1974), Ch. 2.
64. Taira (1970), Ch. 6.
65. Cole (1979), Ch. 1.
66. Sumiya in Okochi *et al*. (1974), Ch. 2.

Select Bibliography

See end of Chapter 8, page 222.

8 THE JAPANESE WAY

After World War II

The greatest disruption in modern Japanese history occurred at the close of World War II. The fabric of society was torn by the catastrophe and shame of national defeat. The regime and its ethics were discredited. In the political and economic arenas all was in disarray. The nation was at the mercy of its conquerors. And the Americans who supervised the re-emergence of Japan during their formal Occupation of the country not only exacted reparations and inaugurated demilitarisation, but also took steps to bury the institutions that were tainted through association with the defeated military regime, and to implant the values and institutions of Western democracy. Changes which might have come at a different pace in different circumstances were greatly speeded up.

The *zaibatsu* were dismantled. The concentration of industry was replaced by a policy of deconcentration. Senior managers were dismissed.[1] The growth of trade unions was actively encouraged. In 1947 an Antimonopoly Law and an Anti-Economic Power Concentration Law were introduced.[2] A policy of recovery and growth of the economy rather than the mere pursuit of profits was adopted by a new generation of young managers who were college-educated, more professional than their predecessors, more idealistic and open, and in their life-styles less extravagant.

Yet disruption did not mean discontinuity. At society's apex the Emperor remained, still the father of the nation, still symbolising the strength of the Japanese heritage, its values and pride. Within industry, if the *zaibatsu* faded, large firms led by the former *zaibatsu* remained; if unions developed, they did so from the base of the embryonic inter-war unions; the employment system for which post-war Japan has become renowned did not emerge full-grown after 1945 but grew from the developing system of earlier periods; even the government's concern for industrial organisation was nothing new, but sprang from earlier practices embarked on in the Meiji Period.

In brief, in the post-war period, the Japanese industrial system evolved in accord with earlier periods of growth and development. It did not mutate. It did not rise like a phoenix from the ashes of defeat.

The government introduced in 1946 a measure of land reform, the Owner-Farmer Establishment Law, to promote land-ownership. Nearly 2 million farmers gained land in a massive redistribution, whereby land was sold by government to former tenants.[3] Owner farmers rose from 36.5 per cent of all farmers to 54 per cent, and tenant farmers declined from 27 per cent to 8 per cent.[4] The agricultural work force declined with the increasing efficiency of the industry from 50 per cent of the employed population in 1947 to 38 per cent in 1955,[5] and then to 13 per cent in 1975 and 10 per cent in 1980.[6] Initially this surplus of labour from the land did not go in large numbers into manufacturing industry;[7] the tertiary sector (which in fact meant the wholesale and retail trades more than government service) took 29.8 per cent of the labour force in 1950, a larger share than either of the other two sectors (37 per cent) in 1960, 51.7 per cent in 1975 and 55.4 per cent in 1980.[8]

The watershed came with the Korean War. The modest recovery of the Japanese economy no longer answered American needs. The building of democracy now took second place to building a bastion against Communism. Reparations were shelved; demilitarisation was suspended; and a Red Purge was initiated to rid the trade unions of Communist leadership. From this point the economy grew spectacularly. The movement of labour from the land became a mass migration. The proportion of the labour force employed in manufacturing industry rose from 16 per cent in 1950 to 21 per cent in 1960 and 27 per cent in 1969.[9] The proportion of the non-agricultural workers who were unionised declined with equal speed: from 55 per cent in 1949 to 35 per cent in 1956. The de-concentration of industry was reversed, and by 1960 only 58 per cent of the labour force worked in companies with less than 100 employees.[10]

The government increased its activity. From 1954 to 1969 government loans to medium-sized and small enterprises increased twenty-fold. The growth points in industry changed: from the manufacture of cameras, sewing machines and scientific instruments in 1950 to the shipbuilding, electrical and electronic industries in 1955.[11] Growth areas were protected by government, changing as the emphasis of manufacturers shifted: electrical appliances, electronics, industrial machinery, cars, aeroplanes, artificial fibres, petrochemicals, and oil refining.[12] The government intervened with import quotas, import licences, protective tariffs, low interest loans, tax limitations and exemptions, and outright subsidies.[13] In the mid-1960s government investment amounted to 30 per cent of gross domestic capital formation.[14]

By the 1960s Japan had overtaken Germany's output of steel. By 1969 she produced half the world's shipping tonnage. By 1969/70 her output of cars became second only to the United States. The Economic and Social Plan for the years 1967–71 forecast growth of the economy of more than 8 per cent per year, but actual growth for these years averaged nearly 13 per cent.[15]

Concentration in industry continued. By 1963 90 per cent of all medium-sized and small companies were organised into more than 1,000 cartels. In place of the *zaibatsu* new groupings of companies appeared, formed round the nuclei of banks and other financial institutions. By 1971 the former *zaibatsu* had re-emerged in new incarnations as networks of companies with interlocking management, mutual stock-holding, jointly planned strategies.[16] By 1973 the 100 largest firms quoted on the Tokyo Stock Exchange had 4,270 dependent firms; that is, the parents either held 30 per cent of the stocks of their dependents or held 10–20 per cent with interlocking managements to secure the link.[17]

It has been the policy of government through the Ministry of International Trade and Industry (MITI) to promote industrial concentration. The Ministry has used the Council on Industrial Structure to achieve this goal, industry by industry, through the voluntary co-operation of the Ministry itself, firms and the major financial institutions. MITI has also encouraged rationalisation of industry by a policy of granting tax privileges and preferential loans. Similarly it has subsidised programmes of research and development in industry.[18]

Societal Characteristics

There are certain characteristics of Japanese society that have so far been no more than hinted at and that need now to be more fully explored. The Japanese have values, attitudes and practices that are strange to the Western observer and of much importance for an understanding of the Japanese industrial system. Almost all are concerned with human relationships.

First, there is the significance of the group, which is not the family group, but the residential, in origin the household, group; in Japanese *ie*.[19] Because the household was more important than the kin, entry was as easy through adoption as by birth, and so the household was a fictive kinship group. It is then the group which decides and the group which acts;[20] and loyalty to the group and the preservation of public 'face' are, in Japanese tradition, of greater importance, more binding, to the individual than following his conscience.[21] And as has been widely commented on, shame — an awareness of bringing dishonour to others — is for the Japanese traditionally more strongly felt than guilt — a sense of having failed oneself.[22] Thus the group is dominant in shaping values and a man's relationship to his salient group is of emotional significance. In nineteenth century Japan an individual had little or no existence outside his identity as a family, household or fictive kinship group member.[23] In contemporary Japan the family group has been replaced by the firm, and in the firm it is group performance that matters. Organisation charts show collective units rather than individual positions or titles, and reporting relationships are indicated in terms of collective units.[24] Workers' obligations and loyalties are to the firm, not to an individual,[25] and workers define themselves as members of firms rather than, as normally in the West, by occupation.[26] Glazer also argues that the educational system, fiercely competitive though it is at entry points, is supportive of the group; there are no drop-outs from school and individual achievement is underemphasised so that the supportive quality of each group of students is promoted.[27]

Second, within the group relationships with leaders are of special significance. The leader is not, as may occur in Western culture, set apart from the remainder of the group, the followers, but is very much a part of the group. Decisions of the group should also be the opinions of the leader (in traditional context, the head of the household), which, in terms of group process, implies first that decisions emerge through extensive consultation, sufficient to convey to the leader what group members think and to other group members what the leader may decide, and second that conformity follows the decision.[28] The object, evidently, is to maintain the cohesiveness of the group and loyalty to its joint actions. The leader who drags his followers *his* way, reckless of their wishes, and the follower whose differences from the majority provoke eccentric loyalty gain no respect in Japanese tradition. Indeed the best leader may well be the facilitator, with interpersonal rather than technical skills, the one best able to elicit consensus rather than the one who in Western parlance 'gives the lead'.[29] Such a consensual style of leadership which on occasion may be sluggish in the making of decisions, especially when it allows for 'acceptance time',[30] has the complementary strength that as the consensus changes the un-making of decisions and the acceptance of change may be rapid.[31]

The Confucian tradition allied to the Japanese conventions of *bushido* placed the strongest emphasis on filial piety and loyalty to the lord.[32] The effects of this value-system have been that the Japanese find their identity not in the pursuit of individual goals but in acceptance of the goals of the group and in strict loyalty to the leader, and also, as a consequence, that deep emotional commitment is involved.[33] The formality and ritual evident in Japanese social relations is thus not an indication of aloofness. On the contrary it is the necessary social front to protect underlying feeling.[34]

In Austin's study of Japanese and Western values he pointed out how much more personal is the Japanese view of leadership.[35] While Westerners accept the authority of an office, Japanese give loyalty to their leaders for their human qualities. While Western firms promote a clear-cut division of labour, in the Japanese firm roles are diffuse and relationships are not fragmented but total.[36] From this it follows, says Austin, that open argument and conflict are painful and hence avoided; and so it is that decisions are taken by the group to avoid placing blame on an individual and provoking the personal distress that could follow.[37] In fact, however, Austin has matters causally reversed, for surely the personal investment follows from the finding of personal identity in the group setting, from a high valuation of interdependence rather than separateness and independence;[38] it is not that emphasis upon the group follows from embarrassment at conflict.

The third long-standing characteristic of the Japanese that is also linked to the first two is their concern for ranking and status. Tradit-ionally the social order has been divided into seniors (*sempai*), peers (*doryo*), and juniors (*kohai*), and has been institutionalised by seniority. Filial piety is owed not only to the lord, the head of the household and the ancestors but to all seniors. Prestige is attributed not only to men and to elders but even more to those with higher status within a hierarchical system. Rank is more important than profits; institutional affiliation matters more than social background.[39]

Hierarchical relationships in Japan, as well as group relationships, are characterised by interdependence. Those of higher rank afford protection to their juniors which leads to mutual dependence, while the greater social power inherent in higher rank maintains the stability of the system just as it outlaws competition and conflict between separate and equal groups.[40] It is in this framework that the *nenko* system of employment in which pay is graded according to seniority and age has its place. Hierarchical relationships may well also be informal. One of Japan's most outstanding post-war entrepreneurs has said, vividly: 'when I meet with my managers it is seldom formal. We communicate knee to knee . . . we must respect the pride of different individuals'.[41]

A view prevails in the West that the Japanese norms of behaviour relating to groups, group leadership and hierarchy are quaint survivals from a pre-industrial phase of history. This leads to the belief that further industrial development will inevitably produce the abandonment of a group perspective and the exaltation of individualism that characterise the industrial relations of the West. The thesis has of course been empirically disproved by the fact that Japan has overtaken most of the Western economies industrially without the forecast shift in values having occurred. But it also misunderstands the role of the group in Japanese cultural development and in the orientation and security of the Japanese personality. We may note that the lack of a recognisable social security system on the Western model in Japan is further evidence for a difference of views about how the individual should be cared for: not by the State, not solely through self-help, but through the collective efforts of the salient groups or institutions of which the individual is a member.[42]

A fourth and final Japanese characteristic that is self-evidently related to industrial success is commitment to work. The point is not that the Japanese workers work harder than those in other nations but that their commitment to work, the significance to them of work in their lives, is greater. In his study of values Austin found work for the Japanese elite to be the essence of a man's self and he noted that so central is work that all fun occurs in a work-environment.[43] Cole notes that workers not only have a high level of identification with company goals but also have a *strong need to find fulfilment at work*. It is this combination that binds management and workers together in a 'community of fate'.[44]

The Society of Industry

The hierarchical ranking that affects individuals is replicated in the industrial system among companies and industrial groupings of companies. Although the *zaibatsu* were dismantled during the American Occupation, the great companies from which they had developed were re-formed as loose alliances of companies, though with less overlap in direction and less mutual holding of each others' shares. These alliances stayed at the top of the society of industry.[45]

Next in the hierarchy come bank-centred groups of companies. Here the companies are linked to the banks concerned, which have their own ranking order, and are not inter-related among themselves. These groupings are followed by those that have formed round recently successful large manufacturing companies (such as Hitachi or Toyota).

In all these groupings there is a sense of community, an industrial gradation and hierarchical organisation, and a degree of specialisation. The companies are thus inter-dependent, and less dependent on individual shareholders and the speculators' market than a Western observer would suppose owing to the high proportion of each company's shares that is owned by other companies[46] and consolidates the groups' independence.

Between the groupings, and between companies within any one grouping, there are recognised distinctions, from those employers which are the largest firms with the greatest stability, the least staff turnover, the highest salaries, the most recognised prestige, the best educated recuits, the greatest credit-worthiness, down through the graded hierarchy to those with the least of these desirable characteristics. The gradation of industrial companies is matched by similar orderings of banks and universities. Naturally the system is rougher and less coherent in practice than in any abstract characterisation of it. None the less the underlying gradations are real and, in crude form, well recognised.

The individual company is specialised in a single industry. When mergers occur, they do so *within* an industry. When firms grow they develop less by the forward and backward integration of the West than by the formation of separate subsidiary companies.[47]

The Japanese Employment System

The Japanese 'system' of employment, since Abegglen's first published description in 1958, has been described and analysed many times. It is found in its fully-fledged form in the Civil Service, in large companies and in some middle-sized companies, and it has five principal characteristics. Employment is life-long, that is, up to retirement at the age of 55; recruitment is at the earliest point in the recruit's career, on leaving school or college; wages and salaries are paid and promotion given according to age and length of service and, to a degree, education; unions are enterprise unions; there is an exchange of commitment — the company provides security and amenities for the employees who in turn offer their loyalty to the company.[48]

The system thus covers employees between the ages of 25 and 55; by definition it does not cover temporary employees of any kind; it cannot be sustained by small companies; and, by far its grossest limitations, it applies only to men. Thus it encompasses government service and, outside, perhaps 28 per cent of men employed in the non-agricultural private sector. Overall, in Cole's phrase, the number of permanent employees is 'limited to the cyclically justifiable minimum'.[49]

Temporary workers are the group at the bottom end of the employment system upon whom the permanent employment of the more fortunate workers depends. Their work is unskilled, their pay and security are low, they are not unionised. In 1959 they formed 12 per cent of the non-agricultural labour force; in 1966 8 per cent; and in 1969 6 per cent. They are in decline.[50] Part-time workers on the other hand are on the increase.

In 1965 women formed about 40 per cent of the labour force and about one-third of the workers in manufacturing industry. On average their wages were 50–60 per cent of those paid to men; their prospects of advancement and their security were far less than in the case of men; they were offered little training and the small number who secured long-term employment had to retire earlier than their male counterparts, at 50.[51] Women are not promoted to supervisor levels. They are in effect expected only to work until they get married, and their turnover in employment is appropriately high. In the bank studied by Rohlen it was 25 per cent per year.[52] Women in effect are outside the mainstream of the employment system: working on low level work, in small companies, and excluded altogether from certain categories of work such as night work.

In fact the system can only be maintained because of the many categories of workers excluded from it. Employers can only offer permanent employment to workers because flexibility in labour management is guaranteed by the high turnover of women workers and by the use of temporary workers, casual workers, home-workers, and subcontract companies.[53]

The pay arrangements pervasive under the Japanese *nenko* system are singularly complex, and sufficiently so as to require an explanation.[54] Basic pay is only a proportion of total income: on Abegglen's estimate in 1958 27 per cent, on Dore's in 1970 42 per cent. This is then enhanced directly by supplements, allowances and bonuses, and indirectly by an impressive array of fringe benefits. Supplements are likely to be for merit and job level. Allowances are given for family, for housing, for commuting, for living in a certain region. Bonuses are usually paid twice yearly. Welfare benefits include the provision of dormitories, houses and hostels, recreation facilities, holiday arrangements, group outings, medical services, and a variety of amenities for self-development. Companies even offer to pay a higher rate of interest than the banks on their employees' savings.[55] This reward system is certainly more multiform than any customary Western system, but its further complexities only appear when the allocation of rewards and the criteria for allocation are examined.[56]

The principal factors in determining the allocation of rewards are age, length of service and education. In the past it was understood that an employee would become of increasing value to the firm with growing experience which was directly related to length of service. This was wholly rational as was the retirement at 55 of those whose powers were in decline.[57] Experience was also closely correlated with age. Given the uniform practice of hiring recruits at the point of leaving the educational system, the longest serving would naturally be the oldest employees. The only exception would occur in relation to differing lengths of education, and so provision was made for pay differentials in favour of the more educated given that increased education was taken to signify more developed ability. Thus the seniority system was a wholly rational system, just so long as experience was taken as a measure of worth. It was not a quaint survival from a pre-industrial past.

The gap between large and small firms in what they offer to their employees is most surely shown in wages. The wage differential was at its widest in the 1950s[58] but narrowed in the period 1959 to 1970.[59] From 1970 the gap began to open again. Thus two labour markets have emerged: in Morishima's words, the market for loyalty and the market for mercenaries.[60]

The *nenko* system — the favouring of the older and long-serving worker — was rational also for ensuring stability. The young worker had to stay with his employer in order to increase his earnings; his rewards were deferred. The older worker was somewhat overpaid in order to guarantee long-term loyalty. Furthermore, the increase in reward might well coincide with the increase in boredom (even alienation, in incipient form) with the work itself. Thus satisfaction and commitment might grow with length of service, and the most committed workers be rehired following retirement.[61]

That this description is true to experience is borne out by Clark's research. He found that immobile men aged 25 to 34 were loyal to their companies but somewhat resentful; older workers were fully content, seeing their service to the company as constituting service also to the nation.[62]

In discussion of the Japanese employment system battle has been joined between those who see its distinctive features to be continuous with the pre-industrial past and those who see them as products of a transitional labour market situation.[63] Not surprisingly such a black and white view distorts the truth, in which elements of continuity are combined with elements of change. In other words, given the remarkable success of the Japanese industrial system, no feature of the past is likely to have survived that was not consonant with modern industrialism; likewise no labour market forces could squeeze out of Japanese industry such well adapted features of the past. We may note here the ill-effects upon analysis of assuming that in the modernisation process there is 'one best way' in which the industrial system should be organised and of which other forms are but deviations with only short-term survival value.

The importance to the system of careful recruitment cannot be overemphasised. Traditionally employees were recruited for their personal qualities, their character, and hence the employer habitually made use of regional 'connections' who used personal contacts to investigate family background. This was no doubt entirely sufficient for recruitment of new industrial workers from rural areas. In the post-World War II period personal qualities remain important but education has become a second factor in what is, given recruitment at the immediate post-education stage, an assessment of potential.

The Japanese company also takes responsibility for training, which encompasses technical training, training of character and training for integration in the community. Company affiliation becomes as important to an employee in the determination of identity as family, education or income. In Rohlen's words, a company is 'a community of people organised to secure their common livelihood';[64] the employee feels that he shares a common fate with his company. Again group membership helps to shape the individual.

The stability of the lifetime employment system quite evidently saves the expenses due to labour turnover and consequent training for mid-career recruits. Training can focus on new requirements and changing job skills. New technology can thus be introduced without threat. Looked at nationally the system can be seen as an encouragement to growth; with labour in effect a fixed cost, the slow-growing and inefficient companies pay the penalties.[65]

Even in recession, Japanese companies can avoid dismissing workers by freezing recruitment, by offering early retirement, by transferring labour to subsidiary companies or subcontractors, or by lending employees to other companies.

The Banking System

The Japanese banking system was already of importance before 1900 as a prime source of loans for industry. Although the Tokyo Stock Exchange was established in 1878 it became a mere forum for speculators and fell into disrepute. Hence firms came to obtain their funding from bank loans rather than stock exchange issues.[66]

From 1900 to 1940 the number of banks in the country decreased from 2,289 to 357 as numerous banks failed and others were swallowed up in mergers. In the process all banks grew in size, from the 'Big Five' city banks to the smaller rural banks. For the small saver the failure of rural banks led to a switch of deposits during this period into the government financial system, that is, Treasury Investments and Loans, via postal savings.[67]

In the period after World War II the government again collaborated with the banking system to stimulate investment in heavy industry, especially in the chemical, metals and engineering industries; the available savings of the new industrial labour force grew as a result of bonus payments and in reaction to a low social security provision which encouraged thrift.[68]

Managers

There have been few studies of Japanese managers and their characteristics, and we shall here make use of only two. In 1965 Aonuma published the results of his own survey of the four top executives in the largest 250 manufacturing firms and the largest 125 non-manufacturing firms; his sample thus totalled 1500 senior managers. He also made use of two earlier studies for comparative purposes.[69] Not surprisingly he found a trend away from owner-managers to professional managers; the 1900 sample included 20 per cent professional managers, the 1928 sample 50 per cent, and Aonuma's own sample 94 per cent. What is more significant is the lack of mobility and the senior age of his executives and their high educational level. Of his 1410 professional managers 46 per cent had spent their careers in one firm and 87 per cent were aged 55 or more. While in the 1900 sample only 5 per cent had higher education, in the 1928 group the proportion was 67 per cent and in Aonuma's own study it was 90 per cent. These college graduates, furthermore, had had a relevant technical background: 23 per cent were graduates in engineering, 22 per cent in commerce, 16 per cent in law and 13 per cent in economics.[70]

What Aonuma's study suggests is that educational status is now the most important factor in a manager's career and this is amply confirmed by Dore's research.[71] All his Hitachi managers were graduates, and none had moved into management from apprenticeship or via any mid-career qualification. Dore noted that despite their high educational status the managers in Hitachi were not as privileged as comparable British managers. They were also closer to their workers in two other respects: they supervised them more closely and junior managers were unionised — in the enterprise union.[72]

These studies at least suggest that Japanese managers owe their status to achievement and that they gain advancement through long service to their companies, which in a few cases is even rewarded by a place on the board of directors.[73] Both these factors might be expected to lead to more harmonious management-union relations than are customarily encountered in Western countries.

Managerial Decision-Making

Japanese management is known for its *ringi* decision-making system, though it seems fair to comment that its procedures are more known of than fully understood. The Japanese word *rin* means submitting a proposal to a superior and receiving approval; the word *gi* signifies deliberations and decisions. Hence the system of *ringi seido* implies that decisions are submitted to deliberation and approval by a group of managers before being implemented. In the case of major decisions a proposal for action (*ringisho*) emerges from one manager and is circulated to all other managers in a position to comment on the proposal and annotate the papers. Thus it reaches the top of the managerial hierarchy complete with an expression of relevant views; the chief executive then announces the decision. In this way all major decisions involve all relevant managers and can be presented as collective decisions even if opposition has been expressed at some level.[74] Lewis Austin writes: 'For Japanese, to decide is *matomeru*; to gather, to collect, to bring together like a flock of birds in a tree. Legitimate decisions are the sum of the contributions of all'.[75]

Western commentators have noted that this system discourages the initiative and autonomy of middle-management and is awkward for quick decisions on the one hand or long-term and planning decisions on the other. They suggest also that the introduction of operational research, new controls and corporate planning will reveal the awkwardness of *ringi* decision-making and most probably render it obsolete.

This view fails to take account of the fact that many important decisions, and certainly those requiring rapid judgement, have always been taken outside the *ringi* system. But more significantly it treats the system as a quaint anachronism from the pre-industrial past. Two quite distinct comments need to be made. First, while the system is a product of the past it has a clear political value. It serves to maintain the homogeneity of the company and binds closer the various levels of the hierarchy. It emphasises the group rather than the individual and, as we have noted, in Japanese culture the group is paramount over and defines the individual. Thus the *ringi* system reflects a core value in the society and is no fad or relic to be thrown away like yesterday's lunch-time menu. Second, it presents a much more modern style of decision-making than that embodied in the independent snap-judging autocratic entrepreneur. In fact today major decisions are frequently group decisions, not only within Japanese culture.[76]

The Zaibatsu

The *Zaibatsu*, as already noted, had a long history, but they emerged as a formidable power on the economic scene only in the last years of the 19th century. The normal development was for the founder firm to form a holding company and to control through this a central core of perhaps 12 companies which would include a bank, an insurance company, a trust company and a trading company. The holding company might control from 40 per cent to 100 per cent of the capital of each major member company.[77] In the inter-war period their power and influence were a source of envy and they were obliged to co-operate with government. By 1945 one-third of all industrial capital was in the hands of the largest ten firms; in banking approximately one-half was held by the largest four. The 'Big Four' *zaibatsu* — Mitsui, Mitsubishi, Sumitomo and Yasuda — controlled 51 per cent of coal production, 65 per cent of aluminium production, 60 per cent of the shipping industry, 70 per cent of bank loans, one-third of Japan's foreign trade, and 69 per cent of the manufacture of locomotives. In these powerful groupings ties were secured by cross-holding of stocks and underpinned by financial support from *zaibatsu* banks. The range of activity of the *zaibatsu* went well beyond the familiar vertical and horizontal integration of large firms in the Western world: the *zaibatsu* not only controlled manufacture in a variety of lines but also shipping and ship-building, banking and insurance.[78]

In 1945 the *zaibatsu* were finally broken up: family ownership was severed, holding companies were dissolved, each subsidiary company was given independence. None the less, as already noted, although the old family empires disappeared the *zaibatsu* model of industrial grouping was approximately modelled. The new groups were bank-centred, greatly reliant on debt-financing. As a result the banks place representatives on client firms' boards of directors, own a large proportion of their stock, and readily provide long-term and short-term loans. The groups are confederations of diversified undertakings, loosely knit: enterprises may be either related to larger firms through majority ownership or control, or affiliated through ordinary business connections, principally on a subcontract basis. Linkages, looked at from the centre, serve to associate the group with suppliers of raw materials, marketing companies, ancillary functions (such as maintenance or transportation), and other subcontracted operations. When the related or affiliated firms are given financial, technical or managerial aid, their dependence on the group is emphasised, but they secure support and stability. The group as a whole benefits from the network of small associated companies because of the flexibility that allows for innovation, for occasional labour-intensive operations and for the placement of retired personnel.

Employers' Organisations

The growth of employers' organisations in Japan coincided with, indeed followed from, the destruction of the *zaibatsu* at the close of World War II by the Allied Powers, who removed at one stroke the dominating influence of ten clans and 56 families and delegated management to professional executives.[79] In the organisational vacuum four employers' associations were formed.[80] In 1946 the *Keidanren* (Federation of Economic Organisations) and the *Keizai Doyukai* (Japanese Committee for Economic Development) were both founded. The *Keidanren* is a federation of 102 financial, industrial and trading associations and more than 800 leading corporations. It is thus an association of the largest enterprises and represents the major voice of business. In contrast the *Keizai Doyukai* has a membership of individual managers. It started with 70 members and has grown to more than 1000. It represents the younger post-war professional managers from industry and banking, and has stuck to an ideological stance of being managerial in outlook rather than capitalist.[81] In 1948 appeared, or rather re-appeared, the *Nikkeiren* (Japanese Federation of Employers' Associations) a powerful voice in the area of labour and labour-management relations. It had had an earlier existence after World War I when it had secure influence in the political arena. In its new era it again collaborated with the political powers and was strongly supported to take a militant stand against labour by the Allied Powers. In 1949 alone it was instrumental in securing 370,000 dismissals.

Finally, in 1953 the fourth organisation was formed to represent the interests of small and medium-sized enterprises. This was the *Nissho* (the Chamber of Commerce and Industry of Japan) which represented 448 local and regional chambers. It has been principally influenced by the policies of the large firms.

The Unions

Unions of workers are a product of Western European capitalism and hence they first became known about in Japan when Japan was deciding to emulate the Western economic powers in industrial development and modernisation. At that time unions were less institutionalised in the West than they have since become and they were perceived in Japan as politically radical and dangerous, a by-product of Western materialism, and irrelevant to the Japanese tradition of ties of loyalty, affection and harmony between masters and men.[82]

The new labour force was recruited in rural areas, most early factories were small and most workers were women, all of which tended towards a paternalistic system. And despite the many efforts to launch unions to defend and enlarge workers' rights, employers and government remained adamantly opposed to their function. The result was to radicalise union organisation, which merely confirmed the original judgement that unions were dangerous and political organisations out of place in industry.

In the 1920s union membership grew steadily, from 125,000 in 1923 to 325,000 in 1929. Inter-war membership peaked in 1931 with its highest membership rate of 7.9 per cent of the non-agricultural labour force and in 1936 with its highest overall membership of 421,000.[83]

In the inter-war period the unions grew and disappeared, but even in 1936 only one-third of trade union members were covered by collective bargaining agreements.[84] Then in 1938 the military government outlawed all unions in favour of *Sampo* (the Association for Service to the State through Industry), a tool of government. Membership of unions was zero by 1945.

It was thus not until the end of World War II and the American Occupation that unions became securely established. In 1945 the development of unions was suddenly perceived as a necessary part of the campaign to secure democracy. The 1945 Trade Union Law guaranteed the rights of workers to organise, to bargain collectively and to strike. The 1947 Labour Standards Law established minimum working conditions. The unions came in from the cold,[85] and by 1949 56 per cent of the industrial labour force was unionised.[86]

In 1973 total union membership was 12.1 million which represented 33 per cent of wage and salary earners.[87] There were 29,600 enterprise unions, 96 per cent of recognised unions being in enterprises with more than 1,000 employees. Of these unions (in 1967) 21 per cent were of blue-collar workers only, 32 per cent were white-collar only, and 47 per cent were for all workers.[88] While 38 per cent of workers in manufacturing industry were unionised, the proportion was much less elsewhere: 18 per cent in transport and communication, 11 per cent in service industries, and 10 per cent in government and other public employment.[89] Union membership varied more dramatically according to firm size. In 1973 65 per cent of workers in firms with 500 or more employees were unionised, 31.5 per cent in firms with 100–499 employees, 9 per cent in firms with 30–99 employees and only 3.4 per cent in firms with less than 30 employees.[90]

As already noted, the majority of unions are enterprise unions,[91] which has advantages for the union side as well as for management. All regular employees in a company are union members, whose dues are automatically collected by deduction from wages.[92] Not only are white-collar and blue-collar workers in the same union but also included are several levels of supervisors, workers on the edge of management. The company offers offices and other facilities to the union, and the leaders of the union are always elected from the regular local work force rather than being from other companies and localities. In a multiplant enterprise a union federation is formed.

Management nationally focuses on the enterprise for purposes of consultation and welfare provision and, given the low public invest-ment in housing development and social security, this concern benefits the workforce. In many cases the posts of union officers come to be seen as jobs in the company, of special attraction to white-collar workers.

Beyond enterprise level the unions are federated within a given industry and, at a national level, may be members of four national centres. *Sohyo* (the General Council of Trade Unions of Japan) claimed in 1973 39 per cent of all organised workers; its membership derived 36.5 per cent from private firms and 63.5 per cent from public employment. *Domei* claimed 19 per cent of organised workers, 90 per cent of whom worked in small or medium-sized enterprises. *Churitsuroren* (the Federation of Independent Unions) covered 12 per cent of the workers and *Shinsanbetsu* (the National Federation of Industrial Organisations) a mere 0.6 per cent; the remaining organised workers (32.2 per cent) evidently had no national affiliation.[93]

The picture that emerges is of most organised workers being in enterprise unions, most of these in large firms. Workers in small and medium-sized firms are much less likely to be unionised, and part-time and casual workers are effectively not unionised at all. This latter group apart, the workers most in need of unionisation are those in public employment, whose working conditions are laid down by government legislation.

It is *Sohyo* that has raised the banner of militancy in struggles for a national minimum wage, for shorter working hours, and for other causes. *Domei* has been politically moderate in throwing its support behind the Democratic Socialist Party since 1959. The other unions have supported the Japanese Socialist Party which is dependent on them.

The government's attitude to the unions was shown shortly after World War II when in 1948 strikes were prohibited throughout the civil service including the railways, the power and telecommunications industries and the tobacco industry. In 1952 the Public Corporation and National Enterprise Labour Relations Law extended this ban to include other national industries such as forestry, the mint and the alcohol monopoly. In 1953 came the Strike Restriction Law to safe-guard the coal and electricity industries from the threat of distur-bance by strikes.[94]

The Japanese unions act as do unions in Western nations: bargaining over wages, promoting worker education, giving assistance in strikes, carrying out research, organising the unorganised and manning political campaigns. But except in the annual *Shunto* offensive they have only modest impact upon the public and they have very little participation in government. In the words of Hisashi Kawada, the labour movement 'is not yet accepted as one of the major forces in society; rather, it is accepted negatively as a necessary evil in contemporary Japan'.[95] Or as Taira has more succinctly put it, the unions are legal but not legitimate.[96]

In the enterprise the union has strong and weak elements. It is strong in its first-hand knowledge of the company and as a result of the close links between union leaders and the rank and file; the workers are secure in their employment. But they are inherently conservative. Candidates for union office are named by the executive board of the union, and then approved by the company personnel department. They are often elected and then re-elected unopposed, and paid by their employers. Thus the enterprise union is not independent of the enterprise; its own fortunes are manifestly tied to the fortunes of the company. It is indeed part of the company's administrative apparatus.[97] When strikes occur they are often as short as a day and merely as a prelude to bargaining, in Galenson and Odaka's phrase 'ritualistic fist-shaking'.[98]

The ambiguity of the union's position is exemplified by a recurrent cycle of union life that is widely observed. The older workers become accustomed to close co-operation with management. Young rank and file unionists mobilise to oppose their acquiescent leaders. The young militants take over the leadership. Then the management side-step the existing union by encouraging a union split and the formation of a second (more co-operative) union, often led by white-collar workers. The militant rump of the union fades and the regime of acquiescence is restored.[99]

Management prefers consultation to confrontation and where possible seeks to see established labour-management deliberation committees dealing with major questions: working conditions, grievance procedures, training, job transfers, the supervisory system, and the introduction of new technology. Such arrangements deal with salient issues and at the same time emphasise the common interest of all members of an enterprise in growth and production. In 1972 90 per cent of all firms with over 1,000 employees had consultation systems.[100]

The effect of the enterprise union *system* is to increase differentiation between firms. The larger the firm, the more organised is the union and the more efficient and better paid the labour force. The union knows the business conditions of the firm almost as well as the management and this leads to a wage structure which is related to the unions' knowledge of what their firms are able to pay. Enterprise unions reinforce differentials in wages, productivity and profits.[101]

Shunto

In 1955 an attempt was made by national unions in eight industries to launch a joint struggle to back wage demands. A schedule of strike action was worked out according to the rank of each enterprise by size, while actual negotiations at each enterprise were handled by the enterprise union. Thus was launched the *Shunto Kyoto Kaifi* (normally known as *Shunto*) — the Joint Action Committee for the Spring Offensive, which was repeated annually up to 1974 with much publicity and varying degrees of militancy. It was a pace-setting endeavour, providing support from established unions for workers in small and medium-sized firms. In 1956 830,000 workers were involved but by 1970 6 million were taking part in *Shunto*, the great majority of them workers in public employment.[102] The customary offensive has faded somewhat since 1974 owing to the effects of the 1973 oil crisis.

Social Security

The history of social security in Japan is a sorry one by the standards of Western Europe.

The first attempt at a Health Insurance Law led in 1926 and 1927 to industrial disputes because the workers, poorly led, protested against their compulsory contributions while employers were exempt from any liability and government subsidies were meagre. In 1931 the Workmen's Accident Compensation Insurance Law provided for employers' liability insurance, but only in the case of public works. Other employers preferred voluntary payment. In 1938 the National Health Insurance Law established voluntary state-aided health insurance societies. In 1947 a new Workmen's Accident Compensation Insurance Law introduced an insurance scheme mandatorily to cover employer liability for industrial accidents. The workers' health insurance scheme evolved as a dual structure, with health insurance societies for workers in large enterprises and a government scheme for all others. By 1961 a further structure had emerged as every municipality developed a scheme for its inhabitants. None the less by 1973 social insurance payments only amounted to 6.7 per cent of national income as compared with 8.1 per cent for the US, 15 per cent for the UK and 19.7 per cent for France.[103] Thus social security matched the industrial structure, with differing provision for government servants, for employees of large firms and for employees in other small industrial enterprises. There is little provision for the underprivileged and adequate provision only for those who stay loyal to large companies.[104]

Medical care is provided through social insurance or social assistance. Unemployment insurance is compulsory in establishments with more than 5 employees, and voluntary elsewhere. There are no family allowances. Finally, the real Cinderella is the provision of pensions. Since the 1954 Workers Welfare Pension Insurance Law pensions have been payable after 20 years of contributions to those aged 60 or more, at the rate of 9 per cent of average wages paid monthly,[105] and in 1965 came permanent disability pensions. Since the 1959 National Pension Law everyone is covered by a contributory scheme but it has not yet developed to the point where funds are generated by the employed population and transferred to the retired.[106] The bald fact is that retirement benefits are so low that beneficiaries are compelled to continue in work as long as possible.[107] The explanation of this weak development is not, however, simply the malignity of *laissez-faire* doctrine firmly held by a hard-faced government, although Japan took a clear 'production first' approach to its industrialisation, leaving society to bear its social costs, relying, in Bennett and Levine's phrase, on 'the reservoir of discipline and conformity in the existing social system.'[108] It is, first, that social security obligations have been honoured by many, and at least the larger, employers; they are contractual to, and institutionalised within, the firm.[109] Lifetime commitment guarantees the most direct form of social security,[110] and, not unwittingly, ties the employee loyally to the firm. But, secondly, the Japanese, spurred by an ideology lauding traditional asceticism and frugality, have become the unmatched savers of the twentieth century. In 1960 personal savings amounted to 20 per cent of disposable income, as compared with 7 per cent for the US and 5 per cent for the UK.[111]

Labour Market Changes

Since 1965 there has been a decline in the 15 to 19 age group at the same time as an increased proportion of the age group has been going on to higher education.[112] Thus middle-school and high-school leavers have been in short supply. In 1970 middle-school graduates were 19.2 per cent of employed graduates of the educational system and Galenson and Odaka predicted a decline to 17 per cent in 1975, 15 per cent in 1980 and 11 per cent in 1985, as the proportion of college graduates among the newly employed rose from 14.5 per cent to 20.9 per cent.[113] This has made it easier for young workers to change jobs in their first five years of employment.[114] Clark gives figures, for 1973, of 72 per cent of male middle-school leavers changing jobs in their first five years and 59 per cent of male high-school leavers; his figures for women are 73 per cent and 78 per cent for middle- and high-school leavers respectively.[115]

Clark identified as mobile groups young less-educated men, young women and, not unexpectedly, temporary and irregular workers (who were mostly students, retired workers and seasonal workers). The immobile groups were graduates, older women (employed in small, family firms) and older men (employed in large firms).

Cole confirms these same trends. With declining population and the drying up of the supply of new labour from the countryside, the labour market became tighter in the period 1959–68 and mobility increased from 2.7 per cent in 1959 to 4.4 per cent per annum in 1968. The proportion of voluntary separations was 68 per cent in 1956, but rose to 82 per cent in 1966. A 1965 study of 950,000 middle-school leavers showed that 20 per cent left their jobs in the first year and 52 per cent within 3 years.[116] Between 1963 and 1970 the turnover of workers aged 30 to 49 employed in firms with more than 500 employees rose from 3 to 6 per cent.[117]

It was in 1970 that the population of working age (15–59) peaked at 65.4 per cent, giving a dependency ratio of 53. But not only is the working-age labour force in decline, the proportion of the 15–19 age group at work is decreasing, as already noted, with educational expansion. In other words, the labour force participation rate has been declining, from 71 per cent in 1955 to 64 per cent in 1980.[118]

These trends put increasing labour market pressures on the system, which are felt more by smaller firms. Larger firms, for example, better resist the ageing process. Cole shows that firms with more than 100 employees, 5.2 per cent of whose work force was over 50 years of age in 1960, employed only 6.6 per cent over 50 in 1970; in contrast, firms with from 10 to 99 employees had 9.3 per cent of their work force over 50 in 1960 and 16.8 per cent in 1970.[119] Such pressures accumulate and in the eyes of many observers put the present system at risk. Drucker notes that while there were seven or eight adult workers for every over-65-year-old in 1970, there were five in 1977 and there would be only three in 1980. Hence the burden on the working population and the wages bill are both bound to grow dramatically.[120]

Pressures for Change

Observers have for many years been alert to signs of change in the Japanese system. Some, in the West, have doubtless held the technological determinist's belief that all industrial systems must in due course converge and some also the parochial belief that the Western path of development is the pre-eminent way. However, putting this issue to one side, changes have of course occurred in Japanese industry in recent years.

First, new pay schemes have been introduced, as the equation of age and experience with merit has become more often invalid and as the coupling of length of service and the reward system has been seen to be unfair. New technology has made new demands upon the work force, for higher educational qualifications and for the adaptability of youth. This has led to schemes whereby workers are paid according to the jobs they do or according to their level of skill or ability, assessed by performance appraisal.[121] In 1972 job-related wages amounted to 30.6 per cent of total cash earnings, as against 8.9 per cent in 1966.[122]

In Marsh and Mannari's study of workers' opinions in the early 1970s they found that workers thought the determinants of pay should take the following order: (a) ability, (b) job or skill classification, (c) seniority, (d) performance, in the sense of contribution to profit, and (e) education. In the three companies that they studied they found differentials based on education, age and seniority to be narrowing.[123]

Second, recent labour shortages have led to intense competition between firms for new recruits. This has pushed up the wages of new recruits, lowered entry qualifications, and reduced differentials in wage payments. Differentials have shrunk between blue- and white-collar workers, young and old, different educational levels, large and small firms and between the civil service and the private sector. For example, between 1964 and 1970 male blue-collar middle-school graduates in manufacturing moved from earning 66 per cent of the monthly earnings of male university graduates to earning 75 per cent.[124] Third, in line with the trend in all advanced societies, competition for labour has led to more casual attitudes among the young who now tend to see a job as a right rather than a favour, and the importance of 'connections' in the recruitment process has noticeably declined.[125] Fourth, there has been an increase in the mobility of workers and the mobile workers have suffered no disadvantage. Some mid-career recruitment now occurs by invitation,[126] especially for the research and development function and on company diversification. Mobility has increased among workers in large firms and among older, more educated, employees, even though it is less easy as family responsibilities grow for other workers. Readier mobility gives greater bargaining power.

More generally, observers note a growth of consumerism and the pursuit of individual economic goals, both providing new definitions of social status and both developments damaging to the ethic of the group.[127] Cole goes on to note the impact of those other general features of modernity familiar to sociologists: urbanisation, education, economic growth, bureaucratic impersonality, capital-intensive technology, material abundance and a growing freedom leading to 'a loss of sense of belonging to and identification with nature, clan, and religion'.[128] To this list of forces for change Bennett and Levine add reactions to it, namely, increased consciousness of deprivation on the one hand and individual rights on the other, and growing expectations that society must provide, as it has not hitherto done, for every individual's basic life security.[129]

No one can indeed doubt that the industrial system that flourished in the period 1948–73 and saw Japan's GNP grow by a factor of ten will have to change.[130] With no knowledge of Japanese society anyone interested in its fate would expect it to change, and someone with knowledge, aware of what has happened in Japan since 1868, should have no qualms about it. It has been made clear in this chapter how resourceful the Japanese have been in adapting to change, and in modifying traditional attitudes and values to suit modern needs. As the needs change so surely will new adaptations be found.

From a Western perspective Japan is an advanced industrial society of high income and low wealth, notably lacking the social infrastructure and amenities that have been painstakingly developed in other nations.[131] And the Japanese know it.[132] Thus a shift from a production-first approach to a new concern for social welfare, the consumer, and the leisure society is undoubtedly occurring. Yet this has no necessary implication of some kind of convergence with other industrial systems. The Japanese system has been different from Western models hitherto, and there is no hint of evidence that its response to the new needs of Japanese society will be any less idiosyncratic than its unique leap into the process of modernisation in the period following 1868 and its unprecedented industrial expansion in the period after World War II.

Given Weber's attempt to relate the impetus for scientific advance and the surge into industrialism to a set of values peculiar to the West, there has been a temptation for commentators to search for values in traditional Japanese culture that can be deemed to have played a part in the industrialisation of Japan similar to the part played by the Protestant ethic in Western societies. The search is entirely misconceived,[133] however, because Japan was not a leader nation in the pursuit of industrialisation; it has been a most eminent follower.[134] As a follower, and a deliberate follower, it might have been expected to seek to retain its traditional values so far as they were found to be compatible with the processes of industrial change, and so it has done. The result, which cannot be surprising and which we have amply documented here, is that the Japanese path has been unique. This path is no doubt being followed even now by South Korea and Taiwan; but if so, these nations will in their turn find forks in the path that lead off in ways that better suit their own particular cultures. In the future evolution of industrial societies Japan may well be a leader not only to Asian but to all industrial societies. What is certain is that its way forward will continue to be guided by its unique past.

Notes

1. Between 1946 and 1948 3,600 top managers were purged. Hirschmeier and Yui (1975), Ch. 4.
2. See Mikio Sumiya, 'Contemporary Arrangements: An Overview', Ch. 3. of Okochi *et al.* (1974).
3. Yoshino (1968), Ch. 2.
4. Morishima (1982), Ch. 5.
5. Allen (1972), Tables III and IV. The proportion in agriculture had been as low as 41.5 per cent in 1940 but had risen thereafter.
6. Fukutake (1982), Table 8, p. 86.
7. Indeed the number of workers in manufacturing industry was substantially less in 1950, at 5.7 million, than it had been in 1940, at 7.2 million. Allen (1972), Table III.
8. Fukutake (1982), Table 8, p. 86.
9. Allen (1972), Table III.
10. Hirschmeier and Yui (1975), Ch. 4. The figure in 1930 had been 79 per cent. See Chapter 7, p. 189.
11. Allen (1972), Supplement.
12. By 1980 workers in the metal industries, machinery and chemicals constituted more than 50 per cent of the manufacturing labour force, and heavy industry and chemicals accounted for more than 60 per cent of total output. Fukutake (1982), Ch. 10.
13. Morishima (1982), Ch. 5.
14. Allen (1972), Supplement.
15. Ibid.
16. Mitsubishi, for example, was a network of 86 firms, Sumitomo of 80, Mitsui of 71. Hirschmeier and Yui (1975), Ch. 4.
17. Ibid.
18. Yoshino (1968), Ch. 6. In 1981 total expenditure on R and D amounted to 2.4 per cent of GNP (that of the US was 2.5 per cent) and has been expected to rise to 3 per cent by the mid-1980s. See Michael Smith, 'Consensus the Key to the Future', *Guardian* (6 Dec. 1983).
19. Nakane (1973), Ch. 1.

20. Rohlen (1974), Ch. 1.

21. Hirschmeier and Yui (1975), Ch. 1. Ben-Dasan comments that the individual's submergence in the group is a 2000-year-old legacy. See Ben-Dasan, *The Japanese and the Jews* (Weatherhill, New York, 1972). The fullest account of the importance to the Japanese of social preoccupations ('the creation and maintenance of smooth and pleasant social relationships') and belongingness as a source of identity is given by Lebra. See Takie Sugiyama Lebra, *Japanese Patterns of Behaviour* (University Press of Hawaii, Honolulu, 1976), esp. Chs. 1 and 2.

22. Ruth Benedict, *The Chrysanthemum and the Sword* (Houghton Mifflin, Boston, 1946). Doi is critical of Benedict but does not seriously dispute her observation. See Takeo Doi, *The Anatomy of Dependence* (Kodansha, Tokyo, 1973).

23. Norbeck, *Religion and Society in Modern Japan*, Ch. 4.

24. Pascale and Tanner (1982), Ch. 5; Yoshino (1968), Ch. 7.

25. Dore (1973), Ch. 10.

26. Cole and Tominaga in Patrick (1976).

27. Nathan Glazer, 'Social and Cultural Factors in Japanese Economic Growth' in Patrick and Rosovsky (1976). See also Kiefer on the extension of familial emotional habits to the school peer group. Christie W. Kiefer, 'The Psychological Interdependence of Family, School and Bureaucracy in Japan', *American Anthropologist*, vol. 72, no. 1 (1970), pp. 66–75.

28. Nakane (1973), Ch. 2.

29. Pascale and Athos (1982), Ch. 5, give the prime qualification for leadership as acceptance by the group. See also Yoshino (1968), Ch. 7.

30. Pascale and Athos (1982), Ch. 2.

31. See Ezra F. Vogel, *Japan's New Middle Class* (University of California Press, Berkeley, Calif., 1963), Ch. 7.

32. Norbeck, *Religion and Society in Modern Japan*, p. 142; Yoshino (1968), Ch. 1.

33. Nakane (1973), Ch. 2. The role of the essential bar visit on the way home from work which has so much intrigued Western observers is, Nakane points out, to allow emotional exchange rather than discussion, relaxation from *personal* relationships. Nakane (1973), Ch. 4.

34. Austin (1975), Ch. 3.

35. Pointed out also by Rohlen. See Rohlen (1974), Ch. 4.

36. Pascale and Athos point out how the group imposes task roles which are not clear and therefore need revision and the constant investment of emotional capital. Pascale and Athos (1982), Ch. 5.; see also Nakane (1973), Ch. 2.

37. Austin (1975), Chs. 4 and 5.

38. Pascale and Athos (1982),.Ch. 5.

39. Nakane (1973), Ch. 2. For full explanation of the significance of dependence and interdependence in Japanese culture see Doi, *The Anatomy of Dependence*. For the Japanese sensitivity to rank order and status see Lebra, *Japanese Patterns of Behaviour*, Ch. 5.

40. Nakane (1973), Ch. 2.

41. Quoted in Pascale and Athos (1982), p. 49.

42. The intensive competition for entry to favoured schools and universities, with its much publicised occasional suicide victims, does not contradict the position taken here. The competition is for *entry* into a group. Upon admission, competition is subordinated to group loyalty and good fellowship. Universities, like companies, have virtually no wastage. Vogel, *Japan's New Middle Class*, Ch. 3.

43. Austin (1975), Ch. 6.

44. Cole (1979), Ch. 8. Ben-Dasan traces the belief in the efficacy of effort to the traditional Japanese campaign-style approach to agriculture. Ben-Dasan, *The Japanese and the Jews*, Ch. 3.

45. Clark (1979), Ch. III. In 1980 the six largest companies were among the world's

50 largest companies. Fukutake (1982), Ch. 22.

46. While in 1950 the proportion was only 24 per cent, by 1960 it was 53 per cent and by 1973 it was on average 60 per cent. Clark (1979), Ch. IV. A 1965 study by the Fair Trade Commission showed the top 100 non-financial corporations to have 4,270 dependent firms, with an ownership interest of 50 per cent or more in 58.8 per cent of the cases, of 30 per cent or more in 82.4 per cent of the cases and with interlocking officials in 75 per cent of the cases. See Richard E. Caves and Masu Uekusa, 'Industrial Organization' in Patrick and Rosovsky (1976).

47. For the classic account of the typical development of the largest Western companies see Alfred D. Chandler, Jr., *Strategy and Structure: Chapters in the History of the Industrial Enterprise* (MIT Press, Cambridge, Mass., 1962).

48. See Abegglen (1958); Clark (1979); Dore (1973); Taira (1970) and Ernest van Helvoort, *The Japanese Working Man* (Paul Norbury Publications, Tenterden, 1979). It must be remembered that Japan remains a country of medium-sized and small companies. Further, in 1979 58 per cent of the labour force were employed in establishments with fewer than 100 employees; the proportions for the US (for 1977) and West Germany (for 1979) were 25 per cent and 19 per cent respectively. Fukutake (1982), Table 32, p. 189.

49. Cole (1971a), p. 122.

50. Cole (1971a), Ch. 5; Dore (1973), Ch. 12.

51. Cole (1971a), Ch. 5.

52. Rohlen (1974), Ch. 4.

53. Van Helvoort estimates that there were 2 million homeworkers in the 1970s, 90 per cent of them women. See Van Helvoort, *The Japanese Working Man*, Ch. 3.

54. See p. 215 for a discussion of recent changes to the system.

55. Cole (1971a), Ch. 6.

56. In Dore's study basic pay was 42 per cent of the worker's wage, merit supplement was 23 per cent and job level supplement 31 per cent; allowances made up the remaining 4 per cent. Half-yearly bonuses were equal to 3 months' basic pay. Dore (1973), Ch. 3.

57. Life expectancy was 53 in 1920 and remained the same in 1947. Van Helvoort, *The Japanese Working Man*, Ch. 4.

58. Morishima (1982), Ch. 5.

59. Dore (1973), Ch. 12.

60. Morishima comments: 'labour is not regarded as a high-class commodity; it is the spirit of loyalty which is prized'. Morishima (1982), p. 117.

61. Cole (1971a), Ch. 5.

62. Clark (1979), Ch. VI.

63. The battle is most clearly represented as Abegglen vs. Taira.

64. Rohlen (1974), p. 14.

65. Abegglen (1973), Part I.

66. Clark (1979), Ch. II.

67. Teranishi, *'Availability of Safe Assets and the Process of Bank Concentration in Japan'*.

68. G.C. Allen, 'The Causes of Japan's Economic Progress' in *The Price of Prosperity: Lessons from Japan* (Hobart Paper 58, Institute of Economic Affairs, London 1974). For further comment on the social security system see below.

69. Quoted in Yoshino (1968), Ch. 4. The 1900 sample was of 420 executives, the 1928 sample of 500.

70. Morishima observes that the Japanese universities quite simply reflect the needs of business by giving priority to engineering, economics and business administration. The natural sciences are less vigorously pursued. Morishima (1982), Ch. 5.

71. This point is also reaffirmed in Clark (1979).

72. Dore (1973), Chs. 2, 3, 9 and 11.

73. Virtually all directors of Japanese companies are company executives. Yoshino (1968), Ch. 7. As Clark points out, they then have the interests of employees closer to heart than those of shareholders. Clark (1979), Ch. IV.

74. Clark (1979), Ch. IV; Yoshino (1968), Ch. 9. Ben-Dasan notes how important in Japan is the *appearance* of unanimity, whatever the underlying disagreement. Ben-Dasan, *The Japanese and the Jews*, Ch. 6.

75. Austin (1975), p. 135.

76. See Handy for his contrast of management styles. Charles Handy, *Gods of Management* (Pan Books, London, 1979). Here the pertinent contrast is between dynamic entrepreneurs (under the star of Zeus) and organisational problem-solvers (watched over by Athene).

77. Clark (1979), Ch. II.

78. Ibid; Yoshino (1968), Ch. 5.

79. Hideaki Okamoto, 'Management and Their Organizations' in Okochi *et al.* (1974).

80. Okamoto in Okochi *et al.* (1974); Yoshino (1968), Ch. 4.

81. Taira (1970), Ch. 8.

82. This conception of the tradition fitted the merchant house and the farm rather than the band of itinerant workmen, but the latter groups (like the casual workers of the modern age) have never set the norms. See Marshall, *Capitalism and Nationalism in Prewar Japan*, Ch. 4.

83. This represented about 7 per cent of the labour force. Fukutake (1982), Ch. 13.

84. Taira (1970), Ch. 6.

85. Cole (1971a), Ch. 1.

86. Morishima (1982), Ch. 5.

87. Walter Galenson and Konosuke Odaka, 'The Japanese Labor Market' in Patrick and Rosovsky (1976). Government employees were 27 per cent of all union members. By 1980 12.4 million workers were unionised but this represented only 31 per cent of the labour force.

88. Cole (1971a), Ch. 7.

89. Hisashi Kawada, 'Workers and Their Organisations' in Okochi *et al.* (1974).

90. Galenson and Odaka in Patrick and Rosovsky (1976).

91. The only industrial union is the All-Japan Seamen's Union.

92. Dore (1973), Ch. 4. In Dore's account the deduction is more than 1 per cent of wages.

93. Galenson and Odaka in Patrick and Rosovsky (1976); Kawada in Okochi *et al.* (1974).

94. Toru Ariizumi, 'The Legal Framework: Past and Present' in Okochi *et al.* (1974).

95. Okochi *et al.* (1974), p. 261.

96. Taira (1970), Ch. 8.

97. Cole (1971a), Ch. 7. Fukutake writes, 'workers can quite happily exhibit a dual loyalty to both firm and union without any sense of contradiction'. Fukutake (1982), p. 113.

98. Galenson and Odaka in Patrick and Rosovsky (1976), p. 646.

99. Cole (1971a), Ch. 7.

100. Galenson and Odaka in Patrick and Rosovsky (1976).

101. Taira (1970), Ch. 7.

102. Ibid.

103. Cole (1979), Ch. 8.

104. The adversity of the underprivileged is perhaps confirmed by the growth of new religious sects since Workd War II. Norbeck notes that the appeal of religion in Japan is to the industrial proletariat and that the new sects appeal to those most beset by the

industrial sytem. Norbeck's estimate in 1970 was of 150 newly formed religious groups with 10–12 million followers. Norbeck, *Religion and Society in Modern Japan*, Chs. 2 and 5.

105. Cole (1971a), Ch. 1.
106. Takeshi Takahashi, 'Social Security for Workers' in Okochi *et al.* (1974).
107. This is so, despite pension increases and index linkage introduced in 1973. Fukutake (1982), Ch. 23.
108. John W. Bennett and Solomon B. Levine, 'Industrialization and Social Deprivation: Welfare, Environment, and the Postindustrial Society in Japan' in Patrick (1976).
109. Dore (1973), Ch. 10.
110. Pascale and Athos (1982), Ch. 5.
111. Cole (1979), Ch. 8.
112. By 1980 95 per cent of the age group were going on to high school after the compulsory period of education; nearly 40 per cent of the age group were attending university. Fukutake (1982), Ch. 20.
113. Galenson and Odaka in Patrick and Rosovsky (1976). By 1982 approximately 95 per cent of all 15-year-olds finished their compulsory education and went on to some form of higher education and 30 per cent of high school leavers went to university. Michael Smith. 'Consensus the Key to the Future', *Guardian* (6 Dec. 1983).
114. In 1969, according to Cole (1972) 70 per cent of all job-changers were under 34 years, most shifts occurring between firms of equivalent size.
115. Clark (1979), Ch. V.
116. Cole (1971b).
117. Hirschmeier and Yui (1975), Ch. 4.
118. Cole (1976). The 1980 figure is Cole's estimate.
119. Ibid.
120. See Peter F. Drucker, 'Japan: The Problems of Success', *Foreign Affairs*, vol. 56, no. 3 (1978), pp. 564–78.
121. Yoshino (1968), Ch. 8.
122. Galenson and Odaka in Patrick and Rosovsky (1976).
123. Robert M. Marsh and Hiroshi Mannari, *Modernization and the Japanese Factory* (Princeton University Press, Princeton, N.J., 1976), Chs. 6 and 12.
124. Cole (1976). Bonuses were excluded from the calculation.
125. Cole noted that while 44 per cent of recruits came via connections in 1955, the proportion had fallen to 27 per cent by 1965. Cole (1971), Ch. 6. See also Clark (1979), Chs. V and VI.
126. Clark (1979), Ch. V.
127. Hirschmeier and Yui (1975), Ch. 5.
128. Cole (1971a), p. 278.
129. Bennett and Levine in Patrick (1976).
130. Kahn and Pepper note that this growth was two and one-half times the world's average. Herman Kahn and Thomas Pepper, *The Japanese Challenge: The Success and Failure of Economic Success* (Harper and Row, London, 1979), Ch. 1.
131. In 1978 Japan spent 11 per cent of GDP on social security as compared with 14 per cent in the US, 21 per cent in the UK and 27 per cent in West Germany. Fukutake (1982), Ch. 23.
132. The new concern for the costs of industrialism and new demands for more participatory politics and for disengagement from political parties are discussed in Taketsugu Tsurutani, 'Japan as a Postindustrial Society' in Leon N. Lindberg (ed.), *Politics and the Future of Industrial Society* (David McKay Co., New York, 1976). There was even a 'down with GNP' movement in the 1970s. Kahn and Pepper, *The Japanese Challenge*, Ch. 2.

133. And would surely not have been pursued by Weber, who of all the theorists referred to in this study was most at home with cultural relativism. Perhaps second to Weber, by implication, was Aron.

134. We may say that all nations that since 1900 have sought to become industrialised have been followers and deliberate followers. In other words, they saw the fruits of industrialisation in Western Europe and North America, including those that were apparently distasteful, and they chose to follow the path.

Select Bibliography

Abegglen, James C. (1958) *The Japanese Factory: Aspects of Its Social Organization* (Free Press, Glencoe, Illinois)

_____ (1973) *Management and the Worker: The Japanese Solution* (Sophia University, Tokyo)

Allen, G.C. (1972) *A Short Economic History of Modern Japan* (George Allen and Unwin, London)

Austin, Lewis (1975) *Saints and Samurai: The Political Culture of the American and Japanese Elites* (Yale University Press, New Haven, Conn.,)

Clark, Rodney (1979) *The Japanese Company* (Yale University Press, New Haven, Conn.)

Cole, Robert E. (1971a) *Japanese Blue Collar: The Changing Tradition* (University of California Press, Berkeley, Calif.)

_____ (1971b) 'The Theory of Institutionalization: Permanent Employment and Tradition in Japan', *Economic Development and Cultural Change*, vol. 20, no. 1, pp. 47–70.

_____ (1972) 'Permanent Employment in Japan: Facts and Fantasies', *Industrial and Labor Relations Review*, vol. 26, pp. 615–30.

_____ (1976) 'Changing Labor Force Characteristics and Their Impact on Japanese Industrial Relations' in Lewis Austin (ed.), *Japan: The Paradox of Progress* (Yale University Press, New Haven, Conn.)

_____ (1979) *Work, Mobility and Participation* (University of California Press, Berkeley, Calif.)

Dore, Ronald (1973) *British Factory – Japanese Factory* (George Allen and Unwin)

Fukutake, Tadashi (1982) *The Japanese Social Structure: Its Evolution in the Modern Century* (University of Tokyo Press)

Hirschmeier, Johannes and Yui, Tsunehiko (1975) *The Development of Japanese Business, 1600–1973* (George Allen and Unwin, London)

Morishima, Michio (1982) *Why Has Japan Succeeded? Western Technology and the Japanese Ethos* (Cambridge University Press)

Nakane, Chie (1973) *Japanese Society* (Penguin Books, Harmondsworth and London)

Okochi, Kazuo, Karsh, Bernard and Levine, Solomon B. (eds.) (1974) *Workers and Employers in Japan: The Japanese Employment Relations System* (Princeton University Press, Princeton N.J.)

Pascale, Richard Tanner and Athos, Anthony G. (1982) *The Art of Japanese Management* (Penguin Books, Harmondsworth and London)

Patrick, Hugh (ed.) (1976) *Japanese Industrialization and Its Social Consequences* (University of California Press, Berkeley, Calif.)

_____ and Rosovsky, Henry (eds.) (1976) *Asia's New Giant: How the Japanese Economy Works* (The Brookings Institution, Washington, D.C.)

Rohlen, Thomas P. (1974) *For Harmony and Strength: Japanese White-Collar Organization in Anthropological Perspective* (University of California Press,

Berkeley, Calif.)
Storry, Richard (1960) *A History of Modern Japan* (Penguin Books, Harmondsworth and London)
Taira, Koji (1970) *Economic Development and the Labor Market in Japan* (Columbia University Press, New York)
Yoshino, M.Y. (1968) *Japan's Managerial System* (MIT Press, Cambridge, Mass.)

PART FIVE

THE FORKING PATHS

9 THE EVOLUTIONARY TRENDS AND THE NEEDS OF HUMANITY

The Argument for Evolution

In the field of social theory it is of greater importance that a theory or a set of ideas or a mode of conceptualising a certain sphere of social life should be displaced than that it should be disproved.[1] The mark of significance of a social theorist is that his sense of what is salient in shedding illumination on a set of social phenomena prevails over the views of others as to what is salient and that the set of social phenomena should be one associated with admitted moral concern. If the concern is lacking, the phenomena will not engage sufficient attention for explanatory attempts to be made. If the sense of salience is not shared, the theory in question will never achieve currency.

This approach may explain why no attempt was made in Chapter 2 to subject the ideas of the various social theorists considered there to test or careful scrutiny. The ideas were taken more as indications of social concern and for their suggestiveness for further reflection and analysis than as testable propositions. We shall none the less return to them in this final chapter in formulating a viewpoint from which to conceptualise the future of industrial systems.

The Lack of Discontinuity

The first step, however, is to offer the hypothesis that in the absence of compelling evidence to the contrary in specific instances we should assume that societal change occurs in an evolutionary manner, without major discontinuities. In this we must oppose Bell, Habermas, Galbraith, and both Marcuse and Mandel.

Bell has contended that industrial societies develop into post-industrial societies, given that, in his view, the United States has moved from industrialism to post-industrialism. But the proposition is only of interest if a qualitative societal change occurs with this progression, and the case is not made. For Bell the indications of the development are the changes in occupational structure consequent upon the preponderance of service employment, the new eminence and salience of theoretical knowledge, information and scientific institutions, and the rise of a new scientific, professional and technical class. The objection is not that these developments have not occurred, but that their significance is quite unclear. Bell asserts that a society in this new phase of development merits a new name, but even the title post-industrial is misleading given that the United States remains an industrial society.[2] The existence of the new scientific class is asserted, but whether this carries a Marxist sense of shared consciousness or the implication of a new social group with its own social, economic or political power is not clear. Bell states that knowledge and information are sources of power but he does not document the proposition. As Lasch notes, he 'simply deduces political power from functional indispensability, without demonstrating the influence of "expertise" on actual decisions'.[3] It is far from proven that the power accruing from the advance of science is wielded in substantial part by the scientists themselves rather than by those who employ and use scientists and their knowledge.

It seems prima facie more probable that new knowledge serves and will serve those in power just as old knowledge has always done; and that the scientific and technical elite, with the increasing specialisation of knowledge, the proliferation of professions and their employment in large-scale organisations, will become progressively diffused and their political power weakened.[4]

Habermas claims that advanced capitalist society has encountered a series of crisis tendencies which cannot be overcome without a major social transformation. This claim contains two assertions, neither of them substantiated: that advanced capitalist societies are experiencing crises that threaten their continued existence and that these can only be overcome by major transformation.

We may accept the existence of recurrent economic crises and of increasingly evident crises of rationality and legitimacy for the capitalist state, but it is far from clear that these are as disabling as Habermas supposes. Capitalist institutions have shown remarkable resilience in the last hundred years and the historical record would suggest an alternative null hypothesis of continuing survival and adaptability. This is reinforced by the observation that no social group in contemporary capitalist society has plausibly been identified by non-Marxists (and is not by Habermas) as the standard-bearer of societal transformation and renewal.

Habermas also hypothesises a motivation crisis whereby individuals no longer have a sense of participation in society's shared norms and values. Hence social integration and social stability are threatened. But the conclusion does not follow from the premiss. As Held points out, Habermas romanticises the past, overestimating the individual citizen's historical integration into society.[5] There is no gainsaying the lack of consensus concerning norms, values and beliefs but there is no warrant for asserting that this is the prelude to societal disintegration. On the contrary, it might equally be asserted that value dissensus weakens the impulse to social transformation and permits the dominance of a powerful and politically mobilised elite.[6] And as far as the individual is concerned, 'an acceptable flow of system-conforming rewards', in McCarthy's words, may suffice to legitimate the political system '*for the reason* that nothing better seems practically possible in the given circumstances'.[7] There may be reasons (however deplorable to some) for acceptance of the system.

Galbraith lacks a similar sharp sense of discontinuity but it is there, if veiled, behind the twin ideas of the emergence of the technostructure and the recognition of the economic and political dominance of giant corporations and the planning system. He implies that he is pointing to the occurrence, hitherto unnoticed, of a qualitative, systemic change. Unfortunately, he does not show in what way the planning system exists *as a system* and it is unclear, following the discussion in Chapter 3, that it does so exist in the sense implied by Galbraith. A network of financial institutions and large shareholders with great potential influence over the largest corporations could sustain a coherent system of linked institutions, but it has yet to be shown that it does so and in what ways the system as a whole, as against individual giant companies, exercises power over the market and the government. Even less satisfactory is the notion of *the technostructure*, the reification and exaltation of what might more reasonably be supposed to be separate and disparate groups of technical specialists working in a range of companies. Even within one company the power of the technostructure, a group of technical specialists, over company decision-making is unproven.[8] A more plausible hypothesis is that individual executives and top management groups[9] remain more ascendant in decision-making in large capitalist companies than do groups of specialists of whatever kind. The need for large corporations to deal with government, to which Galbraith himself draws attention, itself supports this hypothesis.

Neo-Marxist thinkers all expect discontinuous, that is revolutionary, change to occur in capitalist society. Marcuse and Mandel are no exceptions but their views are markedly different. In contrast to Habermas, for Marcuse it is not the crisis tendencies evident in advanced capitalist societies but the lack of them that lead to the vision of a major and necessary transformation. In a context in which 'there is no reason to insist on self-determination if the administered life is the comfortable and even the "good" life', Marcuse yearns for the promised land of liberation.[10] But although the revolution, catalysed (rather than led) by students now that the working class has been incorporated into capitalist society,[11] for the moral good *must* come, Marcuse is no determinist: 'there can be no blind necessity in the tendencies that terminate in a free and self-conscious society'.[12] Notwithstanding his claims and visions, Marcuse's analysis of capitalist society is not of a revolutionary character. Mandel, a far more orthodox Marxist than Marcuse, still believes that revolution, led in capitalist societies by the industrial working class and in the international sphere by the semi-colonial masses, will come to pass, but his prediction is of long-run rather than imminent upheaval. No doubt that ultimate upheaval will be revolutionary and violent but it will be preceded by a period of *evolutionary* change in which capital will become more internationalised, multinational companies will grow, the profits of capital will be less stable, the educational level and the qualifications of the work force will rise and automation will spread. Mandel may believe that he is a revolutionary thinker but all his precise predictions concern the outcome of merely evolutionary development.

We are left then with the undramatic propositions that advanced industrial systems have witnessed: a shift to service employment; the continuing advance of science, and the consequent emergence of new groups of scientists and professionals; recurrent economic crises and, more recently, administrative crises with implications for the legitimacy of government; the increasing importance of ever larger business corporations; and the apparently disarming (and possibly oppressive) incorporation of the industrial working class into the elite-dominated culture of the affluent society. These are noteworthy trends indeed, but steadily developing trends are precisely what they are.

The Absence of Convergence

The social theorists whose views we have examined have not put forward the thesis that the industrial systems of West and East, of capitalist and socialist societies, are converging. Indeed Aron argues persuasively that this is not the case. Similarities there must inevitably be in the development of industrialism since, following the industrialisation of Britain, every other society has had prior examples of the process to imitate and to adapt to its own circumstances. In Part IV we noted the Japanese very deliberate and self-conscious pursuit of just this process; and we also noted the Japanese retention of their own cultural differences alongside the achievement of Western-style industrialisation and modernisation. It is rather obviously a fallacy to suppose that each newly industrialising society 'recapitulates' the growth and development processes of its forerunners.[13] Divergence between systems is as certain as are similarities. A more plausible hypothesis surely is that industrialism in different societies is likely to take the course of parallel evolution;[14] lines of historical development will show similarities but remain obstinately different.

The evidence of Parts Three and Four provides compelling support for this hypothesis. Of course no evidence could disprove the notion that the logic of industrialism will *in the long run* lead to the convergence of the more advanced and developed systems, but the burden of proof must be placed firmly on the proponents of the notion. It is the conclusion of this study that the advanced industrial systems are now encountering developments that manifestly have elements in common, but they are responding to them in different ways and will continue to do so. The assumption of alternative paths of evolution is the most plausible assumption.

A Reassessment of Enduring Themes

In Chapter 2 we reviewed questions that had been of common concern to a number of the theorists that we have been considering. It is now time to reassess these in the light of contemporary thinking and our own evidence.

The Issue of Social Dominance

The moral concern that is the counterpart of this analytical issue is of course with social injustice, and especially with the inequitable distribution of society's goods and the economic exploitation of the many by the few. In the moral sphere the issue endures, but in the contemporary constitution of advanced industrial systems it has become in large measure masked, as some of the greater inequalities and deprivations of past historical periods have been reduced.[15]

Habermas observes that class division underlies the crises of advanced capitalism but he also notes that the most conspicuously deprived groups (such as the old, the sick, and the unemployed) are no longer class-based and he contends that science (and not capital) has now become the leading force in production; in this way the inequalities of class are shrouded by the imperatives of science and technology.

The truth is that while class-based inequalities remain in all advanced capitalist societies, they now compete with many other grounds upon which groups are formed, common consciousness is developed, and social and political action is mobilised; and while they remain the hope of the few they are not judged by the majority to be the most probable source of a future societal transformation. Only in exceptional historical circumstances has social deprivation provided a basis for political mobilisation and societal transformation, and there is no warrant for supposing that the greater development of industrial society promotes an environment congenial to this occurrence.[16] Given that this is so in the capitalist societies of the West, it is even more so in Japan where, while great inequalities and deprivations exist, the opportunity for working class mobilisation is greatly attenuated by the stratification of industry, by the system of company unions and by the lack of development of individualistic ambition owing to the salience of the group as an element in the formation of identity.

The shift of attention in capitalist societies is now to the respective roles of the state, the giant corporations and, in some general sense, 'bureaucracy'. Their little-bridled power is seen to lack legitimation and their potential for oppression is widely judged to be a greater source of moral danger, and to the citizenry as a whole, than that of any economic or social group. And we may suggest that in the leading socialist country, the Soviet Union, whose existence is a monument to the power of an ideology founded on deep class divisions, the threats to the individual and to the system itself derive from the centralised power of government and the organisational complexities that attend it in an advanced industrial society.

The Nature of Work

The traditional moral concern related to industrial work has been that for most workers it generates alienation and anomie; that it provides little or no fulfilment and is conducted in a manner that is demeaning and dehumanising. Without question these concerns remain, as the evidence of Chapter 4 amply demonstrates, despite all the efforts of management theorists, social scientists and others who have attempted to expose the dispiriting reality of most industrial work with a view to its amelioration or abolition. Their conclusion is phrased in contemporary style by Morison: 'no labouring man, or almost no labouring man, at a modern machine in a modern plant uses more than a small part of himself in his work: to that extent he endures a subhuman condition which neither high wages, nor shorter hours, nor the displacement of his feeling and energy outside his job can rectify'.[17] The same conclusion is expressed by Mandel: 'In the long-run, the worker will never be satisfied with hours of work which seem a loss of life, with a labour process which appears forced labour, and with an enterprise whose structure accords him no more than subject status'.[18]

But the evidence of Chapter 4 also revealed a grimmer prospect yet: the abolition of degrading work without the compensation (for some at least, even if not for the workers actually displaced) of the creation of alternative employment elsewhere in the economy. The advanced capitalist economies of the West face three prospects: work that is unfulfilling in itself, work that is demeaning in the way in which it is organised[19] (in that the worker lacks control over his work), and work that is disappearing without net replacement. The Japanese worker, we may infer from Chapter 8, is protected from the worst effects of industrial work, at least in the larger firms, by aspects of the social and cultural system which promote the solidarity of the work group and the loyalty of all workers to the firm. The victims of Japanese society are temporary and occasional workers and workers in small companies.

The Soviet worker is likewise protected by the social system. On the one hand he lacks the Western worker's sense of Us and Them, the competition for advantage continually pursued between workers on the one side and owners or managers on the other. On the other hand his employment is protected by all parties concerned with economic life. It is no doubt true that the full impact of the most advanced forms of automation and mechanisation known in the West has yet to be experienced in the Soviet Union. While Soviet ideology pays greater tribute to the dignity of the worker than does capitalist ideology and we may thus hypothesise for Soviet workers less alienation and less displacement from work than experienced in the West, the moment of truth still lies ahead. It is certain that all advanced industrial systems still have to face in their acutest forms the social and human problems due to the alienating nature of work and the disappearance of work.[20]

The Process of Rationalisation

The process of rationalisation, that is, the progressive application of science and technology to new facets of human affairs, is of moral concern because it narrows the capacity for independent judgement and decision-making and the personal responsibility of the individual. As knowledge becomes more technical and specialised, more esoteric, new spheres are placed beyond the understanding of the individual and the expert practitioners in those spheres become less easy to call to account. The individual is diminished.

But the worry goes well beyond the individual to the citizenry at large. Advancing technological complexity, writes Henderson,

> destroys the conditions necessary for democratic political governments to function, since legislators and even heads of state, let alone the average voter, cannot master sufficient information to exert popular control of technological innovation, while the hazardous nature of new technologies often requires societal regulation and policy that erodes or abrogates civil liberties.[21]

Here succinctly Henderson encompasses Bell's observation of the emergence of a new knowledge elite, Galbraith's concern for the power of the technostructure and Habermas's humanitarian revulsion at technocratic decision-making, but she goes beyond to touch the circle of relationships most significant for the evolution of industrial systems, that between science and technology, government, and organisation. Science and technology require government subvention and large-scale organisation for their development and yet as the development occurs the progress of science and the decision-making in government and large-scale organisations become either more esoteric and unaccountable or more private and remote and unaccountable. This is the paradox of the next phase of evolutionary development, and will be returned to below.

The Development of Bureaucratic Organisation

The moral anxiety induced by 'bureaucracy' concerns the arbitrary, irresponsible and ultimately illegitimate exercise of power by faceless men behaving as unfeeling puppets at the behest of a system which is the organisation itself; in short, the nightmare experience of Kafka's K.[22] As noted in Chapter 2, Weber himself recognised the danger that bureaucracy could evade democratic control,[23] and the worry about the accountability of large organisations has been voiced by Galbraith and yet more strongly by Habermas.

This cycle of anxiety endures, but it is also joined with the fear that bureaucracy may not even be efficient, precisely what Weber argued was its pre-eminent characteristic. Here the argument is that the bureaucratic form of organisation may well be suited to the handling of routine and repetitive tasks in a secure environment but it is not appropriate to uncertain and changing tasks, whose completion requires imagination and flexibility, in a turbulent and even hostile environment.[24] Henderson again takes the argument further yet by suggesting that the traditional bureaucratic organisation grown ever larger and more complex may even cease to function. Some flexible organisations succeed in changing themselves but, she writes,

> other organisations become too complex and diverse and begin to spend more effort transacting with themselves than in producing their desired output. They create so many interdependent variables and interfaces that they can no longer be modelled accurately, and any system that cannot be modelled accurately cannot be managed. Corporations, government bureaucracies, and even nations are susceptible to this syndrome — 'the entropy state' — in which an organisation's own weight gradually winds it down into a state of equilibrium where no further useful work or output is possible.[25]

This Cassandra-like prophecy may appear to have force but the evidence of earlier chapters does not support it. Neither the state bureaucracy of the Soviet Union nor the giant capitalist corporations of the West show signs of terminal seizure, whatever the organisational difficulties they encounter. On the contrary the Party and governmental bureaucracies of the USSR demonstrate a very evident ability to survive, despite the increasing complexities of information-processing and decision-making in that highly centralised system; they have even undertaken regular, if modest, attempts at reform of both procedures and structures.

Indeed what is remarkable is how little the advantages of bureaucratic organisation and the fears of it have changed since Weber's time. The prime argument in favour of bureaucracy today remains the original one, that routine and standard procedures are pervasive; they may even need to become more so in a society that grows in complexity. There are enduring needs for a division of labour, for co-ordination, for information-management, for rationalisation and monitoring, for impersonal procedures. But during this century in the advanced societies there has been another tendency that favours bureaucracy, namely the increasing size of organisations.[26] Greater size permits greater division of labour (with an increase in hierarchical levels) which in turn tends to lead to greater formalisation (and more codified procedures). There is no evident tendency, *pace* Henderson, for large organisations to grow fewer, nor for governmental bureaucracy to shrink. There is then an understandable warrant for the individual's fear of bureaucracy.

The place of organisation and organisations in what we have already called the circle of relationships with science and technology and with government will be explored below.

Solidarity and Moral Consensus

The moral concern related to the Durkheimian theme of loss of solidarity and moral consensus is quite evident: apprehension for the individual who lacks social support and fellowship and for the group which lacks integration. The demand is for a sense of belonging, a source of meaning, that membership of collectivities can alone provide. We have already commented upon Habermas's apparently exaggerated fear of lack of moral consensus[27] but even if societal disintegration does not swiftly follow a decline of solidarity, the absence of the benevolent features associated with real integration and consensus is still lamented and worried over.

Chapters 7 and 8 suggest that Japan, being a less individualistically inclined society than other capitalist societies, is better defended against the threats of the decline of significant groups. Japanese identity is still in large degree secured by group membership and the Japanese worker is a member first of a work group and second of a company that takes the care of its employees with the utmost seriousness and conscientiousness. The Japanese virtually combine the two solidarities contrasted by Durkheim, the mechanical — based on ascription — and the organic — based on achievement and the role differentiation and interdependence of an advanced division of labour.

In the case of the Soviet Union there is a higher degree of ideological consensus spread powerfully throughout the society by the agency of the Party, the trade unions, the Komsomol, the schools and other centrally controlled bodies than could conceivably exist in any contemporary capitalist society. This assertion rests upon the known pervasiveness of state and Party agencies in the Soviet Union and the conspicuous lack of an agreed and elaborated ideology in capitalist countries. Against this, the existence of (an unknown but probably small number of) political dissidents is of small consequence.

But the Soviet worker, whatever may be the degree of his job satisfaction, also has a work situation that is free from the particular Them and Us tension characteristic of worker-management opposition in most capitalist countries, since the owner of capital and of the means of production is the state itself to which workers and managers have equivalent relationships. He is a member of a work group, an enterprise and a trade union whose principal interests are by definition congruent.

What this evidence suggests is that Japanese and Soviet societies both have a greater cohesion than do the advanced industrial societies of the West. At the same time *all* advanced societies show a capacity for survival that it would be a mistake for reasons of moral queasiness alone to underestimate. There is no sound theoretical basis for supposing that a certain (and unmeasured) loss of solidarity and consensus is the forerunner of dissolution or revolution. It is more prudent to suppose that a seemingly minor recovery of consensus can firmly secure a society that is only subjectively judged, or for ideological reasons supposed, to be verging on disintegration (whatever that may mean). This, after all, is what Marcuse appears to have believed, and to have feared.

The Circle of Relationships

We have already used the phrase 'circle of relationships' to refer to the connections that the theorists we have examined have noted between the advance of science and technology, the growth of government and the development of, variously, large-scale organisations or 'big business'. They have also voiced concern for the growth of 'bureaucracy' whether this has occurred in government or in the business sphere. This is the set of relationships that may seem to hold the key to the evolution of industrial systems and it deserves a fuller exposition and a more thorough probing than it has hitherto been given.

First, however, we may recapitulate some of the aspects of these relationships. At the heart of Galbraith's analysis of the industrial state is government expenditure on research and development. The vast growth in this expenditure in the United States[28] leads Galbraith to assert both the power of the scientists and technical specialists (whom he calls the Technostructure) and the symbiotic interrelationship of government and the giant corporations. Mandel sees government acting as the servant of the corporations, budgeting for major industrial projects and taking responsiblity for crisis management of the economy and for providing a secure social context for production. Habermas comments, 'large organisations strive for a kind of political compromise with the state and with one another, excluding the public whenever possible . . .'[29] Additionally, the emphasis on the massive promotion of science suggests to Galbraith the consequent emergence of an educational and scientific estate. Bell is in fair agreement with Galbraith, that the government-aided advance of science is producing a new knowledge elite. They differ in that Bell's emphasis is on the development of universities and research institutions rather than upon the growth of large corporations or government. Habermas's focus is different again, upon the scientisation of decision-making in government accompanied by reliance on experts who act behind the closed doors of the bureaucracy beyond the layman's comprehension, sphere of debate and democratic control; the consequences are a decline in rational decision-taking and a loss of legitimacy.

Between them these theorists have made prominent the circle of interdependencies. Scientific research is now so expensive that it has to be funded by government; thus as science advances, government and governmental power grow. Science is predominantly pursued in large organisations; thus corporations also grow[30] and large corporations become interdependent with big government. Governmental decision-making is dependent upon experts and especially upon scientists; experts are similarly powerful in business corporations. Thus the power of government, of large organisations and of science and scientists grows; science comes to be depicted as the entirely neutral source and justification for this growth. The progress of science and technology comes to be perceived as quasi-autonomous and as the single factor upon which economic growth and the future development of society depend. 'When this semblance has taken root effectively', comments Habermas, 'then propaganda can refer to the role of technology and science to explain and to legitimate why in modern societies the process of democratic decision-making about practical problems loses its function and "must" be replaced by plebiscitary decisions about alternative sets of leaders of administrative personnel'.[31]

From the citizen's point of view, however, the individual is, with every increment of governmental/administrative/organisational/ bureaucratic power, himself diminished and no increment of power is legitimated by prevailing norms. The citizen needs, therefore, to know who controls the experts, to whom the controllers are accountable (the time-honoured *quis custodiet ipsos custodes?*) and how the system of control is legitimated. We shall keep in mind such questions, but we must first examine further the elements in the circle of relationships.

The Control of Science and Scientists

Heilbroner has written that the major problem for industrial society to solve is 'the far reach of science and technology'.[32] But the issue is very obviously mis-stated: what is significant for the development of society is not the advance of science as such but the use to which science and technology are put and the institutionalisation of the social role of scientists. Industrial societies are all of them committed to the promotion of science and its social uses and therefore also to the growth of scientific, technical and professional groups. Thus the roles allotted to the new specialists and the incorporation of their work into the occupational and social systems are matters of vital importance. Are the scientific and technical specialists becoming a new knowledge elite replacing politicians, entrepreneurs and managers, or are the new men simply serving the old?[33] Or are the new men in effect controlling their apparent political and industrial masters while seeming to serve them? Or is knowledge now so complex and fragmented and are the new men so specialised and so little cohesive among themselves that they cannot be considered as a group or an elite with the potentiality implied by the singular nouns for common action? Is political power being dissipated, then, between rival cliques and coteries of experts and between lay pressure groups with access to specialist advice?

The soundest assumption in face of questions that require empirical testing for their proper answering is that nothing has changed, that power belongs, as ever, to the politicians.[34] Of course there are well-documented instances of politicians being persuaded and influenced by scientists and other specialists. There are also instances of politicians receiving contradictory advice from specialists and of politicians reversing decisions made at the behest of one set of advisers when later convinced to do so by another set. Nor is it unknown for specialists, scientific or otherwise, to take government posts or political offices. But decisions are made and unmade by decision-makers, and there is no uniform trend for decision-makers to be drawn from technical specialists. Such a trend is conspiciously absent in the advanced industrial societies.

There remains an argument that Heilbroner's formulation is in fact correct, that technology, in particular, has a life of its own, that 'technology as one of the artifacts of culture embodies the dominant values contained in that culture'. This idealist view provides a warning to socialist governments that wish to borrow the technology of capitalism. 'As a product of its particular historical circumstances', runs Fleron's presentation of the argument, 'the technology that developed under capitalism is a reification and concrete material manifestation of the dominant capitalist idea of maximising control over labour in order to maximise profits. This control function is reflected not only in the machine itself, but also in the accompanying forms of technical rationality and technical infrastructure'.[35]

The onus of proof for this proposition must surely rest with the proposer, especially when it is at variance with the evidence and argument of Chapter 4 that the technology is neutral in itself but the social organisation and social arrangements surrounding its use are not. The argument there was that the diminution and dehumanisation of the worker associated with some technology is due to its mode of use.[36] Jones strongly supports this view by extensive demonstration that every technological change has equal capacity for the degradation or enhancement of life, depending on its use.[37] And the use of technology in industry is securely in the hands of industrial decision-makers and not in those of scientists.[38]

The evidence from the Soviet Union suggests that the technology of Western capitalism can readily be borrowed, just as Lenin maintained, without undermining progress toward socialism.[39] The argument was sustained in Chapter 6 that while the State and the Party allow functional specialisation and varying degrees of organisational and administrative autonomy, give leeway to managers, scientists and the military, and promote measures of reform in economic management, none the less they provide the co-ordinating and integrating elements in a system which remains heavily centralised and in which politics and political decision-making are firmly in control.[40]

The Control of Large-Scale Organisation

Although we have rejected all other theories of convergence, are we, face to face with the continuing growth of large-scale organisation, to be persuaded by Meyer's suggestion that the industrial societies, socialist and capitalist, in East and West, are converging in bureaucratisation? Is it that in the Soviet Union, for example, bureaucratisation of the whole society is occurring while in Western capitalist societies the process is one of multiple bureaucratisation?[41] The idea is worth airing, since it emphasises the pervasiveness of large-scale organisation in all types of advanced industrial society, but it confuses several issues which we are at pains here to separate.

The control of large-scale organisation as a matter of social concern can be split into three issues: the control, by government or citizens, of large-scale organisations, usually business corporations; the control, by citizens, of government, treated here as the largest and most recalcitrant of all large-scale organisations; and the control of the very process of bureaucratisation or organisational development with its tendency to increase as the size of the organisations in which it occurs itself increases.

The Control of Corporations. The first issue we have treated in Chapter 3 and found that large corporations in the West have grown to the point at which they present a challenge to governments (and especially to those in societies which are not themselves industrially advanced, in Third World countries). Their decision-making, potentially at least in the hands of a small elite of individuals and a small group of other equally anonymous (financial) institutions, is largely beyond the rational supervision of government or the democratic control of the electorate.[42] We concluded that their powers have grown to be in excess of their legitimacy. In Barber's concise phrase, 'business has gone international, the countries of the world have not'.[43] In contrast, in the Soviet Union large-scale industrial enterprises (*firmy*) have been deliberately created and fostered.[44] They remain very firmly under state control and their legitimacy is not in question.

The Control of Government. The second issue, that of the control of government, has been raised in relation to Habermas's theoretical concerns and apparently ignored in Chapter 6 in relation to the Soviet Union.

In relation to Western capitalist societies, it is difficult to gainsay the now conspicuous role of government in policies of economic intervention and of social monitoring, the individual's greater sense of dependence upon government, the increase in the number and importance of decisions taken through executive or administrative means rather than by the legislature, the growth in activity and effectiveness of pressure groups[45] which are even less accountable to the electorate than government itself, and the new dissatisfaction with a system of regular but intermittent change of elected leaders as a means of exercising control over their government by the citizens at large. It is equally hard to deny that these developments have been associated with the evolution of advanced industrial systems.

The case of the Soviet Union is little different in terms of the above description of developments except that there is little public evidence there of the effective operation of pressure groups. The difference between the systems is in terms of legitimacy. In the Soviet Union the activities of all agencies in the industrial system, from enterprise to ministry to *Gosplan* itself, are under the constant scrutiny of organs of the Party. In short, the government controls the system, and the Party, at all levels, monitors the government. Furthermore, there is a clear and elaborate ideology to underpin the system and provide its legitimation. It is a paradoxical fact that the system within which the government is most massive, most powerful and most pervasive within its own dominion is that which is ideologically the most secure. Put another way, it is the systems that are most open to challenge that receive the most challenges.

The Control of Bureaucratisation. Organisational development in the capitalist systems of the West has in recent years been continuous. As Meyer notes, 'the post-Weberian student of organisation is aware of the waste and inefficiency, the inflexibilities and conservatism, the immunity to feedback, the misdirection of effort and skewing of goals that mark the performance of bureaucracies'. Hence organisations have been developed in which are promoted the free and informal exchange of knowledge and views, openness to changes in interests and in the environment, the participation and involvement of those most affected by the organisations' decisions, the sharing of responsibilities, the creation (and later dissolution) of problem-solving groups and teams of specialists, the development of new and more flexible structural forms (such as matrix structures), the encouragement of innovation and of individual autonomy, and other changes surprising in any context that could be called bureaucratic.[46]

None the less, despite all such developments, the large-scale organisation, the bureaucratic organisation in the classic sense, is here to stay. It is, as Weber said, 'the most rational known means of carrying out imperative control over human beings' and 'the choice is only that between bureaucracy and dilettantism in the field of administration'.[47] It is essential in a society in which individuals are confronted by uncertainty and unpredictability to reduce as many processes as possible to the routine and the predictable.[48] It is also inevitable with the growth of scale of organisations of all sorts, and their ensuing complexity,[49] that newer, deliberately evanescent forms of organisation are in no position to replace the classic form predicated on stability and continuity. Even the bitterest opponent of large-scale organisation recognises this. 'Without order, planning, predictability, central control, accountancy, instructions to the under-lings, obedience, discipline', writes Schumacher, ' — without these, nothing fruitful can happen because everything disintegrates'.[50]

The process of bureaucratisation is not in itself, therefore, to be seen as a threat. It is not the existence of bureaucracies that social theorists or individual citizens should fear. It is their tendency to escape accountability.

In this case Soviet experience reinforces each stage in the argument. The heavily bureaucratic nature of Soviet government and the management of Soviet industry is clear and, as noted in Chapter 6, it is this aspect of the system that depresses commentators such as Cocks who look for signs of adaptability in the system.[51] But the bureaucracy is inevitable in so large a system regardless of its particular mode of government and underlying ideology. Indeed through the Party machinery the Soviet system may have found a means of monitoring itself that prevents the disabling arteriosclerosis predicted by some observers. Accountability to the Party may not satisfy critics of the system who would prefer accountability to the people, but it may suffice to maintain its capacity for survival.

We conclude, then, that the issues related to the control of large-scale organisation exist in all advanced industrial societies but that they take different forms; once again, the idea of convergence is rejected. Large business organisations cause anxiety to the citizenry and pose a threat to governments in capitalist (and Third World) societies; they have been deliberately fostered in the Soviet Union. The formidable power of central government is evident in all advanced industrial societies but, while it is apparently open to review through the electoral process and challenged and mitigated by the activities of pressure groups in capitalist societies, it is reinforced and justified in the Soviet Union by the authority of the Communist Party: questions of legitimacy, therefore, vary likewise. Finally, the fear of bureaucracy itself and its apparent evasion of accountability is indeed common to all societies and systems, but again, as we have just noted, the form of the accountability problem differs in different systems.

The questions of control — of science, of government, of large-scale organisation — are surely the major questions requiring solution in the continuing evolution of industrial societies.

The Evolutionary Trends

We have come at last to the point at which the results of the studies undertaken and the residues of the discussions of a number of prevalent theories must be drawn together. Given that the attempt has been made to cut a clean path through areas of obscurity and confusion, the outcome is more notable for its brevity than for its novelty.

On the basis of this investigation of advanced industrial systems, the major factors in their future evolution appear to be:

The Power of Government. This is increasingly exercised in economic management, in social administration and, above all, in the promotion of scientific research and the applications of technology, which is itself enhanced by the progress of science and which, in capitalist societies, has outstripped any prevailing theory of legitimation. This factor is identififed by Habermas, Mandel and Galbraith.

The Activities of Pressure Groups. These have yet to achieve the legitimacy now slipping away from government, attempting to exercise the leverage on the political process that now eludes the traditional democratic processes. This factor is noted by Bell, Habermas and Mandel.

The Power of Large-scale Organisations. Especially in business corporations, which have grown international in scope, this is held in the hands of a small number of individuals and influenced by other allied large organisations and has also outstripped any theory of legitimation. This factor is emphasised by Galbraith and Mandel.

The Progress of Science and Technology. This is leading on the one hand to a short-term displacement of work from industry to service employment and to a reduction in the amount of employment and in the meaningfulness of the work that remains, and on the other to the generation of more and more experts offering increasingly specialised advice to decision-makers who will thereby gain in power rather than be displaced. The significance of this factor is variously expressed by Bell, Galbraith, Habermas, Mandel and Marcuse.

The Continuing Growth of Bureaucratic Organisation. Because of its rationality and efficiency, which is both out of reach of traditional democratic controls of accountability and a source of diminution of the individual's sense of autonomy and self-respect, this factor, first identified by Weber, has been of direct concern to Habermas and indirectly so to Galbraith and Marcuse.

These trends, it is apparent, have been working themselves out over an extended time-scale, but so pervasive is the sense of diffuse and bewildering change in advanced industrial societies that the identification of what can be claimed to be fundamental trends is made to appear not merely hazardous but arbitrary. The method employed in this study has been to pick up some of the classic prognoses relevant to industrial systems and some contemporary commentaries, and to relate these to evidence derived from Western capitalist systems, the Soviet Union and Japan in order to reduce the arbitrariness of a fresh attempt to discern the principal features of continuing industrial evolution. It is at least put forward from within a perception that is shaped by past insights and examined against evidence the scrutiny and presentation of which has been only minimally affected by earlier theoretical concerns. The reader must judge the success of the attempt.

The task of the reader (and the writer) is made more discouraging by the widespread belief that social change now occurs so rapidly that it virtually defies the commentator to describe any societal features before they have already changed. On the one hand is the sense that even a society-wide industrial system is only a 'temporary system';[52] on the other is Schon's contention that conceptualisations of social issues and processes, because they are slow to form, are out-of-date even at the moment of formation — given that they are slow to come into good currency, 'once in good currency and institutionalised, they are slow to fade away'.[53]

But of course Schon does not himself infer that because transformation processes are continuous it is not possible to grasp them intellectually as they occur. The caveats about the rapidity of change emphasise the need to examine *processes of change* in industrial systems and to outline *trends of development* rather than to attempt to depict a particular state of a system. In Oppenheimer's more graceful comment, 'the world alters as we walk in it, so that the years of man's life measure not some small growth or rearrangement or moderation of what was learned in childhood, but a great upheaval'.[54] We must expect continual change and it is that which we must analyse and respond to. There is no need to cut and run.

The Needs of Humanity

The evolutionary trends that we have outlined are not experienced neutrally by the citizens of the advanced industrial societies. On the contrary they sound the bells of moral anguish, as the needs of humanity appear to be less recognised and fulfilled as the trends evolve, and as the individual becomes even more confused, ignorant, powerless, diminished and unheard. We end therefore with some prescriptive notes on the needs of humanity as the systems evolve.

The Need for Disorder

The virtues of classical bureaucracy have been duly noted, especially in an hospitable and stable environment, at several points in this study, but it must be evident that in a context of continual change there are difficulties in routinising innovativeness and the capacity to make creative responses to change. What are needed, in Schumacher's lively admonition, are 'the magnanimity of disorder, the happy abandon, the *entrepreneurship* venturing into the unknown and incalculable . . . the risk and the gamble, the creative imagination rushing in where bureaucratic angels fear to tread'.[55] In short, bureaucracy must maintain a framework of stability to protect the people from uncertainty, arbitrariness and what Marcuse called 'the encroachment of special interests upon the general welfare'.[56] Within that framework creativity is a necessity of life.

The Need for Participation

One prerequisite for individuals to keep some control over the nature and direction of change in any society is, in Morison's words, that they 'must feel that they are particpating in the way affairs are ordered, that they have the power of choice. Second, to make this sense of participation and choosing real, the members of the society must have available the kind of evidence required to make judgement among possible alternatives'.[57] The individual's participation, autonomy and control must be maximised;[58] and it is the duty of the powers-that-be to abet the process and of central government to promote the diffusion of information and the decentralisation of decision-making.[59]

In organisations, given the pressure for growth, the promotion of real participation must be joined by the effort, in Schumacher's words, 'to attain smallness within bigness' since practical people have 'a tremendous longing and striving to profit, if at all possible, from the convenience, humanity and manageability of smallness'.[60]

The Need for Public Debate

Habermas's fear is that the transformation of practical into technical questions legitimises their withdrawal from public discussion and deprives the public sphere of its critical function.[61] But since the process only *seems* to be legitimised, it must be resisted and declared illicit; and the public sphere must retain its critical function for the rational attainment of consensus, since the basic human interest is in communication free from domination and in which there is 'complete mutual understanding by participants and recognition of the authentic right of each to participate in the dialogue as an autonomous and equal partner'.[62]

Habermas's demand for proper communication exactly matches Schon's requirement of public learning. Schon observes that 'the opportunity for learning is primarily in discovered systems at the periphery, not in the nexus of official policies at the centre'.[63] There is of course a clash between the interests of the government and the people, between the demand for order and stability and the demand for public learning and public debate. Balance can only be found if government recognises the changing and experimental character of each phase of development of the governed system, as Morison has put it, 'by consciously supplying a series of reasonable alternatives, varied solutions, for the whole society to think over as it makes up its mind about what it would like to do and, equally important, to be'.[64]

The Need for Purpose

To call for the citizens of societies characterised, as are the capitalist systems of the West, by sharp dissensus in respect of norms and values freely to find a common purpose might seem to be a pointless exhortation. To call for the citizens of socialist systems living under an enforced ideological consensus freely to find a common purpose might seem equally pointless. But the call is not for the sudden attainment of a common purpose, full grown, like Athene born from Zeus' head. It is for taking the path toward the later evolution of a sense of purpose, the path through recognition of the needs for creative disorder within a necessary framework of order, for active local participation and for rational and informed public debate. The path may be hard to find and it may be long, but it would appear to be the only way for men to achieve a measure of control over the evolution of their societies that is recognised by all to be legitimate and that is compatible with the still cherished principles of democracy and with respect for the dignity of all citizens.

Nur um der Hoffnungslosen willen ist uns die Hoffnung gegeben.[65]

Notes

1. In a philosophy of science context this stance implies setting aside Popper's criterion of falsifiability as the proper test of a theoretical proposition as overly demanding in the social field. What is aspired to is a framework of analysis the adequacy of which is judged by its capacity to generate illuminating insights. The goal is closer to Kuhn's thinking than to Popper's, the search for an accepted 'paradigm', a conceptual scheme which defines the objects of investigation and the ways in which they should be investigated. See Thomas S. Kuhn, *The Structure of Scientific Revolutions* (University of Chicago Press, Chicago, 1963) and Karl Popper, *The Logic of Scientific Discovery* (Hutchinson, London, 1959) and other papers.

2. Manufacturing industry remains the prime source of wealth and the main field for the application of science and technology. An industrial society does not, by contrast, remain agrarian, since agriculture is also revolutionised by science.

3. Christopher Lasch. 'Take Me To Your Leader', *New York Review of Books*, vol. xx, no. 16 (1976), p. 66.

4. A Marxist view of Bell's thesis is that state monopoly capitalism remains such, call it what you will. Lumer, for example, comments, 'The concept of post-industrial society is, in fact, but a glorified version of state monopoly capitalism, improved and

reorganised with the scientists and professionals managing affairs'. Hyman Lumer, 'The Ideological Essence of "Post-Industrial Society"', *World Marxist Review*, vol. 15, no. 12 (1972), p. 41.

5. See David Held, 'Crisis Tendencies, Legitimation and the State' in John B. Thompson and Held (eds.), *Habermas: Critical Debates* (Macmillan, London, 1982).

6. Ibid.

7. Thomas McCarthy, *The Critical Theory of Jurgen Habermas* (Hutchinson, London, 1978), p. 377. See also Anthony Giddens, *Profiles and Critiques in Social Theory* (Macmillan, London, 1982); Chs. 7 and 8 concern Habermas's theories.

8. Perhaps a technostructure in the Ford Motor Co. was responsible for the ill-fated production of the Edsel. If so, it certainly displayed no power over the market. See J.E. Meade, 'Is "The New Industrial State" Inevitable?', *The Economic Journal*, vol. 78 (1968), pp. 372–92.

9. Allen, in a criticism of Galbraith, asserts this, and the evidence from Chapter 5 above concurs. See G.C. Allen, *Economic Fact and Fantasy* (Institute of Economic Affairs, London, 1967).

10. Marcuse (1968b), p. 53. For the view that Marcuse's critique of society is essentially religious rather than political see R.N. Berki, 'Marcuse and the Crisis of the New Radicalism: From Politics to Religion?', *The Journal of Politics*, vol. 34, no. 1 (1972), pp. 56–92.

11. We should note that Marcuse's disbelief in the industrial proletariat as the agent of revolution is strongly challenged by his Marxist critics. See, for example, Jack Woddis, *New Theories of Revolution* (Lawrence & Wishart, London, 1972), Ch. 4, 'Marcuse and the Western World'.

12. Herbert Marcuse, *Reason and Revolution: Hegel and the Rise of Social Theory* (Humanities Press, New York, 1963), p. 318.

13. See Ian Weinberg, 'The Problem of the Convergence of Industrial Societies: A Critical Look at the State of a Theory', *Comparative Studies in Society and History*, vol. 11 (1969), pp. 1–15.

14. See James R. Millar, 'On the Merits of the Convergence Hypothesis', *Journal of Economic Issues*, vol. ii, no. 1 (1968), pp. 60–8.

15. This statement touches on an area of central sociological concern and a vast literature. The issue is peripheral to the principal focus of this study.

16. The point is that no twentieth century socialist revolution has occurred in a fully industrialised nation solely as a result of spontaneous internal pressures.

17. Morison (1966), p. 121. A very similar conclusion can be found in Schumacher (1973), p. 30.

18. Mandel (1975), p. 586.

19. This point was brought out in chapter 4, pp. 92–4. In Durkheim's terminology it is the forced division of labour that prevails. See Chapter 1, pp. 11–12.

20. The subject of the future of work in the evolution of the advanced industrial societies is too large and important to be given what could here be only superficial treatment. For a range of approaches to this vast and growing topic the reader is referred to Sebastian de Grazia, *Of Time, Work, and Leisure* (Anchor Books, Doubleday and Co., New York, 1964); Stanley Parker. *The Future of Work and Leisure* (MacGibbon and Kee, London, 1971); Clive Jenkins and Barrie Sherman, *The Collapse of Work* (Eyre Methuen Ltd., London, 1979); and Olya Khaleelee and Eric Miller, *The Future of Work* (Work and Society, London, 1984).

21. Henderson (1980), p. 384.

22. The reference is to *The Trial*. See Franz Kafka, *The Trial* (Penguin Books, 1953).

23. See Chapter 1, p. 11.

24. This touches on a vast literature. To quote from one source, Meyer, 'the post-Weberian student of organization is aware of the waste and inefficiency, the

inflexibilities and conservatism, the immunity to feedback, the misdirection of effort and skewing of goals that mark the performance of bureaucracies'. See Alfred G. Meyer, 'Theories of Convergence' in Chalmers Johnson (ed.) *Change in Communist Systems* (Stanford University Press, 1970), p. 328.

25. Henderson (1980), p. 227.

26. In the USSR the development of *firmy* and production associations was noted above, pp. 138–139. The growth of giant capitalist business corporations was also documented in Chapter 3, pp. 51–2; see also S.J. Prais, *The Evolution of Giant Firms in Britain* (Cambridge University Press, 1976). The increase of governmental bureaucracy is a world-wide phenomenon.

27. See the discussion of Habermas's fears, pp. 228–9.

28. Barber provides figures for 1968 that document Galbraith's case. In that year the US government provided 70 per cent of the R and D expenditure in fields related to defence, space and atomic energy, while industrial firms carried out 70 per cent of the research; 46 per cent of *all* scientists and engineers employed in private enterprise were on Federal contracts; 82 per cent of all *research* scientists and engineers were Federally supported; and in the previous 15 years R and D expenditure had grown by 400 per cent, to more than $25 billion per annum or more than 3 per cent of GNP. See Richard J. Barber, *The American Corporation: Its Power, Its Money, Its Policies* (MacGibbon and Kee, London, 1970), Ch. 9.

29. Jurgen Habermas, 'The Public Sphere', *New German Critique*, vol. 3 (1974), p. 54.

30. For Lasch the process is reversed: 'the production of technical knowledge remains subordinate to the corporation's drive to enlarge itself and expand its influence'. See Lasch, 'Take Me to Your Leader'. This may be taken to reinforce the notion that the relationships under discussion are circular.

31. Jurgen Habermas, *Towards a Rational Society* (Heinemann, London, 1971), p. 105.

32. Robert L. Heilbroner, *Business Civilization in Decline* (Penguin Books, Harmondsworth, 1977), p. 45.

33. See the useful discussion by Straussman: Jeffrey D. Straussman, 'Technocratic Counsel and Societal Guidance', Ch. 5 in Leon N. Lindberg (ed.), *Politics and the Future of Industrial Society* (David McKay Co., New York, 1976).

34. This is a deliberate extension of Schumpeter's observation, 'democracy is the rule of the politician'. See Joseph A. Schumpeter, *Capitalism, Socialism and Democracy* (Harper & Row, New York, 1962), p. 285.

35. Both quotations are from Frederic J. Fleron, Jr, 'Afterword' in Fleron (ed.), *Technology and Communist Culture: The Socio-Cultural Impact of Technology under Socialism* (Praeger, New York, 1977), p. 472. See also Jacques Ellul, *The Technological Society* (Alfred A. Knopf, New York, 1964).

36. See Chapter 4, pp. 93–4.

37. Barry Jones, *Sleepers, Wake! Technology and the Future of Work* (Wheatsheaf Books, Brighton, 1982), Ch. 10.

38. The point here is not that trade unions have no part to play, for clearly they play a part in industrial decision-making even if a minor part in comparison with management; it is that scientists play no independent part, only through access to management.

39. Lenin wrote 'socialism is inconceivable without the technique of large-scale capitalist industry based on contemporary science'. The passage, from *Tax in Kind*, is quoted in William J. Conyngham, *Industrial Management in the Soviet Union: The Role of the CPSU in Industrial Decision-Making, 1917–1970* (Hoover Institution Press, Stanford University, Stanford, California, 1973), p. 3.

40. For further support for this conclusion see George Fischer, *The Soviet System and Modern Society* (Atherton Press, New York, 1968), especially the Conclusion.

Fischer classifies the system as 'tutelary monism', a category firmly distinguished from any notion of totalitarianism.

41. Meyer, 'Theories of Convergence'.

42. See Chapter 3, pp. 62–3, 65–7 and 71–2.

43. Barber, *The American Corporation*, p. 284.

44. See note 26 above.

45. We may note that while extra-constitutional political activity is often condemned for being illegitimate, the activity arises from the perception that much apparently constitutional activity has itself lost the substance of legitimacy, retaining only the form of it.

46. It is no part of the aim of this study to enumerate the whole range of organisational developments, merely to exemplify some. There are countless sources on organisational theory and practice. For an introductory source see John Child, *Organisation: A Guide to Problems and Practice* (Harper and Row, London, 1977).

47. See Chapter 2, notes 6 and 7.

48. In order, as Morison puts it, 'to keep our complicated, diversified, intricate, and fragile society from shaking itself to pieces'. Morison (1966), p. 65.

49. This is to accept guidance from a biological analogy. Haldane writes, 'the higher animals are not larger than the lower because they are more complicated. They are more complicated because they are larger'. It is contended that organisations are similar: the larger organisations are more complicated than the smaller *because* they are larger. See J.B.S. Haldane, 'On Being the Right Size' in his *Possible Worlds and Other Essays* (Chatto and Windus, London, 1927), p. 21.

50. Schumacher (1973), p. 209.

51. See Chapter 6, p. 167.

52. The phrase comes from W.G. Bennis, 'Beyond Bureaucracy' in Bennis and Philip E. Slater (eds.), *The Temporary Society* (Harper and Row, New York, 1968).

53. Schon (1971), p. 127.

54. Quoted in Bennis, 'Beyond Bureaucracy', p. 53.

55. Schumacher (1973), p. 209.

56. Marcuse (1941), p. 155.

57. Morison (1966), p. 220.

58. See Schon (1971), Ch. 6 for a discussion of the tensions between the centre's pressure for uniformity throughout the system and local counterpressures at the periphery.

59. The political luxury, as Commoner puts it, of 'failing fully to inform citizens of what they need to know in order to exercise their right of political governance' must be given up. Barry Commoner, *The Closing Circle* (Jonathan Cape, London, 1972), p. 296.

60. Schumacher (1973), p. 53.

61. McCarthy, *The Critical Theory of Jurgen Habermas*, Ch. 5.

62. This formulation is Giddens's. See Giddens, *Profiles and Critiques*, p. 88.

63. Schon (1971), p. 177.

64. Morison (1966), p. 223. Commoner has expressed the self-same thought as follows: ' . . . sweeping social change can be designed only in the workshop of rational, informed, collective social action'. Commoner, *The Closing Circle*, p. 300.

65. This quotation from Walter Benjamin is already justly famous: in translation, 'it is only for the sake of those without hope that hope is given to us'. Marcuse used these words to close Marcuse (1968b).

Select Bibligraphy

Henderson, Hazel (1980) *Creating Alternative Futures: The End of Economics* (Perigee Books, G.P. Putnam's Sons, New York)

Morison, Elting E. (1966) *Men, Machines and Modern Times* (MIT Press, Cambridge, Mass.)

Schon, Donald A. (1971) *Beyond the Stable State* (Temple Smith, London)

Schumacher, E.F. (1973) *Small is Beautiful: A Study of Economics as if People Mattered* (Abacus, Sphere Books Ltd., London)

SUBJECT INDEX

253

NAME INDEX